FROM THE LIBRARY OF

Kari Kauffman

_____

Kari — I hope these stories
of faith will help you grow
in strength & wisdom. May
the courage of these "heros"
inspire you to do great
things for God!
Love,
MeMe

FAITH'S GREAT HEROES

VOLUME ONE

EDITED BY

DAVID LINDSTEDT

BARBOUR
PUBLISHING, INC.
Uhrichsville, Ohio

FAITH'S
GREAT
HEROES

VOLUME ONE

ISBN 1-57748-445-2

Edited by David Lindstedt.

The contents of this book have been edited and abridged from the following "Heroes of the Faith" biographies, all published by Barbour Publishing, Inc.: *Billy Graham, The Great Evangelist,* by Sam Wellman; *Corrie ten Boom, Heroine of Haarlem,* by Sam Wellman; *Martin Luther, The Great Reformer,* by Edwin P. Booth (edited and abridged by Dan Harmon); *Sojourner Truth, American Abolitionist,* by W. Terry Whalin; and *Watchman Nee, Man of Suffering,* by Bob Laurent.

Published by Barbour Publishing, Inc., P.O. Box 719, Uhrichsville, Ohio 44683
http://www.barbourbooks.com

Member of the
Evangelical Christian
Publishers Association

Printed in the United States of America.

CONTENTS

INTRODUCTION

What distinguishes a "hero of the faith" from you and me? Is it possible that *we* could also be heroes? Reflecting on the lives of great Christians, it's easy to see how God used them for His glory, and we might be tempted to think that their lives were somehow ordained in a way that ours are not. But if we could go back in time and walk along with these people as they grew, we would gain an entirely different perspective on how God raises up people for His purposes. The remarkable similarity among each of the five individuals profiled here is how unremarkable their early days were:

—A miner's son, whose father wanted him to become a lawyer, but who answered God's call into the monastic life. As he studied the Scriptures, he discovered the truth of salvation and challenged the decadence that was consuming the Roman Catholic church. His preaching and writing sparked the Reformation and brought about a resurgence of the gospel throughout Europe and the world.

—A watchmaker's daughter, who never married, but who influenced the lives of hundreds of young Dutch women through the girls' clubs that she founded. Then, in her fifties, God used her and her family to shelter Jews and others from the Nazis during World War II. After the war, she established homes that met the needs of war-devastated people.

—A freed African-American slave who, though she lacked a formal education and could neither read nor write, went on to become an eloquent and influential advocate for the rights of African-Americans and women.

—A dairyman's son who channeled his boundless energy into a career as an evangelist. His efforts continued to grow throughout the years, until he had preached the Good News to more people around the world than anyone else.

—A well-educated young Chinese man, who chose the life of a preacher and evangelist over certain success in business. He went on to lead the establishment of an indigenous Chinese church that continued to thrive despite Communist persecution. He also wrote several books that continue to build the faith of many, both in China and abroad.

As we look into the lives of these men and women, several common elements emerge. Without exception, they faced hardship, uncertainty, setbacks, illness, persecution, and misunderstanding. But because they trusted God to do more through them than they were able to do themselves, God took them as they were and accomplished His purposes. In the process, each one learned a new and powerful reliance on God through prayer; they experienced a growing awareness of God's life-changing presence and power; and they developed a willingness to be faithful to God's call in their lives.

Just as He did throughout the Bible, God takes the ordinary, and by His power and grace accomplishes the extraordinary. As you walk with these men and women through the pages of their lives, may your vision be enlarged as to how God might want to use you. Along the way, you will discover that a simple willingness to follow God regardless of the cost is what makes these men and women five of *Faith's Great Heroes*.

—David Lindstedt, editor

BILLY
GRAHAM

Childhood Days

Every day just seemed chock full of school and work and fun. Some days, Billy felt like he had been awake for a week. But he never got tired. When he went to bed he was asleep so fast he couldn't remember ever trying to fall asleep.

On Saturdays, his daddy often drove him and Catherine over to Grandma Coffey's. There they played under long rows of sagging plum, pear, and apple trees. Eventually, Grandma Coffey would sit them down to milk and cookies and tell them stories.

"One fall day in 1918, your mother had picked butter beans, then started having a baby that night," Grandma Coffey told Billy. "It was not until late afternoon the next day, November 7, that you were born, Billy Frank Graham, kicking your legs like a wild frog."

"Did they have to tie a rope to my legs and yank me out?"

"No. Folks don't pull stubborn babies out like they pull out stubborn calves." Billy was like a different boy in school. He knew his parents couldn't believe it, compared to the way he acted at home, but in class he hardly said a word. School was stiff, formal, and boring. But one second off the school bus in the afternoon and he was raring to go. On his way to the barn to milk the cows, he thought of tricks he could teach his menagerie of goats and dogs and cats.

"It's such great fun being back on the farm again and being free," said Billy. "Even if I do have to do chores and play with Melvin."

The dairy was doing very well, with five or six dozen cows, and more every day it seemed. The red barns trimmed in white were a landmark to the kids on the school bus. His daddy built a new two-story brick home with white pillars, complete with city water and electricity, landscaped in front with oaks and cedars.

Billy's mother kept a ledger of how much money the dairy brought in and how much money was spent. When Billy asked why his daddy didn't keep the books, he found out that his mother had one year of college, but his father had only made it through the third grade. It didn't seem to make any difference to anyone.

When Billy was ten, he finally memorized the Catechism, and he got to hang around and listen to his daddy and Uncle Simon talk about God. On Sundays, the Grahams listened to "The Old-fashioned Revival Hour" on their new radio, but the preaching got boring for Billy and he would begin to fidget. They weren't allowed to play games on Sunday, so Billy traipsed into the woods and took his sweet time picking flowers for his mother. It was a good way to get out of the house.

Billy muddled through school. His father grunted indifference at his report card, unless there was a poor grade in deportment. Then the belt came out.

Billy always could fall back on his smile. He wasn't so sure of his looks, but it seemed like kids just warmed up to his smile. The girls seemed to like him plenty. The older Billy got, the more sure of himself he became.

Growing-Up Years

During the Depression, Billy didn't notice any change on the farm. The Grahams lost their savings, but not their livelihood, and the cows still needed milking twice a day. His mother said, "We have four hundred regular customers and most of them will keep paying us. Folks with kids won't give up their milk."

One day when Reese Brown, the dairy's black foreman, was sawing a plank of wood with a power saw, a knot flew off like a cannon ball, striking Frank Graham in the mouth. His face was smashed in from the nose down and all of his front teeth were gone. But those were the least of his injuries.

At the hospital, Billy's mother held baby Jean and comforted the three older children. "Don't you remember your father saying the Lord 'is my refuge and my fortress; my God, in him will I trust' from Psalm 91?"

Even after Frank's terrible accident, the world didn't cave in on the Grahams. The dairy ran fine, thanks to Reese Brown and the able hired hands.

By the following spring, Billy's father was back, physically fit, but not the same as he was before. His thin, sad face was even droopier, even more woeful. And he, too, seemed connected with the world Billy couldn't see. He became even more active in the Christian Men's Club, which had formed after Billy Sunday's visit ten years earlier.

One morning, to Billy's amazement, the men in the club gathered in the Graham's pasture by a pine grove for an all-day prayer meeting. Their wives walked up to the house to spend the day with Billy's mother.

That night his father was glowing. "What a day with the Lord! This fall we're going to build a tabernacle. We're going to have a real revival. Get us a real old-time preacher!"

Mother said, "I heard that a man at your prayer meeting implored the Lord to let Charlotte give rise to a preacher who would spread the Gospel to the ends of the earth!"

"Maybe Charlotte is the end of the earth," said Billy with a smile. But his parents were not amused. Billy didn't know who that man from Charlotte would be, but he was sure it wasn't him.

Billy began to stretch his horizons. He drove the family's dark blue Plymouth sedan to school, but he drove it like a sports car and challenged other kids to drag races. His interest in girls had advanced beyond talk and he was hugging girls at every opportunity. The privacy of the car gave him plenty of opportunity, but he remained very polite and never tried to go much beyond hugging. A few times he kissed a girl, but going beyond kissing, outside of marriage, was just unthinkable. He knew it happened, but it seemed more depraved than drinking alcohol.

It seemed that almost every girl would let him hug her, if no one was watching. Maybe his mother was right after all. His bony cartoon of a face was no drawback at all. After a while he grew certain he had a charm over girls.

Billy had two great interests: girls and baseball. He thought he was a natural-born first baseman, with windmill arms that snapped balls out of the air like a bullfrog snapped flies. It was just a matter of time before he started connecting with the bat. Milking cows had given him a grip that could make a grown man cry. And his long, farm-strong arms blurred the bat when he swung. If he hit the ball squarely, the horsehide soared. The problem was, he didn't often hit it squarely.

Billy was not enthusiastic when he heard that a preacher named Mordecai Ham was coming to Charlotte late that summer in 1935 to hold the revival meetings his father had talked about.

"Too bad the local preachers won't help us," Billy's father said at supper.

"How come?" asked Billy absently. He was thinking about a girl named Pauline, who was just about the most sophisticated young lady in Mecklenburg County. He had met her at a Bible camp in the mountains last summer, and could she ever kiss!

"Mordecai Ham makes it plenty hot for preachers," said his father, with as much of a smile as he ever mustered. "Skins the local preachers pretty good."

When Dr. Ham finally appeared in Charlotte, Billy was far too busy with Pauline to make time for a revival meeting. But his curiosity was piqued when he heard that Mordecai Ham had accused the kids at the Charlotte high schools of being sinful.

"I've got to hear this Dr. Ham for myself," Billy said. He went to the revival with Albert McMakin, a tenant farmer on the Graham's land. Albert was almost ten years older than Billy and had been a star athlete at Sharon High School.

When Billy walked inside the tabernacle, he was stunned. The place seemed magical. The darkness was lit by dozens of high-swinging sunny bulbs. The air smelled of pine. The floor was sawdust but clean. There were already hundreds of folks sitting on benches and crates and chairs, with plenty of room for more.

Albert sat down near the back.

"Say," objected Billy, "I want to be right down front."

"You sure?" said Albert.

"I'm sure," insisted Billy.

"Let's go then," said Albert, smiling.

They went down as close as they could get and sat right in the middle. "Why, there are plenty of seats up here," said Billy. "I could never understand why folks sit at the back."

The tabernacle filled. Billy had never felt like he did tonight. Regular church always seemed cool with right-eousness, but this tabernacle was a pulsing, sensuous, warm thing. He couldn't put it in words. And there were so many people.

Mordecai Ham appeared on the stage. He was tall, fiftyish, with a fringe of white hair and a thin white mustache. His rimless glasses gave the appearance of a truly colorless man. How was this singularly insignificant man going to take on a crowd of four thousand people and all the preachers in Charlotte? But he did, and the fight was very lopsided. When he spoke, his face seemed to grow redder and angrier. Billy sat up tall so he wouldn't miss anything.

"You are a sinner!" bellowed Dr. Ham, pointing right at Billy.

"Me?" gasped Billy. He slumped in his chair. How did Dr. Ham know about him? What had Billy done? Before the evening was over, Billy was shaken. He really felt like a sinner. How naive he had been about revivalists. He had almost pitied Dr. Ham when he first appeared, but now he felt thrashed from head to toe.

Billy went back again and again. He was thrilled by the pulsing warmth in the tabernacle and Dr. Ham's power. Billy had heard some pretty good preachers over the radio, but he had never heard anyone who could speak like Mordecai Ham. In person, with all the senses tuned in, his preaching was soul-shaking. But Billy made sure he never sat in Dr. Ham's line of fire again. He joined the choir, which stood behind the preacher. He sat next to the Wilson brothers, T. W. and Grady.

Every night, Mordecai Ham ended his preaching by calling folks to the altar to accept Jesus as their Savior. Of course, Billy was already a Christian. But after several nights he began to wonder if he was really in Christ.

Finally, one night after Dr. Ham invited sinners to the altar and the choir began singing "Just As I Am," Billy felt the presence of the living Christ. Was Jesus telling him to go to the altar? Billy resisted. He had been baptized as a baby. He was already a Christian. Wasn't he?

When the choir started another hymn, Billy glanced at Grady Wilson. Grady was very troubled. "I thought I was already saved," he stammered. "Maybe I'm not." As the choir sang the last words of the hymn, Billy found himself trudging to the altar, head down, suddenly painfully self-conscious of his gangly height.

"I'm a changed boy," Billy told his mother that evening, but he was uneasy. He felt a tremendous burden. Where were the fire and the joy? Billy felt no farther along than Christian at the beginning of *The Pilgrim's Progress* as he started his perilous journey to salvation. Billy saw his imperfections now magnified. Wasn't he supposed to be already saved? Maybe he didn't really understand what living in Christ meant.

Weeks later, his mother said, "You've calmed down, Billy. You seem more tuned in to other people. I know you have always loved other people, but sometimes you were moving too fast."

Billy had changed, but not everyone appreciated it. He had to remind himself not to be self-righteous with kids at school, telling them right out if they did something wrong. He began hanging around with the Wilson brothers, who went to different high school. Some kids started calling them the Preacher Boys.

Completely spellbound by the power he had witnessed in Mordecai Ham, Billy impulsively went to Belk's Department Store in downtown Charlotte and began preaching on the sidewalk. He waved his arms and jabbed his finger at sinners as they fled past him. Afterward, he had to admit that his evangelizing was a dismal failure. But strangely, he wasn't embarrassed or sorry.

The family started talking about Billy becoming a preacher. He began to look for a suitable college that he could afford to attend. His father had planned on Billy working the dairy farm full-time after high school, but he agreed to help Billy with his college expenses.

"Maybe Billy will be that preacher from Charlotte who spreads the Gospel to the ends of the world," said his mother.

"God willing." Billy's father looked pained.

"T. W. Wilson went out west to Tennessee to that college run by Dr. Bob Jones," volunteered Billy. "He likes it."

"I never heard of it," said Mother.

"Don't you remember? Jimmy Johnson went there," said Billy brightly. Jimmy Johnson was a young itinerant preacher who had stayed with the Grahams. Billy thought he was an excellent preacher. "I would be a preacher in a twinkling if I could preach like Jimmy Johnson."

"What's it cost?" asked his father.

"Well, you know T. W. couldn't afford much, Daddy."

"That's it then. It's Bob Jones," said his father, looking like he could make no better bargain than that. "Come on, Melvin." The two of them left to do chores.

Suddenly, Billy was out of high school with a diploma in his hand. What was he going to do for the summer? His quandary didn't last long. Albert McMakin had left the farm to work for Fuller Brush. He invited the three Preacher Boys to come to South Carolina to sell brushes door-to-door.

"I thought you were going to help me on the farm this summer," Billy's father said.

"I can save up money for college this way, Daddy," gushed Billy.

"You'll be back in two weeks," scoffed Uncle Clyde.

On that encouraging note, Billy left for South Carolina with the Wilson brothers.

New Horizons

B illy opened his case, grabbed one of his cheapest brushes and knocked on the door of his first potential customer. The door opened. An exasperated face appeared in the doorway. "Yes?"

"I'm Billy Graham, ma'am. Your Fuller Brush man. I'd like to give you a free brush today. . . ." He held out the brush. "All you have to. . ."

"Thanks, sonny." The woman snatched the brush out of his hand and slammed the door.

He learned fast. At the next house, he took his sweet time digging in the case for the free brush, while launching an unstoppable avalanche of words. And Billy made sure his customer was blinded by his smile. Billy threw himself into his sales job, heart and soul, and he never doubted for a moment he was going to sell every brush in his case.

Albert McMakin was amazed. "You're selling more brushes than I am, Billy." By mid-summer, Billy was clearing fifty dollars a week after expenses, but he liked to spend his money on gabardine suits and hand-painted ties. At the end of the summer, he had a fine wardrobe.

Billy crossed paths with Jimmy Johnson during the summer, and he never missed a chance to hear Jimmy preach. One Sunday afternoon in Monroe, North Carolina, Jimmy took Billy and Grady Wilson to a jail. Facing the cells full of grumbling prisoners, Jimmy suddenly pointed at Billy. "I have a young fellow here who was just recently saved. Give our friends your testimony, Billy." It was an old trick on would-be preachers.

Billy froze. He noticed Grady squirm. Jimmy was amused. "Help me, Lord," prayed Billy. Hadn't he practiced a hundred times? "Get me started, Lord."

"I'm glad to see so many of you turned out," said Billy. Then he shouted, "I was a sinner!" A weak "Amen" wafted from a cell. "I was no good!" He punched the air. "I forgot God!" He began to pace and punch the air as he spat out his testimony in clipped sentences. "Finally, I accepted Jesus!" His voice caromed off the walls, each word as loud and clear as a church bell. "Jesus brought me joy!" He was sweating now and his sentences got longer, louder, more fluid. "Amens" rolled out of the cells after every sentence. Finally, he stopped, trembling in a state of joy he had never felt before.

"So that's what preaching is really like," he gushed to Grady later.

All summer long, Billy sold brushes and evangelized. When he returned to Charlotte, his father drove him and Grady Wilson to Tennessee. The boys were champing at the bit. They hatched a plan to take over the freshman class. Billy nominated Grady for president of the class and he won the election. But when it came time for Grady to nominate Billy for an office, he found out officers couldn't nominate candidates.

"Thanks, buddy," said Grady afterwards. "The first part of the plan worked great."

At first, Billy thought the school was wonderful, but within a few weeks he felt burdened by the Bob Jones regimen. Boys couldn't talk to girls. Mail was monitored. Billy felt like a prisoner, and with his impulsive energy he piled up demerits at a record pace. Finally, he began to become frantic like a jungle cat in a small cage.

One day in math class, Billy realized he hadn't the slightest idea what the instructor was lecturing about. Was this a class in Medieval Icelandic? Impulsively, he stood up. "Professor, is it possible to drop this class?"

"Certainly, if you want an 'F'," answered the professor, expecting Billy to sit down.

"It's a bargain," said Billy and strode out of the room.

When Billy returned home for Christmas vacation, the Grahams drove south to visit his mother's sister in Florida. At a gasoline stop south of Jacksonville, Billy was the first one out of the car.

"So this is Florida," he gawked. "Feel that balmy air." He clapped his hands. "What a paradise!"

While in Florida, they took a side trip to the small town of Temple Terrace to survey the Florida Bible Institute. Pale stucco buildings with red-tiled roofs overlooked tennis courts and a sprawling golf course. Nearby, the Hillsboro River crept along under moss-hung cypress trees.

"It's beautiful," gushed Billy.

"It's a former resort hotel and country club," said his mother casually. "Now it appears to be a fine institution to study God's Word, I read about it in *Moody Monthly*." Billy suddenly realized that the whole Florida trip had been engineered by his mother to show him another school. Billy had no problem imagining himself striding across campus in balmy sunshine, resplendent in his lime gabardine suit and hot pink tie, free to smile at any pretty girl he saw.

When he returned to Bob Jones College, he tried to talk the Wilson brothers into coming with him to the Florida Bible Institute. They refused. Bob Jones was all they could afford. So Billy talked his friend Wendell Phillips into going with him.

Bob Jones was not pleased when Billy and Wendell

announced they were leaving. "If you boys don't fit in at my college, you won't fit in anywhere, not even at some tiny school in the swamps. You'll end up poor old preachers out somewhere in the cane fields."

Billy returned to Charlotte and his father drove him to Florida in February of 1937. Billy flourished like an orchid at Temple Terrace. The Institute had rules against smoking, drinking, and "heavy" dating, but these were common virtues for the students, and Billy felt free.

Many evangelists came to vacation and lecture at the Institute, and wide-eyed Billy absorbed their lectures. It seemed that every evangelist drew inspiration from two great preachers from the past.

"Dwight Moody and Billy Sunday," said Billy.

D. L. Moody had softened the message of earlier evangelists into an earnest rapid-fire plea for redemption from the God of love. And Moody was a master organizer, enlisting the help of local churches in city-wide revivals, and creating seminaries, rescue missions, and an outstanding Bible school.

Billy's real idol became Billy Sunday, who, like Moody, had preached to one hundred million people. Young Billy Graham had been impressed by Billy Sunday years ago. Who could forget a man who stomped his feet and pounded his fists like Billy Sunday did? Who could forget how he raced across the platform and slid like he was stealing a base? Who could forget how he screamed at the "bull-necked, hog-jowled, weasel-eyed, sponge-spined, mush-fisted, yellow-livered, hell-bound sinners"?

Billy Sunday was flamboyant, but he was not just a performer. He was as shrewd as a fox, organizing men's luncheon groups and prayer groups to help get huge turn-outs for his revivals.

"How could anybody ever top Billy Sunday?" asked

Billy Graham every time the subject of great preachers came up.

Billy was in paradise at Florida Bible Institute. The curriculum was no better than at Bob Jones, but students were urged to practice preaching whenever possible. Billy polished four sermons he borrowed from a book—a common practice. Who knew when he would be called?

He got his first opportunity at a small church near Palatka that numbered about thirty members. Billy got wound up and hammered out his four sermons in less than ten minutes. John Minder, dean of the Bible Institute, deftly filled in the remaining time. Billy felt miserable. Why couldn't he slow down and be like a real preacher? When they returned to campus, Dean Minder asked him to be the youth director at the Tampa Gospel Tabernacle.

Billy threw himself into the job with his usual energy. The Tampa high school kids responded to Billy's loud fervent prayers. They were seeking God and the group grew in number. Billy was thrilled.

Billy made many new friends at the Bible Institute, and life was wonderful. The only missing ingredient was a girlfriend. And then he met Emily, a pious and talented dark-haired beauty, whose family lived in Tampa. Billy was so smitten that he took her home to meet his parents in North Carolina, and at one time even proposed marriage. But Emily ultimately fell in love with another student and broke Billy's heart.

Billy was tempted to slide into bitterness. What was God's purpose in having a young person crushed by such injustice? Was it to show that only love for Christ and love from Christ were true?

Night after night he lay awake in his dorm room agonizing over his misfortune and doubts. In his loneliness, he sometimes wandered the campus grounds at night. Misfortune had clouded his calling. His misery had evolved into doubts about being a preacher at all.

Finally in 1938, as he sat on the eighteenth green on a cool March night, the veil lifted. It was sudden and definite. Glimpses of rallies, with throngs of people in front of a platform flickered in his mind. He got on his knees.

I let love for a woman fool me. The first commandment is to love the Lord my God with all my heart and with all my soul and with all my mind. I surrender, Lord! If you want me to spread the Gospel by preaching, I will!

Billy threw himself into Christ now. He had been little more than a tourist before. Now he prayed hours on end. He read the Bible as he never had before. He was appointed assistant pastor of the Tampa Gospel Tabernacle. He preached in trailer parks. He preached to Cubans through an interpreter. He preached on the student radio station. He preached on the streets of Tampa.

He returned to Palatka. This time it was billed as his own revival. He was very bold. He now asked fellow ministers to plug him. Cecil Underwood was quoted in a local paper as saying Billy was "causing quite a sensation." Stoked by Underwood, the paper went on with flaming rhetoric that Billy was leading "the greatest meeting in the history of the church." Billy promoted himself all the time now. He had handbills printed, which grew in boldness until they were proclaiming "One of America's Outstanding Young Evangelists."

Ministers in the area had doubts, however. Billy heard the rumors. "His preaching is frenetic," said the whispers. Billy flailed the air with his arms, pointed his finger, bounced around the pulpit like a man swatting flies, and boomed his raw North Carolina twang off the ceilings. Yet his message was plain: "You are a sinner. Christ died to pay for your sins. But you must accept Christ to be saved."

Billy knew what they were saying, but he told himself, "I'm sure God wants me to preach this way."

Still, the question nagged at his mind. Could he, or could he not, bring sinners to Christ and salvation? So far he had never made the call to the altar. That was done by the presiding pastor. If Billy couldn't bring folks to Christ, he might as well give it all up and go back to the dairy or sell brushes.

Called to Preach

In Venice, sixty miles south of Tampa, the night for his first altar call finally came, Billy gnawed at his fingernails, sick with worry. He had prayed all afternoon for God's help.

One hundred people were in the congregation to listen to him preach in a storefront church. Heart pounding, he began. As he preached, he felt very strong, as if the Holy Spirit was helping him. Arms flailing and words exploding like gunfire, he delivered the Gospel. At the end of his sermon, when he made the altar call, his heart was in his mouth. What if no one came?

A man stood up and slowly walked toward the altar. After a moment, a woman made her way forward.

Then another person stood.

And another.

Soon they were rising so fast Billy could no longer count. He wanted to weep. He wasn't worthy of such an outpouring. "Oh, rebuke me, God," he prayed. This was not Billy's sermon. It was not his personal charm. The sinners came to Christ because the Holy Spirit was working through Billy.

"Thirty-two came to the altar," said one of the local churchmen later. "In all my years, I never saw that many come to the altar in one meeting."

By early 1940, Billy was nearing graduation and was considering what to do next. One day he was caddying for two golfers named Elner Edman and Paul Fischer from Wheaton, Illinois.

Billy gushed, "Where is Wheaton College located? What a coincidence. My mother always dreamed of my going there."

Paul Fischer said, "My brother is the chairman of Wheaton College's board of trustees. Mr. Edman's brother is president of the college."

"Wow," said Billy. "You must be proud of them."

Fisher said, "I want you to go to Wheaton, Billy."

"Can't afford it, sir."

"I'll pay your room and board for one year." Fisher looked at Edman. "Elner?"

Edman said, "I'll pay your tuition for a year. After that, I expect you can get a scholarship. Truth is, we want Wheaton College to graduate Billy Graham."

"If that doesn't beat all. Me?" said Billy. "Mother will be so happy."

In the late summer of 1940, Billy Graham arrived at Wheaton College. Like every young man in America, he was keeping a wary eye on Europe, where Adolf Hitler was extending his murderous grip.

At twenty-two, Billy was an ordained minister, yet he was a mere freshman at Wheaton, because many of his Bible Institute credits had not transferred. The gangly, smiling southerner, in his gabardine suits and bright ties, was a curiosity at first, but he had something else that could not be seen: the Holy Spirit. Once the other students heard him pray, they never looked at him the same way again.

He majored in anthropology and got a part-time job moving furniture with a senior student named Johnny Streater.

"Say, Billy, my girlfriend has a friend I'd like you to meet," said Johnny.

"I guess that's okay," Billy said politely.

So Johnny Streater introduced him to Ruth Bell, a second-year student who was the daughter of missionaries in China. Her sharp features and wide, thin lips were softened by amber eyes, a creamy complexion and complete innocence. Most girls did a double take with Billy, but not Ruth. She was looking for something else in a man and responded coolly to the young southerner. Billy immediately fell in love with her.

He thought about her all the time, but he had been burned before. In the two years since Emily, he had been cautious. His interest in girls had been platonic, almost priestly. Ruth Bell inflamed him, but he was not going to force the issue. He was going to leave it to God.

"If it is God's plan to pair me with Ruth, then God will make it happen," Billy assured himself.

But after several weeks, he had to admit to himself that Ruth was not going to make the first move. He nervously invited her to a performance of Handel's *Messiah,* and she accepted!

His date with Ruth was both satisfying and disturbing. She seemed compatible spiritually, and though her face clouded slightly at some of his stern judgments of things, that was not the real problem. The problem was that Ruth wanted to be a missionary. Nevertheless, Billy wrote to his mother that very night, telling her he had met the woman he was going to marry.

But the more he thought about Ruth Bell, the more troubled he became. How could her goals ever be reconciled with his own? Could he rob this godly woman of her destiny? Once again he backed off. Let God decide. He saw Ruth at student prayer meetings but remained aloof. Finally, many weeks later, he received a letter from Ruth—an invitation to a party!

They dated for several months, usually going together to prayer meetings or sermons. Sometimes she went to hear Billy's sermons. She was strangely silent afterward, almost as if embarrassed. Billy had to accept that. She wasn't the first one put off by his flailing arms, pointing fingers and window-rattling, non-stop delivery.

Sometimes Ruth talked about her childhood in China, which was awesome to a North Carolina farm boy. Ruth had been embroiled in the civil war between Chiang Kai-shek's Nationalists and Mao Tse-tung's Communists. It was Billy's first real knowledge of the unrelenting godless ambitions of Communists. Then the Japanese soldiers had come, and they were twice as brutal. Added to the constant threat of war was the extreme hardship of life itself. Yet Ruth retained an almost holy innocence. Her worn Bible had notes penciled in all the margins.

Billy had never met anyone as fascinating as Ruth, but he remained aloof until he was certain she was God's choice for him. He had not so much as kissed her.

Then he heard from Johnny Streater that Ruth had started dating other men.

Billy rushed to see her. "Say, I thought we were seeing only each other," he complained.

"You haven't called me in more than a week," she explained.

"Has it been a week? Well, you can date me or everybody but me. Make a choice."

She chose Billy, but he was still troubled by the separate paths he and Ruth seemed to be taking and he prayed for guidance. Then suddenly, Ruth had to drop out of school to nurse her older sister, Rosa, who had tuberculosis.

Billy finally decided he was going to have Ruth as his wife. Longing for her gnawed at him constantly. He decided to ask Ruth to marry him and let God sort the careers out. If God wanted her to be a missionary, then she would be a missionary. Let God's will be done.

When the students left Wheaton for the summer recess, Ruth still had not given Billy an answer. She was agonizing over it as much as he was. Billy knew that after all his dilly-dallying, he had come on very strong.

Billy went to preach again in Tampa and received her answer by letter postmarked July 6, 1941. "Yes!" he screamed.

It seemed Billy and Ruth were moving toward an inevitable marriage, but late that summer Ruth's health failed. Her father thought she had malaria. He sent her to a sanitarium in Albuquerque with her older sister, Rosa. In the clutches of depression, Ruth tried to break the engagement, but Billy continued to pray long and hard.

On December 7, 1941, the Japanese bombed Pearl Harbor and pulled the United States into the war. Billy's professors talked him out of enlisting as a combatant, but he tried to join the army as a chaplain. He was told by the army that he had to finish his college work first and then serve one year as a full pastor to qualify as a chaplain.

Ruth returned to Wheaton in early 1942, still wearing the engagement ring, but Billy found that she had real misgivings about marrying him. She told him straight out that he was opinionated and domineering. And he told her straight out that his marriage would be biblical. He would be the head of the family. And she had to trust him and follow him.

"Lord, give him wisdom," she muttered in compliance.

Billy's new roommate at Wheaton was none other than Jimmy Johnson, and his old friend Grady Wilson soon arrived as well. Billy would be graduating in the late spring of 1943, and he already had a pastorate promised to him by Robert Van Kampen in nearby Western Springs. The small church, with a mere thirty-five members, was in dire straits, but Billy was undaunted. He could hardly wait to get started, but he had another great event in his life to attend to first.

After three years of courtship, he married Ruth at Montreat, North Carolina, on August 13, 1943. Brother Melvin was the best man. Rosa was the maid of honor. Officiating was Billy's old mentor from the Florida Bible Institute, John Minder. Ruth told Billy she would never remove the gold wedding band, not for a split second. They honeymooned for one week in a cottage high in the Blue Ridge Mountains.

Billy began pastoring at Western Springs more like a tornado than a shepherd. He herded his flock hard. He was a conservative evangelical through and through, but he convinced his flock to change their denominational name to The Village Church, to appeal to more people seeking a church.

Almost overnight, he started a prayer group of prominent businessmen and, before he knew it, three hundred businessmen were coming to prayer dinners! Opportunities seemed to seek Billy out, but usually they found him because he was everywhere, opening doors.

Then Torrey Johnson, pastor of Midwest Bible Church, approached Billy and offered him his "Songs in the Night" radio program. Each step taken by Billy seemed ten times higher than the last, but this opportunity looked like a hundred steps up.

Broadening Horizons

H ow will you find time?" was Ruth's first question when Billy rushed home with the news.

"I will. I have to," Billy said excitedly. "Maybe I can get that terrific bass baritone George Shea who sings on 'Club Time' to sing hymns for our program."

"Your mind is made up and racing one hundred miles an hour," said Ruth. "But where do you fit in?"

"Between songs." Billy smiled. "Don't you worry. We've got forty-five minutes of air time to fill. You'll hear me plenty."

"Where do I fit in?"

"You can help with the scripts. Just like you help me with my sermons now. And I want you in the audience. We'll broadcast right from the church."

The church elders were reluctant. The expense of the show, $150 per week, seemed to be a surefire recipe for financial disaster. But Billy, in his eager forceful way, persuaded them.

On January 1, 1944, Billy welcomed listeners to "Songs in the Night." Interspersed with songs by George Shea and others, Billy burst forth with his dynamic sermons.

Donations began to pour in to the church and things just kept getting better and better. Even when

Billy occasionally tripped it seemed he stumbled straight ahead.

The radio experience helped his preaching. Relying entirely on his voice and the message, he became not quite so frantic. When he preached from the pulpit, however, he didn't abandon his larger-than-life gestures.

Next, Torrey Johnson rented a concert hall and invited Billy to be his principal speaker at a rally for soldiers he called "Chicagoland Youth for Christ." Billy hesitated, but eventually accepted the invitation. After a shaky start, he preached to a hall packed with very tough, very cynical soldiers. After his sermon, forty-two soldiers came to Christ.

The Chicago rally was so successful that others soon followed. Eventually, Billy was traveling to preach to crowds of ten thousand or more. It happened so fast that he never had a chance to be overwhelmed.

By early 1945, Billy was so busy with Johnson's rallies, it was obvious he could no longer pastor the Village Church. It was impossible to be both an evangelist and a pastor. Consequently, he left the church to work full time for Youth for Christ.

Billy knew Ruth was suffering. He was traveling constantly and there was not enough money for her to travel with him. But she joked once that she would rather have a little of him than a lot of anybody else. Ruth soon left Illinois to go live with her parents in Montreat.

In 1945, six hundred leaders showed up at Winona Lake in Indiana to formally start an international organization called Youth for Christ. Torrey Johnson was elected president and Billy became the single field representative.

Once again life changed drastically. Billy lived out of a suitcase and his office was a rail car or a Greyhound bus. He tried to make amends to Ruth, who was now pregnant, on sporadic visits to Montreat, yet somehow the

Youth for Christ movement was always at hand.

Ruth gave birth to a daughter on September 21, 1945, not long after Billy left North Carolina for a speaking engagement in Alabama. They named her Virginia after Ruth's younger sister, but Ruth nicknamed her GiGi, which is Chinese for "sister."

By early 1946, the Youth for Christ movement was a national phenomenon. With the war ended, Torrey Johnson decided it was time for the organization to become international. Teams left for Japan, Korea, China, India, Africa, and Australia. In March 1946, Johnson led a team to England that included the organization's two most dynamic speakers, Chuck Templeton and Billy Graham, with Cliff Barrows and his wife, Billie, leading the music. They spoke to one hundred thousand people in three weeks.

English clerics were appalled by Billy. They had never seen a preacher in a bright red bow tie, who stalked the platform—bending down, bolting upright, flailing his arms—and delivered the simple message of sin and salvation at 240 words per minute. Even more stunning was the stream of sinners answering the altar call.

Billy returned to Britain and Ireland in the fall of 1946, this time for six months. Ruth met Billy in London and accompanied him for part of the trip. His song leaders were again Cliff and Billie Barrows. In the back of his mind, Billy felt like he was building a team.

In Wales, Billy met Stephen Olford, a Welshman. "You are filled with the Holy Spirit, Stephen," Billy said. "I want the fullness of the Spirit, too."

The two secluded themselves in a hotel room to pray and pore over the Bible. Olford taught Billy to use "quiet time" every day to completely absorb the reality of Holy Scripture. He next urged Billy consciously to surrender hourly to the sovereignty of Christ and the absolute authority of the Bible.

"This will bring the fullness of the Holy Spirit," counseled Olford.

Billy believed him totally. "This is the turning point of my ministry," he cried. That night he spoke to his largest audience in Wales. Tonight there seemed more real authority in his voice. He was speaking for God. Daniel, chapter 5, came alive.

Finally, he invited the Welsh sinners to come to Christ.

Stephen Olford was shocked. "Virtually the entire audience is coming to the altar!"

Billy's next great test was in Birmingham. After his first sermon, which drew a paltry two hundred people, Billy hunkered down in his hotel room and telephoned local clergymen with humble appeals for help. One by one, he melted their resistance. Before long, the campaign was restored and the city auditorium was filled every night.

Billy now wanted to work American cities like he had worked Birmingham. He started in Grand Rapids, Michigan. By fall, he was to be in Charlotte. At Billy's citywide campaign in Minneapolis, eighty-six-year-old William Riley pestered him "like the persistent widow" to become president of Riley's Northwestern Bible Schools. Billy refused. When Riley wouldn't let up, Billy promised to assume the role of president if anything happened to Riley within a year.

The preparation for Charlotte was another of Billy's black moments. What if he failed in his own backyard? Billy's nervousness spurred an advance campaign that went far beyond the usual billboards, bumper stickers, radio commercials, and placards. Billy had airplanes zooming over Charlotte, trailing banners and dropping leaflets. He gave daily press releases to thirty-one local papers.

In eighteen services at Charlotte, they drew forty-two thousand people, and many of them came to Christ. Billy was very pleased with his team of Bev Shea, the Barrows, and Grady Wilson.

Billy felt so good that he began more and more to think about going out on his own to evangelize. Then on December 6, 1947, while he was evangelizing for Youth for Christ in Hattiesburg, Mississippi, he got a phone call that stunned him to silence. William Riley had died.

Young College President

Since the spring of 1945, Billy had traveled to forty-seven states for Youth for Christ. He had flown more than 200,000 miles. He didn't have time for his own family. Yet he had promised William Riley. In a daze, Billy headed to Minneapolis to become the youngest college president in America. He was twenty-nine.

Like every job he did, he threw tremendous energy into it. Before long, he convinced Grady Wilson's brother, T. W., to take over as administrator.

With T. W. installed, Billy became an absentee president. He would return to Minneapolis often enough to see that the Northwestern Bible Schools flourished, but he refused any salary and went on with his evangelizing.

In Montreat, he bought a house across the street from Ruth's parents, and Ruth was happy to move into her own home. In May, another daughter was born, and they named her Anne.

In late 1948, Billy attended the formation of the World Council of Churches in Amsterdam. The organization espoused an ecumenical spirit that Billy approved of, but a liberal theology that he could not accept. But his attendance was in keeping with his character. Billy would not condemn fellow Christians.

As Billy drew away from Northwestern, he realized that he also wanted to leave the Youth for Christ organization. He wanted to evangelize on his own, but he was falling prey to discouragement. His former colleague Chuck Templeton was giving up evangelizing all together. He had enrolled at Princeton Theological Seminary and his theology was giving way to rationalism. He tried to pull Billy away from evangelizing, telling him he had stopped growing intellectually and his pulpit theology was too literal and simple-minded.

Shaken by Templeton's defection, Billy called his closest friends together in November 1948, to discuss ways to improve their evangelism. What emerged from this meeting with Cliff Barrows, Bev Shea, and Grady Wilson in Modesto, California, was a set of principles, dubbed the Modesto Manifesto, governing financial integrity, sexual purity, and credible reporting of the results of their evangelism campaigns.

He continued to talk to Chuck Templeton, who sank deeper into liberal theology. His doubts about the truth in Scripture shook Billy. How could he doubt the Bible?

"Is my theology outdated, intellectually shallow?" Billy kept asking himself. "Are parts of the Bible not true?"

Somehow he bounced back and continued. But depression and doubts returned as his biggest campaign ever loomed on the horizon: Los Angeles in September, 1949. How could he possibly pull himself together?

One month before the Los Angeles campaign was to begin, he was driving with Grady Wilson across Utah to a conference in California. Suddenly, he was overwhelmed with doubt. Tears poured down his cheeks.

Grady was staring at him. "What's the matter, buddy?"

"Templeton says I am committing intellectual suicide. Maybe he's right."

"Pull over on that jeep trail," barked Grady.

A few minutes later, he and Grady were on their knees in the scrubby desert, praying out loud, beseeching God for help. Billy gradually felt his old confidence return.

At the Forest Home conference center, his faith failed again. Chuck Templeton was at the conference, and he and his liberal theologians stumped Billy. Their attacks on the Bible were so dazzling that he couldn't argue with them.

That night he stumbled into the forest in doubt, as he had once roamed the golf course at Florida Bible Institute. He placed his Bible on a stump and knelt. "Oh God, I cannot prove certain things. I cannot answer some of the questions Chuck is raising, but I accept this book by faith as the Word of God." He rose. "From this moment on I surrender myself to God's hands—heart and soul."

In Los Angeles, Armin Gesswein and Edwin Orr had labored mightily for nine months and organized eight hundred prayer groups to pray for the success of the revival. The campaign had the support of more than two hundred and fifty local churches. Dawson Trotman had trained counselors to assist those who would come to the altar. Cliff Barrows recruited a top-notch choir and singing groups, and the dignified Bev Shea was prepared with his reverent hymns. He always preceded Billy's sermon to set the right tone.

Because they now embraced a greater audience than youth only, Billy had toned down the service, so that it was more a church service than a loud show. His gaudy clothing was gone. He now wore dark suits more often, though always with a handkerchief blossoming from the breast pocket.

Billy started with a passage from the black Bible he clutched. "The Bible says. . ." he would bellow, borrowing an old evangelist's phrase, before he went on to quote Scripture. Then began his ringing denunciation of those who disobeyed God's Word. He still stalked the platform and locked his eyes on several hundred people at once. But when he had them squirming, he would soften his tone for a while or move on to lambaste another segment of his audience.

After three weeks it was customary to extend the crusade if success merited it. So far, Billy's success had been marginal. The novelty was wearing off and the crowds were beginning to thin.

"I'll put out a fleece," Billy said somewhat nervously on Saturday, just one day before their last scheduled service. "It has been unseasonably cold or rainy ever since we got here. We'll see if the weather changes."

The weather had been cool every day, but on Sunday, the air was uncomfortably warm inside the tent. Billy announced that the revival would continue.

When a couple of local celebrities made publicized confessions of faith, interest in the revival began to grow. "We may need a larger tent," replied Billy, gnawing his fingernails. "I need to call Armin Gesswein. This is getting awfully big awfully fast now."

Celebrities like Gene Autry and Jane Russell began to attend the revival. Suddenly, the crusade was being touted in two Los Angeles newspapers, the *Herald* and the *Examiner,* with full page stories and photos of Billy haranguing the crowd like John the Baptist. Both Los Angeles newspapers were owned by William Randolph Hearst, who according to stories at the time had instructed his editors to "puff Graham."

The Canvas Cathedral overflowed at his last meeting, November 20. The seating inside had been expanded to nine thousand, but the crowd overflowed into the street. In eight weeks, Billy had drawn 350,000 listeners, of which three thousand had come to the altar to inquire.

"It will be kind of nice to get away from all the hub-bub for a while," said Billy to Ruth as they boarded the train to Minneapolis the next day. But the train was no refuge. Everyone seemed to know him now. The conductor and porters treated him like a celebrity, which embarrassed Billy. At Kansas City, reporters rushed inside the train, asking questions and popping flashbulbs. He wanted to tell them to back off, but wouldn't he be betraying his friends? Wasn't this publicity what the revival movement needed? Billy was suddenly overwhelmed by what happened in Los Angeles.

Overnight Celebrity

The next campaign was scheduled for Boston, and Billy's team could not have picked a tougher city to evangelize. Boston was dominated by Catholics, and its Protestant clergy were so stodgy they had refused to sponsor a Youth for Christ rally that Billy had once tried to hold there. Billy was scheduled for ten days, but there had been little advance work. Everyone had been too busy with Los Angeles.

The first night Billy preached to six thousand at Mechanic's Hall. When he gave the altar call, one hundred and seventy-five responded.

Bolstered by such success, the team announced an impromptu meeting the next afternoon. The only other notice of the meeting was in a few hastily amended Sunday morning church bulletins. Nevertheless, Billy preached to another six thousand. At the regularly scheduled meeting that night, two thousand had to be turned away. The next night they turned away seven thousand!

The response was stunning. Mindful of how success could corrupt, Billy invited his hosts to prayer. He beseeched them, "Pray that the Lord will remind me that this is His Glory! I must not take the tiniest bit of credit or His hand will leave me."

The Boston rallies grew. Billy was invited to open the state legislature with a prayer. Shifting auditoriums to accommodate the much larger than expected crowds, Billy's final meeting was at Boston Garden, where the Celtics played basketball. The revivalists jammed sixteen thousand inside, with another ten thousand standing outside.

The crowds inspired Billy to new heights. Yet he reminded himself constantly that he was speaking through the Holy Spirit. He must not take credit. He really believed that if he did, his power would end as suddenly as it did for Moses when he struck the rock at Kadesh.

Next, he preached for three weeks in Columbia, South Carolina. Willis Haymaker had organized prayer groups, which was standard operating procedure, but he seemed to do it better than anyone else had before. He also got local churches to block out certain nights so every meeting had the core of a good audience. Haymaker was the first to call the revivals a "crusade" to imply it was an ongoing effort that would not end when Billy left town.

Forty thousand people crowded inside a football stadium for the final rally in South Carolina. Ten thousand more were turned away. Billy preached about Noah and the flood as God's judgment. And there was a great flood of people who came to the altar. How could he top that?

He returned to New England and preached to a crowd estimated at fifty thousand by the Boston police. No one could doubt Billy had risen to prominence when he received an invitation to the White House after the New England crusade.

Grady Wilson was giddy. "The White House? President Truman?"

On July 14, Billy, Cliff Barrows, Grady Wilson, and Jerry Beaven, the newest member of the team, met with the single most powerful man in the world. After a cordial twenty-minute meeting, during which Billy asked Mr. Truman to declare a national day of repentance, the men prayed briefly with the president and were ushered out of his office.

Outside the White House, the four were besieged by reporters. Billy told them what he had said to the president and, after much cajoling from the assembled members of the press, the four men knelt on the White House lawn to offer a prayer of thanks.

The next day, Billy was criticized in the papers for repeating what had been said in his meeting with Truman. The president was reported to be angry about the incident on the White House lawn.

"Oh Lord, how puffed up we were," said Billy, remembering. "Pride. That's what did us in."

Billy moved on to his Portland Crusade, which was another staggering success. Meanwhile, two friends of the ministry, Walter Bennett and Fred Dienert, were negotiating a weekly radio program with the ABC network. At first, Billy was enthusiastic, but when he realized that the program would cost his organization $7,000 a week, he balked. ABC also wanted $25,000 up front to reserve time on the network.

Bennett and Dienert continued to pester Billy until he finally said, "If the Lord wants me to do this, I will have the $25,000 tonight—before midnight."

Billy waited until after the love offering had been collected before telling his audience about the radio opportunity. In a low-key, almost half-hearted way, he told them that if anyone wanted to encourage this kind of evangelism, they could donate money after the service.

Unbelievably, people lined up afterwards, coming one by one to contribute. When the money had all been counted, they had a total of $23,500.

"It's a miracle!" someone said.

"It's not enough," said Billy. "The devil is tempting us."

When the team returned to their hotel, they picked up their mail at the desk. When they opened the envelopes up in their room, they found checks totaling exactly enough to bring the sum to $25,000.

Billy wanted to call the radio program "Deciding for Christ," but Ruth volunteered "Hour of Decision." The team preferred Ruth's name and "The Hour of Decision" went on the air November 5, 1950, on over 150 ABC stations.

The program typically featured a Scripture reading by Grady Wilson, Jerry Beaven reading the news, Bev Shea singing a hymn to set the mood, and a sermon by Billy.

Expanding Vision

Finances were getting complicated. Billy had to be incorporated now that so much money was pouring in. He was given the salary of a minister of a large church. No more and no less. It was crucial to remain clear of any suspicion of money-grubbing. He objected to calling his organization the Billy Graham Evangelistic Association (BGEA), but even Ruth insisted that his name had to be in the title.

Within months, the number of radio stations carrying "The Hour of Decision" doubled. BGEA, headquartered in Minneapolis, grew larger and added people to write scripts and take care of a thousand details. The organization began compiling a mailing list of sympathetic supporters.

"BGEA won't use the list to hound folks for money," vowed Billy. But it didn't hurt to keep supporters informed of their opportunities and to drop the gentlest reminder that evangelism required money.

In 1950, Ruth gave birth to their third daughter on December 19. The infant was named Ruth Bell, but was almost immediately nicknamed "Bunny."

In 1951, Billy was talked into sponsoring Christian films. He formed World Wide Pictures, which made two movies called *Mr. Texas* and *Oiltown*.

Despite stinging criticism of the film as hopelessly amateurish, Billy shrugged and prayed their efforts would get better.

Billy also launched a weekly television show called "The Hour of Decision." The show aired stirring clips of his crusades. Other times, Billy sat in a comfortable chair as if in a home library and delivered a calm, reasoned, low-key message.

His radio and television shows inspired money to pour in to the Minneapolis office. Billy continued his citywide crusades, but he stopped all love offerings. Never again would he be embarrassed by a photograph showing his ministry carrying away what appeared to be bags of money after a crusade.

The crusades were still far from perfect. One great need was follow-up. Far too often, inquirers flooded to the altar, then waited in vain for counseling. It took many appeals by Billy, but he finally convinced Dawson Trotman, founder of the Navigators, to train his counselors full-time.

Another need was gnawing at him. He had always called everyone to the altar together, even calling out pointedly, "The ground is level at the foot of the cross. I want all white folks, all colored folks to come forward. . . ." Yet he was still setting aside sections for blacks. Wasn't it time for that to end? How could he approve of any form of segregation? He knew in his heart that segregation was not in Christ. But he was pragmatic. The Bible cautioned one to be wise in the worldly ways of men. White folks had to be won over gradually. Billy wasn't a hypocrite. He was committed to do something about segregation, but it would be slow and cautious.

In his crusades, Billy now praised the movers and shakers that he thought could be instrumental in stopping Communism. He wrote a letter to General Dwight

Eisenhower urging him to run for president.

After four years as president of Northwestern Bible Schools, Billy resigned to make way for a full-time replacement. He turned his attention to mounting a crusade in Washington, D.C., in early 1952. President Truman refused to endorse the crusade, but everything else fell neatly into place. One-third of the senators and one-fourth of the members of the House requested special reserved seating, and Speaker of the House Sam Rayburn arranged for Billy to hold his final rally on the steps of the Capitol. The crusade drew more than three hundred thousand in five weeks. Billy met General Douglas MacArthur and made many friends among politicians in both parties, including Lyndon Johnson and Richard Nixon.

Billy expanded his organization during 1952, adding a weekly newspaper column to his radio and television shows.

His son Franklin was born July 14, 1952. With four children now, Ruth accompanied Billy less and less. Billy purchased two hundred acres of wooded mountain behind their house, and Ruth seemed interested in building a home in a more secluded setting.

In November, Eisenhower ran for president as a Republican and won the election. Ike really seemed to like Billy and he picked him as his religious consultant for the inauguration.

During the Truman administration, Billy had tried to arrange a trip to war-torn Korea. In December, right before Truman left office, permission was abruptly granted. Billy's team flew overseas to an unexpectedly warm welcome. Commanding General Mark Clark personally greeted them. Billy was treated like a VIP, but his joy soon ended. Unlike Ruth, he had never before seen men mangled by war. One soldier, lying face down and totally helpless on a contraption in a hospital, begged to see Billy.

Billy crawled underneath to lie on the floor and pray with him. By the time Billy visited the combat zone, he felt no urge to be a drummer leading the charge. He wanted only to give the soldiers hope. And he prayed for the war to end.

Billy had to think about issues of race again. The Korean experience had really sobered him. Black soldiers were dying right beside white soldiers. In March 1953, at his Chattanooga crusade, Billy could not deny the truth of the Gospel any longer. He was angry when he saw ushers putting up ropes to separate blacks and whites. Why hadn't he noticed before? He strode back and ripped down the ropes himself. But it had an ironic result. The turnout of blacks was the poorest he ever had. They were uneasy sitting with whites.

In Dallas, where Billy fought unsuccessfully to prevent segregated seating, thousands of blacks attended. The answer to the race question was very complicated indeed. Hearts had to be changed.

In 1954, Billy decided to proceed with a crusade in England, despite severe criticism of him from across the Atlantic. The British press decried the "big business" American evangelist who was spending a staggering sum for the time—fifty thousand English pounds—to promote the crusade. While the team was enroute by ocean liner, a controversy erupted in Parliament over Billy's frequent criticisms of socialism, which he used almost interchangeably with communism. Members of Britain's Labour party sought to deny Billy admittance to the country.

It was not like Billy to go where he wasn't wanted, but Ruth reminded him that two key ingredients to a good crusade, prayer and publicity, were working for his success already.

Reports in the London newspapers were uncompromisingly vicious. Even the photographs of Billy were snide, one captioned: NO CLERICAL COLLAR, BUT MY! WHAT A LOVELY TIE!

The unrelenting hostility crippled Billy. The day of the first meeting he had one of his darkest moments. The ride to the meeting hall was somber. When they arrived, the dog racing track next door was lit up and thronging with patrons, but the parking lot to the Harringay Arena was almost empty. Billy trudged dejectedly inside.

Evangelist to England

I nside the arena, Billy had to blink his eyes. It was packed to the rafters! "Oh God, forgive me," he prayed, "for not trusting You. This is Your glory, not mine." Because the crusade was in London, many people had apparently taken the Underground to the meeting hall.

In the first sermon, Billy jabbed the air. "There's a hunger for God in London!" And he was right. Londoners flocked to the arena day after day. The Church of England quickly came into the fold, now realizing that not sponsoring Billy was a horrible blunder. They offered their own clergy as counselors, and Billy gratefully welcomed their participation.

By the end of twelve weeks, even the press fell under Billy's unrelenting sincerity and goodness. One of his most vicious detractors was a columnist named William Conner, who wrote for the *Daily Mirror* as "Cassandra." Billy countered his caustic criticism by writing him a letter, praising his ingenuity and offering, as he always did, to meet him for a "chat." Conner mocked Billy by inviting him to a pub. Billy not only showed up, but he won Conner's praise through friendliness and humility.

On the last day of the crusade, Billy spoke to crowds of 67,000 and 120,000 in stadiums at White City and

Wembley. The colossal success at Wembley triggered a prize invitation to meet Winston Churchill.

At noon on May 24, 1954, Billy found himself inside Number 10 Downing Street. After a brief exchange of pleasantries, Churchill suddenly asked Billy, "Is there any hope for this world?"

Billy was shocked. Was this the same man whose memorable speeches gave the British people and the world hope against the Nazi war machine? Had Churchill succumbed to pessimism? Or was he testing Billy?

Billy reached in his coat pocket and pulled out his New Testament. "Mr. Prime Minister, this fills me with hope!"

Churchill listened as Billy explained the message of Christ in his simple, direct way, and the two men exchanged views on the future of the world.

As they parted, Churchill said, "I do not see much hope for the world unless it is the hope you are talking about. We must return to God." Then he added, "You will keep this conversation private, I trust?" After his experience with President Truman, Billy was quick to assure Churchill of confidentiality.

After briefly considering the possibility of staying longer in Great Britain, Billy and the team pushed on to Scandinavia. He preached successful one-day meetings in Helsinki, Stockholm, and Copenhagen. He went on to Amsterdam and then Germany, where the European trip began to unravel.

In Düsseldorf, Billy awoke in the night with wracking pain. A doctor diagnosed a kidney stone and prescribed rest. But Billy couldn't pass up his next stop: Berlin. It was too important. The symbolism was gigantic.

He realized that God was sending him a message. Though he was weak and in pain, he would be spiritually strong through the Holy Spirit. That afternoon he preached to 80,000 at Olympic Stadium, including 20,000 East Berliners. Billy's short punchy sentences were ideal for translation, and thousands of Germans surged forward when Billy invited them to the altar. Knowing that the crusade team would not be able to counsel so many at once, Billy urged the inquirers to write letters, so local pastors would follow up.

A few days later in Paris, in spite of searing pain, he preached well again. His sermon was so well received, the team began planning a crusade for Paris. After that he returned to North Carolina where he had an operation for the kidney stone. Mercifully, the doctor ordered him to rest at home for six weeks. He was rundown and underweight, but the results of the Berlin crusade speeded his recovery. Sixteen thousand letters had been sent in by inquirers!

In March of 1955, Billy once again crossed the Atlantic, this time for his All-Scotland Crusade. This crusade was officially supported by the churches, and Kelvin Hall in Glasgow was booked solid for all six weeks.

The crusade never wavered. The response night after night was so gratifying that the organizers expanded by telephoned broadcasts into England, Ireland, and Wales. The climax was the Good Friday meeting where Billy was accessible by BBC television to virtually all of Britain! The media were saying that only Queen Elizabeth's coronation had been watched by so many Britons.

Communicating the Gospel

After a subsequent seven-day crusade back in England, Billy and Ruth were invited to meet with the queen mother and Princess Margaret. Five days later, in strictest confidence, he was allowed to preach to young queen Elizabeth and her retinue at Windsor Castle.

Billy moved on to Paris for five meetings, then blazed through twelve cities in Switzerland, Germany, Scandinavia, and Holland. He returned to America, then Canada, to hold a crusade in Toronto for three weeks.

In early 1956, Billy traveled to India. Measured by the size of the crowds he attracted, Billy was successful, but in his own mind the trip was successful because he recruited a man named Akbar Abdul-Haqq. Billy would bring him to America and train him to lead his own crusades in India. Turnouts of 100,000, with little advance preparation, proved the Indians were receptive.

Billy made one-day stops in the Philippines, Korea, Hong Kong, Formosa, Japan, and Hawaii on his return to America.

Back at Montreat, Billy got a surprise. Ruth and the children were in a new home, which Ruth called Little Piney Cove, on the property Billy and Ruth had bought on the mountain several years earlier.

GiGi was almost eleven, Anne eight, Bunny five, and Franklin three. Billy knew their family life was unusual. When he came home, Ruth deferred to his idea of discipline, but after an incident with GiGi, Billy became far more lax.

He had entered GiGi's room to scold her for rudeness after she slammed her door at the end of an argument, and she had snapped, "Some dad you are! You're never here."

Billy felt like she had slapped his face. His heart ached. What could he say? She was right. He was rarely there. After that he felt like a hypocrite trying to discipline the kids the strict way his father had disciplined him. His father was always there.

It was a long hot summer. The issue of racial injustice was simmering. Blacks no longer would submit to separate seating, separate water fountains, separate schools, and high poll taxes to discourage them from voting. Billy phoned the governors of North Carolina and Tennessee to urge them to address the racial problems from a spiritual point of view and promote justice.

His viewpoint became well-known and response to his moderation was swift. He was attacked by integrationists on one side and segregationists on the other.

Since Christmas of 1954, Billy and his father-in-law, Nelson Bell, had talked about a magazine for evangelicals similar to *Christian Century*, the magazine that liberal Christians had published for many years.

In the fall of 1955, Nelson Bell resigned his surgical practice to ramrod the magazine, already called *Christianity Today*. By the middle of 1956, Carl Henry was appointed managing editor, and the first issue was scheduled for the fall.

In many ways, Billy felt that *Christianity Today* was the last cog in the evangelical machine he had built, even if the magazine was semi-independent. People were even calling Billy's movement the New Evangelicalism to distinguish it from Fundamentalism.

In November of 1956, Eisenhower was re-elected easily over Adlai Stevenson. Billy still had a good friend in the White House. He became totally absorbed in getting ready for his New York campaign in May of 1957. BGEA reserved Madison Square Garden for several weeks. The Protestant Council of New York, representing thirty-one denominations and 1,700 churches, had presented a united front in inviting Billy to New York, but Billy was immediately attacked from Fundamentalists on the right and the liberal theologian Reinhold Neibuhr on the left.

It was soon obvious the results in New York were going to be staggering. Night after night Billy preached to nearly 20,000 people. After it was clear he was going to pack the Garden every night, BGEA approached ABC to buy airtime for nationwide Saturday night specials. The first one on June 1 competed with television giants Jackie Gleason and Perry Como on the other two networks. Billy got only twenty percent of the total viewers—a distant third—yet he reached an astounding six million viewers! The power of television was awesome.

BGEA began to get 50,000 letters a week. Billy topped himself in New York week after week. He appeared as a guest on all the network news shows. And in an inspired move, Billy invited Martin Luther King, Jr., the black civil rights leader, to open one service at the Garden in prayer.

He preached to more than two million people, drawing 55,000 inquirers for Christ. After drawing 100,000 into Yankee Stadium, he drew 200,000 people into Times Square for his finale.

To the Ends of the Earth

As 1958 began, a second son, Nelson Edman, was born, and immediately dubbed "Ned."

The team went to Central America for three weeks, San Francisco for seven weeks, Sacramento for one week, and Charlotte for several weeks. Those crusades sprouted more opportunities.

That fall, racists bombed a high school in Clinton, Tennessee, that had just been desegregated. Billy stepped forward to declare, "Every Christian should take his stand against these outrages."

One day in January, 1959, when Billy was playing golf, his club head kept missing the ball. "The ground has ridges in it," he explained to Grady Wilson.

"Lord have mercy," Grady chuckled. "That's a new excuse, buddy."

Suddenly, pain stabbed Billy's left eye.

At the Mayo Clinic, doctors found that Billy suffered edema in his left eye and ordered him to rest. Meanwhile, crusades were scheduled to begin in Australia and New Zealand in just a few weeks. Billy rested in Hawaii with Ruth, but he was not idle.

When he opened in Melbourne in February, the crusade had to move immediately from a 10,000-seat facility to a sprawling outdoor amphitheater where crowds swelled to 25,000, and finally to 70,000. At Melbourne's finale at the Cricket Ground, turnstiles admitted 130,000 before police simply opened other gates to relieve the incoming flood of people.

In Sydney, Billy preached to 70,000, with speakers reaching another 80,000 in an adjacent show ground. In just four weeks, Billy preached to one million Australians.

Back in America, Billy held two rallies in Little Rock. Racist groups mounted hate campaigns, but Governor Faubus shrewdly urged segregationists to leave Billy alone.

The next year, 1960, was a year of great temptation for Billy. Oh, how he wanted to meddle in the presidential election! Since 1956, Billy had indulged in political strategies with Richard Nixon, confiding what he thought would happen if Nixon were to run against this Democrat or that Democrat. But Billy knew that dabbling in politics was wrong for his ministry.

He started an African crusade in January, but they skipped South Africa when Billy found out that blacks could not attend his rallies there.

He opened to small crowds in Liberia and Ghana, but had better attendance in Nigeria, where Billy drew more than 100,000 in one week. In Nigeria, he was invited to a leper colony and witnessed firsthand the ravages of that disease.

When the Muslims managed to have his invitation to the Sudan withdrawn, he went on to Kenya, Tanganyika, and Rhodesia.

He was received with open arms in Ethiopia, a country with a Christian tradition back to the Apostle Philip. In Egypt, Billy learned that a full-scale crusade might be possible, but he decided it would be too provocative in an overwhelmingly Muslim country.

In Israel, he was not allowed to hold public meetings,

and he was warned not to mention the name of Jesus to any Jew. But Billy made the most of his time. He felt he convinced influential Israeli politicians Abba Eban and Golda Meir that he was a true friend of Israel.

Back in America, Billy was nagged by the temptation to support Nixon publicly in the 1960 election. Finally, he offered to come out openly for Nixon on "Meet the Press" in June. Nixon demurred. "Stay out of politics," he advised.

Nevertheless, the election drew him like a moth to a flame. He couldn't keep out of it. And other religious leaders were drawn to it, too.

"We're not leaving for Europe any too soon," said Ruth.

In Switzerland, where Billy would crusade for one month, the entire Graham family were guests of Ara Tchividjian, a wealthy man converted through Billy's book *Peace with God.* Billy preached one-week revivals in Berne, Basal, and Lausanne, followed by two days in Zurich.

After Switzerland, Billy returned to Germany. At the finale of a one-week crusade, Billy preached to 25,000 Germans, many from East Germany. He resisted speaking out against Communism. He had learned to speak the truth while avoiding fruitless provocations.

When Billy returned to America he busied himself with a three-day crusade in New York for Hispanics and publishing the first issue of *Decision,* the new official magazine for BGEA.

Billy became so worried about the election, he offered to write an article for *Life* magazine, not denigrating Kennedy but building up Nixon. Ruth was appalled that he was going so public. Within days, Billy regretted it himself and tried to get Henry Luce to pull the article. But Luce only pulled it after Kennedy got wind of the article and personally complained.

Family Changes

When Kennedy won the election, Billy had no time for lamentations. Within two weeks, he was invited to play golf with the president-elect in Florida, but the meeting was delayed when John Kennedy, Jr., was born. Billy finally met Kennedy in January for their game of golf. That evening, Kennedy held a press conference and unexpectedly called on Billy to address the religious questions that were still surfacing. Billy said truthfully that Kennedy's election had bridged the gulf between Protestants and Catholics, and that religion might never be an issue in a presidential campaign again.

After four months in Florida, including a three-week crusade in Miami and shorter revivals in other cities, Billy headed to England for a crusade in Manchester. The crusade drew an average of 30,000 every night—even though Billy was sick the first week.

During that summer, President Kennedy met with the Russian leader Khrushchev, and in August, the Berlin Wall was erected to keep East Germans from fleeing to the west.

Back in America, Billy crusaded during the fall in Philadelphia, then attended one of the rare assemblies of the World Council of Churches in New Delhi, India.

Although he was still not a member, his presence reflected the attitude of his new evangelicalism: All Christians must all work together for Christ.

The following year, he crusaded in El Paso, Chicago, and South America. The South American crusade, split into two separate campaigns, lasted a total of nine weeks. Billy blazed through the Catholic bastions of Colombia, Venezuela, Paraguay, Uruguay, Chile, Argentina, and Brazil. Every city was an adventure.

Sandwiched between the South American trips, Billy held a very successful crusade in Chicago in June, drawing 40,000 night after night to the McCormick Place. At the finale in Soldier Field, he spoke to 116,000, one of his largest American audiences ever.

In August 1962, Billy's father died. For several years Frank had suffered small strokes, each time surviving but a little weaker, a little shakier. Finally, one morning in the hospital, while calmly talking to his doctor, he quietly expired.

In September, Billy and Ruth got a letter from Stephan Tchividjian, the son of Ara Tchividjian, the man who had been their host in Switzerland. Stephan very formally asked for GiGi's hand in marriage.

In the second half of 1963, Billy crusaded in the Los Angeles Coliseum, drawing more than 130,000 at the finale.

Billy was playing golf the day that Kennedy was assassinated. When he heard the news, he and T. W. Wilson went on the air at a radio station owned by BGEA. Billy tried to reassure the listeners.

Within hours the nation knew that President Kennedy was dead and that Lyndon Johnson was flying back to Washington.

Billy was allowed to sit with the Kennedy family at the funeral, and he offered his services to Lyndon Johnson.

Johnson had a long history as an overbearing, arm-twisting, loud-mouthed legislator from Texas. He had never expected to become President. Powerbrokers like Johnson just did not get elected.

Billy was invited to the White House within one week. He was not surprised when he was allowed only fifteen minutes. Billy tried to bring LBJ the peace of God. Fifteen minutes became five hours.

Billy cemented the friendship by telling the press, "Lyndon Johnson is the most qualified man ever to take on the presidency."

BGEA now got millions of letters. Billy had millions of supporters around the country. His pavilion at the World's Fair in New York drew millions of visitors.

He resumed his crusades, the most notable being in Boston.

A meeting was arranged with Cardinal Cushing. The Cardinal shocked Billy by urging Catholics to go to the crusade meetings. "I'm one hundred percent for Dr. Graham," said the Cardinal. "The hand of God must be upon him."

Billy and Ruth became grandparents. Billy was just forty-five when GiGi gave birth to the first grandchild, and Ruth a mere forty-three. Ruth still had six-year-old Ned at home herself!

Billy launched 1965 with a crusade in Hawaii, followed by Copenhagen and Denver. Then, at Lyndon Johnson's request, he visited Selma, Alabama. On Easter Sunday, he held a large, integrated rally in Birmingham.

Billy had another book published. *World Aflame* sold 100,000 copies in the first three months. The title was apt for current events in America. Never had America seen so much rebellion. Some blacks had tired of the American process and now spouted Communist rhetoric. College students were violently opposed to fighting in Vietnam.

Critics of this new rude behavior, like Billy, seemed old-fashioned. The turn had been so sudden and so ugly, Billy and many others were flabbergasted.

When Billy went to England in 1966, he saw further proof. The deterioration of spirit had gone much farther there than in America. Decay was in the very heart of the church. Leading clerics simply could no longer swallow the truths of the Gospel.

By any measurement, the crusade at Earls Court Arena in London was a success. Billy preached in person to more than one million people in only one month, and another innovation was added: closed-circuit television to ten English cities. This state-of-the-art production almost outdid the live event. A giant screen showed Billy up close, something few saw at the real event. The sound was crisp and clear.

Influence and Politics

B ack in Montreat, Anne Graham married Danny Lotz. Bunny and Franklin were at Stony Brook, a boarding school in New York. Only nine-year-old Ned was at home during the school year.

Billy went to Vietnam for Christmas. He preached twenty-five times, often combining talents with Bob Hope. Vietnam was far worse than he had thought. The situation was profoundly depressing.

In his citywide crusades, his preaching had fallen into a very successful format. In his experience, people suffered from four maladies: emptiness, loneliness, guilt, and fear of death. Unless he was speaking to a specific audience, he would tackle one of those main four human miseries. Then Billy called them forward.

He was always very uneasy during the call to the altar. But as dozens of lost souls started to come forward for salvation, he was overwhelmed by his gift. He would plant his chin in his right hand, suddenly very self-conscious, reminding himself they were responding to the Holy Spirit, not Billy Graham.

Nineteen sixty-seven was the first year Billy really cut back. His schedule was limited to an Earls Court follow-up and eight-day crusades in Puerto Rico, Winnipeg, Kansas City, and Tokyo.

Billy spent a lot of time with Lyndon Johnson. Two dozen times he had been a guest at Camp David, the White House, or the LBJ Ranch. The war was crushing Johnson. He had attained the pinnacle, and he had the legislative skills to move the nation any direction he wanted. But the failure of the war drained him.

For 1968, Billy had crusades scheduled for Australia, Portland, Pittsburgh, and San Antonio. While he was in Australia, the world turned topsy-turvy. Johnson announced he would not run again. Days later, Martin Luther King was killed by a sniper. That summer, Robert Kennedy was assassinated in Los Angeles.

Billy intended to stay away from the nomination and election processes for president in 1968, but he was kidding only himself. At the Portland crusade, just before the Republican convention, he introduced Julie and Tricia Nixon. At the convention, he led the delegates in prayer after Richard Nixon delivered his acceptance speech.

Nixon squeaked out the narrowest of victories over Hubert Humphrey. The next morning, Billy met Nixon for breakfast. Nixon asked him to led them in prayer for the great job ahead.

In March 1969, Billy was called to Walter Reed Hospital in Washington, D.C. Eisenhower had been there for almost a year, dying. He had asked for Billy. They talked about eternity. Four days later, Ike died.

Billy continued his crusades during the Nixon years, talking with Nixon occasionally and with Nixon's chief of staff, H. R. Haldeman, weekly. His special status with Nixon's White House thrilled him and bothered him at the same time. God forgive him if he was being used. It seemed Nixon genuinely respected him and used him for a sounding board. It seemed that he and Nixon were truly friends.

On the home front in 1969, Bunny married Ted Dienert, the son of the advertising executive who years before had pestered Billy into starting "The Hour of Decision." All three daughters were now married, every one by the age of eighteen. Franklin had returned home from Stony Brook in New York to finish high school in a local public school. Determined not to be a "preacher boy," he smoked and drank, and topped his image with long hair. He rode a motorcycle and terrorized young Ned.

In October of 1971, Charlotte held a Billy Graham Day and invited President Nixon to speak. Nixon was superb, speaking warmly about Billy without notes.

Billy finally held a meeting in South Africa. For years he had refused to hold a revival in South Africa unless everyone was allowed to attend in unrestricted seating. The government acquiesced in 1973. The crowd of 45,000 at Durban's Kings Park was completely integrated.

Two months later, he campaigned in South Korea, and the first service drew 500,000 Koreans! By the finale, expectations for a huge turnout were extremely high. But the crowd exceeded even those expectations. Never had there been a crowd like this for a religious service. Its respectful silence made the attendance of 1,100,000 even harder to believe. In five days, Billy preached to three million South Koreans.

When the Watergate scandal hit the news in 1973, Billy at first was skeptical. He told Ruth, "It will all blow over."

Family and Business Crises

The summer of 1973 was a sad one for the Grahams. In August, Nelson Bell, eighty and diabetic, passed away. Ruth's mother clung to life, her voice gone from a stroke. In the fall, Nixon's vice president, Spiro Agnew, resigned.

In April 1974, Nixon petulantly released transcripts of selected tapes, and claimed loudly to the nation he was innocent of any wrongdoing. After his Phoenix campaign in May, Billy finally sat down to read the transcripts of the Oval Office tapes. Astonishment turned to horror. The Nixon on the tapes was a man he didn't know. Nixon was foul, cynical, and hateful. Billy prayed several days, then composed a watered-down press release deploring the moral tone of the White House.

On August 9, 1974, Nixon resigned. Billy wanted to console him, but Nixon would not take his calls. Some critics wanted to tar and feather Billy along with Nixon, implying that he was an insider. The truth was that Billy knew more of the inner workings of Lyndon Johnson's White House than Nixon's. As usual, Billy ignored the slander and innuendoes.

In October, Billy crusaded in South America, and Ruth took the opportunity to visit GiGi and the grandchildren. In Brazil, Billy got a phone call from GiGi. Ruth was in a coma in the hospital! She had rigged up a pipe slide for the kids to play on, and had fallen fifteen feet when a wire had broken as she was testing it.

Oh God, prayed Billy, *don't take Ruth yet.* How could he continue without her? Ruth regained consciousness, but her memory was a shambles. What else could go wrong? thought Billy. Then Ruth's mother died. Ruth could barely stand on crutches at the funeral. Over the weeks, Ruth recovered her memory, but her hip deteriorated, and surgery loomed somewhere in the future.

Meanwhile, on a summer trip to Switzerland and the Holy Land, the Lord had become real to Franklin, and he had accepted Jesus as his Lord.

Billy backed away from Washington, D.C. Never again would he delude himself into being unofficial chaplain of the White House—thinking he was advancing the Gospel while he was actually being used as a small political pawn.

He invited President Ford to a crusade, as he had invited every president since Truman in 1952, but Ford declined.

Away from the crusade circuit in 1975, the Billy Graham Evangelistic Association had two major successes: the movie *The Hiding Place*, about the heroic ten Boom family of Holland, and Billy's book, *Angels,* which became a best-seller.

When Jimmy Carter was elected, Billy was quick to announce his full support for the new president, but Billy did not attend the inauguration, the first one he had missed in twenty years. Although he was a guest at the White House within a month, Billy's relationship with Carter was congenial but cool, much as it had been with Ford.

In March 1977, while Billy was crusading in Las Vegas, Grady Wilson suffered a massive heart attack back in North Carolina. Grady had always been the one who kicked Billy in the seat of the pants when his nose was too high in the air. Billy rushed east to visit his old friend. Grady recovered and Billy soon had little time to think about anything but his own reputation.

In the spring of 1977, the *Charlotte Observer* ran a detailed series on the financial structure of the Billy Graham Evangelistic Association. The newspaper reported that BGEA spent as much money every year as it collected, that all financial decisions had to be approved by an executive committee made up of outside directors who did not receive payments from BGEA, and that the executive committee had set up a trust, administered by a bank, to direct the royalties from Billy's books. In short, the *Observer* found BGEA to be squeaky clean.

That summer, however, the *Observer* screamed betrayal and hypocrisy when their investigative reporters discovered another organization connected with Billy that had amassed more than twenty million dollars. The World Evangelism and Christian Education Fund (WECEF) had nine board members who were also directors of BGEA, and the other two WECEF directors were Ruth Graham and her brother Clayton.

Billy now had to devote much time to defending himself. He explained on "The Hour of Decision" that WECEF was a separate organization established to promote three missions: a planned training center for laymen, in Asheville; an evangelism training center in Wheaton, Illinois; and funding for three youth programs: Campus Crusade, the Fellowship of Christian Athletes, and Young Life. The surplus of money had been accumulated to finance construction for the training centers. WECEF was no secret. Billy had announced its creation in Minneapolis in 1970.

Later, Billy remembered that in 1976 he had discussed WECEF candidly with a reporter, who had taped the conversation. When the *Observer* was presented with this information but refused to retract their accusations, Billy managed to get the tape released to the Associated Press. The AP printed the truth about WECEF, as well as several editorials scolding the *Observer* for not setting the record straight.

Although Billy had always been careful with money, he now realized that all evangelical organizations needed to be more diligent. He immediately set about to organize a council which would hold evangelical organizations accountable for the way they handled money. Within two years, the Evangelical Council for Financial Accountability (ECFA) was formed and BGEA was one of the first voluntary members.

Later in 1977, Billy prepared to fly to Hungary for a full-fledged crusade. Access to this Soviet-bloc nation had been engineered in part by Dr. Alex Haraszti, a Hungarian-born doctor who had emigrated to escape Communism.

Haraszti explained that America had two things that Hungary wanted. Since the end of World War II, Hungary's most precious religious symbol, the Crown of St. Stephen, Hungary's patron saint, had been stored at Fort Knox. The United States refused to return it, claiming that Hungary's current government was a puppet controlled by the Russians. The Hungarian government also wanted "most-favored-nation" trade status with the United States.

"These things can only be obtained at the highest level of government," said Billy, but he promised to speak to President Carter about these issues.

By late 1977, Billy opened his crusade in a church in Budapest. At first, the small crowds were mildly hostile, but Billy's preaching won their hearts. By the end of the ten days, he had met with Jewish leaders and government officials and had preached several times, once to a crowd of 30,000. The Hungarian triumph seemed to break down the barriers to eastern European; the following year, Billy preached in Poland.

In 1980, Ronald Reagan was elected president. Billy had known Reagan for more than twenty-five years and knew him to be disarmingly affable but resolute. A friend told Billy, "In many ways, Reagan is just like you, Billy." Both men were masters of communication. Both were honest men who had visions of what the world was about. And both men were not afraid to delegate authority.

Later that year, Billy went to China with Ruth, her brother Clayton, and her sisters Rosa and Virginia. They visited the old Bell family mission in Tsingkiang. Ruth had tried to arrange the trip for years, and the arrangements were finally expedited by Richard Nixon, who had remained a friend of Billy's. They had reconciled several months after Nixon's resignation. The China trip was far more than a venture in nostalgia for the Bells. Billy had been briefed on which officials he had to convince if he ever hoped to crusade in China. He met with them and patiently explained the virtues of Christianity. Then he went home and waited for God's will to be done.

Back in Charlotte, after a series of strokes, Billy's mother, who was nearly ninety years old, died in August, 1981. "I never felt more mortal," said Billy, now sixty-two. Was he, too, winding down at long last? What was left for him to accomplish?

Worldwide Evangelism

I n 1978, Billy had established a genuine rapport with the Catholic clerics in Poland, and in 1981 he met with the pope for the first time. They discussed relations among the great Christian movements, the rise of evangelicalism, and how Christians should respond to moral issues.

Billy now turned his attention to the third great goal of his life: world peace. World peace could never be attained without dealing with Communism. Billy's most immediate goal was to crusade into the very center of Communism.

"To reach the center—Russia—would be a real blow for Christ," he prayed.

Once again it was the uncanny shrewdness of Alex Haraszti that brought it about. Jumpy diplomats at the American State Department urged him privately not to go, hinting that President Reagan was very much against it.

The Sunday before Billy was to leave, he was invited to lunch with Vice President George Bush—and the Reagans showed up. The president pulled Billy aside and assured him that he must go to Russia. In May 1982, Billy and his team arrived in Moscow—to preach the Gospel of Jesus Christ! In Moscow, after a series of changes imposed by the Communists, who were determined that Billy would not draw a large crowd of Russians, he preached at a church, unannounced, very early on a Sunday morning. The sermon still drew an audience of one thousand. The Communists intercepted others trying to get there and kept them behind barricades several blocks away. But Billy was delighted.

The secular press magnified every gaffe that Billy made. When he spoke of religious freedom in Russia, in the hope it would come about, the press chided him for being a backward rube, a dupe of the Russians.

In 1983, Billy spearheaded a world conference for evangelists to instruct them on how to compose sermons, how to draw crowds, how to raise money, how to use videos, and every other aspect of day-to-day evangelizing. The conference in Amsterdam was called the International Conference for Itinerant Evangelists, or ICIE. It drew nearly four thousand preachers from one hundred countries.

During the early 1980s, Billy held crusades in Canada, Japan, Mexico, and England as well as Anaheim, Anchorage, Baltimore, Boston, Boise, Chapel Hill, Fort Lauderdale, Hartford, Houston, Oklahoma City, Orlando, San Jose, Spokane, and Tacoma.

In September 1984, Billy finally got his first full-fledged crusade in Russia, where Billy was allowed to preach over twelve days in four cities: Moscow, Leningrad, Novosibirsk, and Tallinin in Estonia. An added benchmark on this trip came when Billy's son Franklin, newly ordained, preached with him.

In 1986, Amsterdam again hosted the ICIE conference. This time, more than nine thousand evangelists attended and some of the success stories from the previous conference were staggering. A Kenyan who had seen only 130 converts in ten years, was now seeing nearly ten thousand come to Christ each year!

The ICIE also hatched a plan to utilize the newly available communication satellites to broadcast live Billy's London and Latin American crusades. They called this new venture "Mission World."

In 1986, Billy held a Greater Washington, D.C., crusade, enlisting help from the outset from black churches. Other crusades followed in Columbia, South Carolina; Denver; Tallahassee, Florida; and abroad in France and Helsinki, Finland.

In 1987, Billy felt helpless as he watched evangelism tainted by immorality, dishonesty, and bizarre behavior. First, Billy's old friend Oral Roberts solicited funds by saying that he would be taken to heaven if several million dollars were not raised for his medical school in Tulsa. Next, it was discovered that Jim Bakker of PTL Ministries had paid hush money to a church secretary with whom he had had an affair. He was later convicted and jailed on fraud charges stemming from his financial dealings at PTL. The third blow came when popular televangelist Jimmy Swaggart, who had self-righteously condemned Bakker publicly, was discovered with a prostitute.

In the fall of 1987, Grady Wilson finally succumbed to heart disease. Billy never felt more regret than at Grady's funeral. Though overshadowed by Billy's fame, Grady had been a fine preacher. And he was the one who loosened up worriers like Lyndon Johnson and Richard Nixon with his barrage of humor.

Beyond America, the world was changing. The Berlin Wall came down and the Soviet Union dissolved. Billy achieved another goal with a crusade in mainland China. After he and Ruth received a rousing welcome in Beijing, Billy began a five-city crusade, and he spent one hour with Premier Li Peng.

Billy still enjoyed influence with the White House.

He attended state dinners and led prayers at both nominating conventions in the summer of 1988, and he was invited to give the prayer at George Bush's inauguration.

In 1989, he preached in Hungary again, this time in a stadium full of 100,000 nominal Communists. His massive Mission World satellite-broadcast outreach was launched from London live to Britain, Ireland, and ten African countries. Delayed broadcasts were received by another twenty-three African countries. In late 1990, Mission World reached millions in Asia from Billy's live crusade in Hong Kong.

Billy followed up crusades in New Jersey and New York with a massive rally in Central Park, which topped the Times Square rally of 1957 by drawing 250,000.

In 1992, Billy penetrated the most recalcitrant Communist country in the world: North Korea for five days. Christianity was thriving in South Korea, growing at a rate no one could have imagined just a decade earlier. The church was a force to be recognized in Asia.

Over the years, Billy had dealt with many illnesses: kidney stones, hernias, ulcers, tumors, polyps, hypertension, pneumonia, prostate trouble, and broken ribs. He didn't get much sympathy from Ruth, who hid her illnesses like the great Livingstone and had scant sympathy for "hypochondriacs." But during the summer of 1992, even Ruth was stunned when Billy was diagnosed with Parkinson's disease.

Continuing His Course

Billy's symptoms of the progressive nervous disorder were tremors in his hands and fatigue. "God comes with greater power when we are weak," answered Billy to anyone who implied he should retire at age seventy-three.

But when Billy was reminded that his father had lived to be seventy-four, his Grandpa Crook Graham had lived to be seventy, and Grandpa Ben Coffey had lived to be seventy-three, Billy decided he would slow down, just a bit.

He returned to Russia in October of 1992, for a full-scale, city-wide crusade in Moscow. Attendance averaged 45,000. The number of inquirers ran up to twenty-five percent instead of the usual two percent. The Russians had been denied Christ for seventy-five years and Billy had never seen such spiritual hunger. Evangelism continued worldwide by radio, prime-time television specials, satellite networking, magazines, movies, and citywide crusades.

In 1994, Billy ventured into the Far East again. His four-day Tokyo crusade was his best ever in Japan. He followed that success with ten days of preaching in China. And, this time, Billy was allowed to preach in North Korea. In March 1995, Bob Williams implemented his latest version of Global Mission. From San Juan, Billy's three nights of sermons went to thirty satellites that sent them on to 185 countries. Only China did not participate. The goal was to reach one billion people!

In June of 1995, Billy collapsed at a luncheon in Toronto just before the five-day crusade was to begin. At seventy-six, he was now constantly reminded of his mortality. He recovered enough to preach at the fourth night of the crusade to a turnout of 73,500, the largest crowd ever at the Skydome.

In moments of exhaustion, Billy reflected on retiring. He felt fulfilled. Only God knew how many people he had preached to one way or another. More than any evangelist in history, he fulfilled the Great Commission. And though his health was considerably weakened, Billy continued to evangelize. As he had said so many times, "I'll keep opening doors. God will sort it all out."

CORRIE
TEN BOOM

Beginnings

As far back as Corrie ten Boom could remember, her home was *gezellig*, close and warm and cozy—smelling of soup and fresh bread, and sounding of soft laughter and the rustles of Mama and three aunts in long dresses. When she was five, Corrie would have wonderful parties with her doll Casperina under the dining room table. She could even creep down the steps into Papa's workroom behind the clock shop that faced Barteljoris-straat. Silently she sat and smelled his cigar and listened to clocks ticking like hundreds of heartbeats. She watched Papa bent over his bench. Each time he placed some tiny thing in a watch he would pause and say, "Thank You, Lord," as gently as if he were talking to Corrie or Mama. God must have been right there with him.

Aunt Bep called Corrie the "baby" of the family. Corrie didn't like to be called a baby. Out in the alley, Corrie was just one of many children who played there. Corrie skipped rope by herself or joined the other children to play bowl-the-hoop or a game with a ball and stones called *bikkelen.*

By the time Corrie was ten, she had the nickname Kees. It was boy's name because she was a tomboy. Betsie was a tall, delicate, sloe-eyed seventeen-year-old with thick chestnut hair. Nollie was twelve, solid and blonde, with a square face and nose so perfect they belonged on a princess. Both sisters turned the heads of boys like magnets. But then there was Corrie. She was lengthened and strengthened in all the wrong places. She became pigeon-toed and high-hipped. Her lips were wide and so thin they were a cartoon. Her jaw got stubborn and never softened. Her eyes, turned down on the corners, would have seemed perpetually sorrowful if she hadn't smiled so much. Such slight differences between beautiful and homely!

Extended Family

As Corrie grew up, she began to care about her manners. She didn't want to be a tomboy. She knew she would never be beautiful, and she would never have the desire or flair for elegant clothes that Betsie and Nollie had. But she did want to be a young lady. No one could long resist the love of a family so grounded in Christ.

Corrie had three aunts who lived with the ten Booms. Aunt Bep's sour outlook on life was only a mild irritation. Corrie understood that Aunt Bep was to be tolerated and loved. Aunt Jans, on the other hand, was imperious and demanding, but also generous. Her husband, Hendrick Wildeboer, who had died young, had been a minister. Then there was wise Aunt Anna. She was the one who added a sash or ribbon to Corrie's Christmas dress so it would look a little different each Sunday and on every special occasion as she wore it for the obligatory year.

Corrie's sisters and brother were the best of friends. Willem was witty, but too often lapsed into seriousness, even gloom. Nollie was the strong sister. Of all the children, Corrie was the most "normal," rarely ill or in trouble. Betsie was a sleepy-eyed beauty, but had resolved never to marry because she had anemia.

Although barely forty years old, Corrie's mother lived

in white-knuckled pain from gallstones. When the pain became too intense, she resorted to surgery. But after she had a minor stroke, the doctor gave her bad news: The surgery was too dangerous now; she just had to bear the pain of the gallstones. She never acted the martyr, but always the peacemaker. It was Mama who understood what was in someone's mind in a flash and smoothed things over before anyone else even realized what was happening. It was Mama who knitted baby clothes or wrote cheery messages for shut-ins—often from her own sickbed!

And then there was Papa, well-known as the best watchmaker in Holland. But he was much more than a superb watchmaker. He came from a long line of ten Booms who were never afraid to take God's side as revealed in the Bible. Papa's grandfather Gerrit lost his job as a gardener because he spoke up against Napoleon. Papa's father, Willem, the original watchmaker at Barteljorisstraat, had started a Society for Israel—a fellowship to pray for the Jews—in 1844 when it was unpopular to befriend the Jews.

Papa also loved the Jews. In his first years as a watchmaker in the poor Jewish section of Amsterdam, he read the Old Testament—their Talmud—with them and even celebrated their Sabbath and holy days. He lived fifteen fruitful years in Amsterdam, where he met Mama and where all the ten Boom children were born. Aunt Anna and Aunt Bep also lived with him in Amsterdam.

When his father died and his mother needed help with the shop, Papa returned to Haarlem.

It seemed that every evening at the ten Booms' home blossomed with activity. A favorite pastime was reading aloud wonderful books by writers like Charles Dickens or Louisa May Alcott. Often the family would sing—everything from hymns to the Bach chorale "Seid froh die Weil." Willem sang tenor, Nollie soprano, and Corrie alto.

Another favorite was Bible study combined with language study. Mama would read a passage in Dutch. Willem would read the same passage in Hebrew or Greek. Papa or Betsie would read it in German. Nollie would read it in French. And Corrie would read the same passage in English. She learned to read English and German almost as well as her native Dutch.

It seemed every member of the family was a natural organizer. Aunt Jans organized a soldier's center and went there herself to give Bible lessons and sing hymns. Aunt Anna organized a club for servant girls. Every Wednesday, she would meet with her girls for Bible study and hymns. Papa published a little magazine for watchmakers, and he was always involved in civic events such as the annual parade for the queen's birthday.

By the time Corrie was a teenager, she had a perspective on life that never changed. She had Jesus in her heart. She was a lady. She loved Holland and the queen. She knew a good family was a wonderful blessing not to be neglected.

Romantic Notions

Corrie was fourteen years old when she met Karel, a college friend of her brother's. Tall and blond, nineteen-year-old Karel was polite, but his deep brown eyes remained aloof.

It was not unusual for Corrie to be struck by love. She had loved every boy in her class at one time or another—secretly, of course. But this love for Karel was different. Here he was right in her home. That familiarity made him special, as if he, like her family, cared nothing about how she looked but cared only about what was in her heart.

Two years later, Nollie and Corrie visited Willem at the university in Leiden. When Karel stopped by shortly after the girls arrived, he won Corrie's heart. Somewhere in the exchange of pleasant introductions, he looked at Corrie and said, "Why, of course. We already know each other."

Then Karel asked her if she were going to Normal School next year. Corrie blurted, "No, I'm staying home with Mama and Aunt Anna."

Later as they returned home on the train, her childishly weak answer lingered with her. Yet she was needed at home more than ever. Aunt Bep had tuberculosis and lay coughing in her room most of the time. Aunt Anna tended to her, so that none of the others would be exposed. Mama was not strong either.

Corrie finished secondary school and began working at home. One day, she felt hot and weak. When the doctor made his regular call on Aunt Bep, Mama asked him, "Can you examine Corrie? She seems feverish to me."

The doctor examined her and then said, "Corrie has tuberculosis." Her future was suddenly yanked away from her as cruelly as a fish hooked from the North Sea!

The doctor ordered bed rest immediately. Corrie was stunned. How could this be happening? Her life seemed barely started, but tuberculosis for people with little money was a death sentence. Only an expensive sanitarium and special care could save a victim of the dreaded lung disease. How could God do this to her?

She hid her bitterness. In a house full of chronically sick women, such as Aunt Bep, Aunt Jans, and Mama, how could she complain? She didn't want to be sour like Aunt Bep.

Willem came by to sit with her. His exams were coming up. He had her drill him on theology, and he left some books with her. She passed the time reading about church history. She studied her Bible. She read about Paul and his never-ending trials. She found strength in the Gospels.

She prayed, "Deliver me from this affliction, Lord."

She began to sense the living Christ. She prayed more and more. Soon she was praying for hours every day, but she had to keep telling herself she was not losing hope because deep in her heart she felt doomed. Then, as if she did not have enough to worry about, she developed a pain in her stomach.

She had been in bed five months when the doctor paid one of his regular visits to the ten Boom house. "How are you doing, Corrie?" he asked.

Corrie pressed the right side of her abdomen. "I have a pain here, doctor."

He poked and watched her wince. "You have appendicitis."

After the operation, her fever vanished. Corrie was perfectly healthy. She had never had tuberculosis at all!

The time in bed had solidified Corrie's flabby plans about getting out in the world. She began Normal School and eagerly sought things to do outside the home. When her friend Mina invited her to tell Bible stories at the Christian school where Mina was a teacher, Corrie was uncertain and asked her sister Betsie's advice. Betsie told Corrie that she could polish her technique in Betsie's Sunday school class first. Betsie was an experienced storyteller and Corrie learned from her how to make a story come alive for the listeners.

Corrie continued her studies in Normal School, earning diplomas in child care, needlework, and other domestic skills. With her newfound confidence, she was ready to leave home, but she felt guilty. Her mother and her aunts needed her so much.

Then an offer came from a wealthy family that needed a governess for their little girl. With her parents' blessing, she took the job, but it didn't last long.

One day Willem appeared at the mansion. "Aunt Bep is dead. At last her suffering is over. You must come home, Corrie. Aunt Anna is exhausted from caring for her. Mama is getting sicker every day. Betsie must work in the shop. Nollie has a permanent job as a school teacher. And you know Aunt Jans is just Aunt Jans."

She and Willem strolled along the beach for a while before they returned to Haarlem. Willem sang Bach at the top of his lungs.

"How can you sing when Aunt Bep just died?" she asked.

"A true Christian rejoices when a loved one goes to heaven to be with the Lord. Grief is an indulgence for ourselves."

Corrie would have to think about it a lot more before she could bring herself to sing.

Heartbreak

Once again, Corrie was home. Willem had been right. Aunt Anna was worn out. Now Corrie was the housekeeper, but she didn't enjoy cleaning house and cooking like Mama and Aunt Anna did. Her goal every day was simply to finish the work faster than she had the day before.

One day Mama bluntly told her, "Housework is not fulfilling for you, Corrie."

Papa said, "Yes, Corrie. You need more. What about the new Bible school that just opened in Haarlem?"

So Corrie enrolled in school again, tackling the curriculum of ethics, dogmatics, church history, Old Testament, New Testament, Old Testament history, and New Testament history. She studied very hard in her moments outside of housework.

Other activities began to occupy her outside the home, too. Jan Willem Gunning was organizing groups in Holland for foreign missions. All four young ten Booms became active: Corrie, Willem, Nollie, and Betsie. The purpose was to have the Dutch meet real missionaries from around the world and be inspired to support mission work.

But the times were full of bad news too. Europe rippled with rumors of war. Rumors threatened to poison the prayer group that Corrie, Betsie, and Papa met with every week. They took the trolley south to the village of Heemstede every Saturday night. Papa continued to pray for the queen and Holland, but some in the meeting objected now. Christians should not support governments. They should be above the fray. They should seek only the Kingdom of God.

When the "Great War" exploded across Europe in 1914, Holland managed to stay neutral. Although the ten Booms avoided direct exposure to the war, bad news nevertheless flooded their home. Mama was sicker than ever and Dr. van Veen diagnosed Aunt Jans with diabetes—as sure a death sentence as tuberculosis! Aunt Jans had always been preoccupied with death. She had been dismissed as a worrywart by the ten Boom children, but now she faced death for real.

Of course, the news was not all bad in the house. Doctor van Veen's sister Tine, who assisted him as a nurse, caught Willem's eye when he was home from school. He was just months away from being ordained a minister, and he and Tine scheduled their marriage for two months after his ordination. Corrie was happy for her brother, and she also relished the opportunity to see Karel again.

Karel was twenty-six and Corrie was now twenty-one—no longer a schoolgirl. Betsie spent an hour brushing Corrie's dark blonde hair before the wedding. Corrie wore a very elegant silk dress that Betsie had made. Karel was attracted like a moth to a flame.

He was attentive. He flattered her. Could anyone doubt his intentions? Corrie could hardly remember Willem and Tine's wedding, she was so shaken. She thought her heart would explode.

But as surely as she soared into the clouds with that event, Aunt Jans's death soon brought her plummeting down.

Four months after Aunt Jans's funeral, Willem gave his first sermon as a pastor in the tiny village of Made, at the southern end of Holland.

No family would miss a minister's first sermon. The ten Booms and Aunt Anna arrived in Made on the train. Three days later, Corrie's wish came true when Karel arrived. He was an assistant pastor himself and free to marry, a fact that was emblazoned in Corrie's mind.

Karel again showed interest in Corrie. Soon the two were walking farther from Willem's rectory each day. They talked about what they would do to decorate a rectory, what furniture they would have, and a hundred other things. They never actually spoke of marriage, but who could doubt that matrimony was in the offing?

Willem doubted, and he let Corrie know it. "I went to school with him for many years, Corrie. I know how he thinks. I know how his family thinks. He must marry well. Even my sister is not good enough for him."

Gloomy old hard-nosed Willem, fumed Corrie to herself. How she resented his pessimism sometimes.

One November day, Corrie answered a knock on the door to the alley.

"Karel!" she cried.

"Hello, Corrie. I came to introduce my fiancée."

Watchmaking

Karel stayed only a short time to proudly introduce his fiancée to the rest of the family. After they left, Corrie slipped away to her bedroom.

Papa followed her. "Love is the strongest force in the world," he said. "And when it is blocked there is great pain."

"It's excruciating."

"We can kill the love to make it stop hurting. Or we can direct the love to another route."

"I will never love another man. I know that for sure."

"Give your love to God."

After Papa left her, Corrie prayed that her love would go to God. She was only twenty-three years old. Her unmarried status was hardly glaring. Betsie was thirty and single, and Nollie was twenty-five and still unmarried. Corrie had had two aunts who never married at all. She could not feel sorry for herself very long.

She began studying her Bible school subjects again and tried to fine-tune her housework like a virtuoso. She still gave Bible lessons at the public school, and she used her earnings to improve the home. It was Corrie who paid for two toilets that actually flushed the waste into the sewer system. Before that, city workers had to come and empty the waste. It was Corrie who bought a bathtub for the home. Before that, they sponged themselves out of small wash basins.

"What luxury we have now!" praised Mama.

Good news or bad, nothing remained the same very long in the ten Boom house. Mama had a stroke so severe she went into a coma. For two months, around the clock, Corrie, Betsie, Anna, Papa, and Nollie watched Mama in shifts. And one morning Mama woke up!

They moved her bed into Aunt Jans's front room, so she could watch the activity on Barteljorisstraat. She recovered enough to walk again, but only with help. She could not use her hands to write or knit. She spoke only three words: "Corrie," "yes," and "no." Corrie believed her name was one of the words only because she was with Mama in the kitchen when she had her stroke.

The Great War ended. Much of Europe was devastated and many children were destitute. It wasn't long before the ten Booms welcomed Willy and Katy, urchins from the streets of Germany. Soon they were joined by Ruth and Martha, sisters from Germany. So there were four children ranging in age from ten to four in the home. The children adapted well. Even Mama was up and about, fussing over the newcomers.

The next months were blessed for the ten Booms. The four foster children became so healthy again, they returned to relatives in Germany. Corrie took the exam at the Bible school and passed. And Nollie met a fellow teacher named Flip van Woerden and they were married. At the end of the wedding ceremony, they sang Mama's favorite hymn: "Fairest Lord Jesus."

Corrie was stunned to hear her mother's hoarse voice singing every word of the song. At first, it seemed a miracle, but after the wedding Mama relapsed and within a month she passed away.

Christmas time that year was a great turning point for Corrie. She was twenty-eight years old. The change started innocently enough. Betsie got the flu, so Corrie helped Papa in the shop. She greeted customers and worked with the bills and correspondence. As Betsie got better, she began picking up Corrie's duties in the house. Sensitive, artistic Betsie was much better at housework than Corrie. She had a special touch, like Aunt Anna. But the reverse was true too. Corrie was much better at working in the shop than Betsie had been. Better yet, each sister loved her new role. Without a moment's hesitation, they exchanged duties.

Corrie was amazed at Papa. He was known far and wide as the best watchmaker in Holland, but he was so inept at business that Corrie was flabbergasted. He had no bookkeeping system. He forgot to make out bills. He did not price his watches low enough to sell. He closed his shop just as people began to stroll the streets in the evenings after work.

Corrie established a bookkeeping system, and she served customers in the shop, but soon she was looking for something more. She asked Papa if she could work on watches.

"You're the only one of the children who ever asked me that," he answered in surprise. "Of course you may. I will teach you."

So Corrie was trained by the best watchmaker in Holland. Papa even sent her to Switzerland to work in a watch factory for a while, but soon she was back. With Papa's help, she became the first woman watchmaker licensed in Holland.

Encouraged by a wealthy ladies' club concerned about lack of activities for teenage girls in Haarlem, Corrie and Betsie started taking a few girls for walks before church on Sundays. They ran a blunt ad in the newspaper:

DO YOU LIKE TO GO ON WALKS? IF YOU WANT
TO MEET OTHER GIRLS AND HAVE FUN, COME TO
THE TEN BOOM SHOP AT BARTELJORISSTRAAT 19.

It seemed like a small thing, but Betsie's and Corrie's
club soon had forty other ladies, each with a troop of
eight girls. Corrie and Betsie made sure that the Gospel
was always sandwiched in between fun things to do.

Their three hundred girls became quite a presence in
Haarlem. Once a year, they rented the concert hall to show
a thousand friends and relatives the skills they were learning
in the clubs. Corrie was a fearless public speaker by now.
Always, right in the middle of the show, she offered the
Gospel in talks with catchy titles like "God's telephone is
never busy," or "Do you have your radio tuned to the right
station?" Her organization became officially the Haarlem
Girls' Clubs. Soon they were welcomed into the Christian
Union of the Lady Friends of the Young Girl, with headquarters in Switzerland. Everyone now wore uniforms!

Then faithful Aunt Anna died, and only Papa, Betsie,
and Corrie remained in the house which had once
resounded with nine people living in seven bedrooms. But
the ten Booms were not ones to waste empty bedrooms.
They began to take in children left in Holland by missionaries. This was no small undertaking. Even though
they were the offspring of missionaries and usually eager
to please, many were at a difficult age.

The first ones to arrive were eleven- and twelve-year-
old sisters Puck and Hans, and their brother Hardy, fourteen. Soon a girl named Lessie arrived. And not long after
that Miep and another girl came to live with the ten
Booms. The new children named the house "Beje," pronounced bay-yay, after the initials of Bartel Joris, for whom
Barteljorisstraat was named. Betsie and Corrie became
their "Aunts." Papa became "Opa," Dutch for grandpa.

After many years of blessed health in Beje, Papa ten Boom was struck down by hepatitis in 1930. He was within days of reaching his three-score-and-ten years of life. His beard turned white as snow as he clung to life in small inconspicuous Saint Elizabeth's hospital. What would Corrie and Betsie do without Papa?

Corrie prayed that God's will be done.

The Third Reich

Papa ten Boom recovered.

Upon his return to Beje, he was visited by a committee of shopkeepers, who gave him the latest invention: a radio, a table model with a speaker on top like a giant morning glory.

"What joy it will bring the ten Booms, as much as we love music," said Papa in thanks.

Papa's illness was a wake-up call for Corrie. He was seventy years old. It was time to get him some help in the shop. They had already hired a bookkeeper, a surly woman named Toos, who seemed to like no one in the world except Papa. But, unfriendly as she was, Toos really helped Corrie more than she helped Papa.

One day, in walked a shabby man who introduced himself as Christoffels. "I am looking for work," he added.

After only a moment or two, Papa hired him. "Don't judge him by his ragged clothing. He's the old-style clock man, the kind who roams the country fixing any kind of watch or clock you can name. He will be invaluable to us."

Corrie's girls' club evolved into the Girl Guides, another international organization. Although relieved of her many duties, Corrie became unhappy with the Girl Guides when they began to squelch the teaching of Christianity.

Before long, it was impossible for Corrie to remain with Girl Guides and she pulled her girls out of the organization and formed a new local group called the Triangle Club. The triangle represented social, intellectual, and physical skills. But the triangle was inside a circle, which stood for being in the right relationship with God.

In 1937, the watch shop celebrated its centennial. Christoffels and Toos continued to work diligently, and it was a golden age for the three ten Booms at Beje. Troubles seemed in the distant past.

The day of the hundredth anniversary, people rapped constantly on the alley door to the shop. Flowers, flowers, and more flowers arrived. It was going to be a great day for Papa. All day long, guests flowed in and out of Beje. One of Corrie's favorites was Herman Sluring, a man the ten Boom sisters had dubbed "Pickwick" after the Charles Dickens character. Sluring was grossly overweight, and his wide-set eyes darted different directions like a chameleon's.

Meanwhile, on the eastern horizon, the Nazis were strengthening their grip on Germany. The poor, the old, the feebleminded, and the handicapped were seen as enemies of progress. Soon the Jews and Communists were included as enemies.

As the months passed, Adolf Hitler's influence began to be felt in the countries that bordered Germany. The ten Booms now had two radios. The table model was in Aunt Jans's big room, and they had a small portable radio on the kitchen table, a present from Pickwick. Almost all the time the speakers carried blissful concerts carefully selected by Betsie from radio schedules, but every once in a while, as a member of the household searched the dial for a station, the speaker would erupt with fiery screams from Germany. This man Hitler sounded like the devil himself.

Papa's young apprentice, a German named Otto,

brought the message home to Beje loud and clear. One day he attacked Christoffels. His reason was that Christoffels was old, decrepit, and worthless. Papa fired Otto immediately. Later Papa made excuses for him: He was young and confused. Gloomy Willem said that Otto was a typical German these days.

In 1938, the radio brought news that Germany was meeting with Italy, France, and Britain in Munich to discuss Hitler's demand for an area of Czechoslovakia called the Sudetenland.

After Hitler got what he wanted, Papa said, "The bully got his first piece of the pie. He will soon be after another."

Surely it isn't that bad, thought Corrie. But six months later, Hitler's army walked into Czechoslovakia and took over the entire country.

In 1939, Germany signed a pact with Russia. "That is very bad," said Papa. "Hitler just made sure the Russians will stay on the sidelines." One week later, Germany invaded Poland and split the territory with the Russians.

The French and British declared war on Germany, but the United States declared its neutrality. Which was worse? To fight or to be neutral? Who could know?

Nothing more happened for weeks, until suddenly, in April 1940, Hitler invaded Norway and Denmark. In early May, the prime minister of Holland came on the radio to reassure the Dutch: *Holland is neutral.*

Papa snapped off the radio.

"Don't you want to hear him?" objected Betsie.

"I'm sorry for all the Dutch who don't know God, because we will be attacked by the Germans, and we will be defeated."

Corrie went to bed, and for the first time in her life she prayed that Papa was wrong. Surely this nightmare couldn't be happening.

She awoke hours later to lightning and thunder.

"No! That is not a thunderstorm!" she cried.

Other noises popped and boomed and crackled. She raced down the stairs and checked on Papa. He was asleep. She dashed into Betsie's bedroom. Betsie was sitting up, terrified. They hugged each other.

"Most of the big explosions seem far away to the east," said Betsie. "I'll bet the Germans are bombing Amsterdam."

It was the worst shock of Corrie's life. She seemed plunged into hell. In the hours that followed, she and Betsie prayed for Holland. Betsie even prayed for the Germans.

While praying, Corrie had a vision. In the town square she saw four enormous black horses pulling a farm wagon. In the wagon was Corrie herself! And Papa. And Betsie. She realized the wagon was crowded. There was Pickwick and Toos—and Willem and Nollie! Even her young nephew, Peter. None of them could get off the wagon. They were being taken somewhere. What could the vision mean?

Finally, the bombing stopped.

After dawn, the Dutch people of Haarlem walked the streets in a daze. The radio had urged them to tape their windows, but there was little else to do. In Haarlem there were no craters, no shattered windows, no crumpled bricks. But there were damaged hearts, especially among the Jews. Fear was written on their faces. This was a bad time for the Jews. Everyone knew what Hitler had been saying.

On May 13, the queen of the Netherlands fled to Britain. Within two days, the Dutch army surrendered. Soon, German soldiers arrived in Haarlem and Holland became part of the glorious Third Reich.

At first, the occupation seemed tolerable to Corrie.

The German soldiers had money. They bought things at the shop, including clocks and watches that had been in the shop for years. There were a few inconveniences, such as a ten o'clock curfew at night, and every Dutch citizen had to carry an identity card in a pouch hanging from a necklace. Food and merchandise had to be purchased with coupons from ration books. The Germans were very well-organized.

"This occupation is seductive," said Papa after a few weeks. "The Nazis are more patient than I thought."

Then the Dutch were ordered to turn in their radios. Willem insisted that without their radios, the Dutch would soon be hopelessly lost in a world of never-ending lies and deceit. Corrie decided to turn in the portable radio and lie to the Germans about the other one. She told herself she was only being as wise and shrewd as a snake but as innocent as a dove.

Next, the Dutch lost use of their bicycles, the primary mode of transportation for many. German soldiers began stopping riders and confiscating their tires. The tires were shipped back to Germany to be used in the war effort. Rubber was precious. The practical Dutch quickly learned to wrap the rims with cloth and ride the bicycles anyway. But soon the soldiers were confiscating the bicycles. The Nazis didn't want the Dutch moving around. Soon the Dutch hid thousands of bicycles inside their homes.

Corrie had to disband her girls' clubs. The Nazis were not about to allow a well-organized network of three hundred Dutch teenagers to exist. Gradually the ten o'clock curfew was moved earlier and earlier. Nighttime was just too convenient for Dutch troublemakers to move around.

Corrie Smit

The German occupation of western Europe became more evil every day. Soon Jews were made to wear a large yellow star of David with *Jood*, the Dutch word for Jew, sewed inside.

For a year and a half, the three ten Booms tried to live their normal lives. One November morning in 1941 changed that. Corrie was on the sidewalk folding back the shutters on the watch shop when four German soldiers with rifles rushed into the furrier's shop across the street from Beje. Moments later, a soldier prodded the owner, Mr. Weil, into the street with a rifle muzzle.

Corrie ran inside Beje. She and Betsie watched through their shop window in horror as the soldiers smashed up Mr. Weil's shop and stole his furs. One soldier opened a second-story window. Clothing cascaded to the sidewalk. Mr. Weil stood on the sidewalk in a daze.

"We must help Mr. Weil," cried Corrie.

She and Betsie ran out to help him gather his clothing off the sidewalk, then quickly they ushered him down the alley and up into their dining room.

"Mr. Weil!" exclaimed Papa happily, not realizing what happened. He cherished visitors.

"I must warn my wife," worried Mr. Weil. "She's

visiting relatives in Amsterdam. She must not come home."

"Willem will know what to do," Corrie said. And almost as if in a dream she found herself walking to the railway station, then riding the train through Amsterdam all the way to Hilversum. She got off the train at midday and walked to Willem's house.

Tine was home with her grown son Kik, who told Corrie, "Have Mr. Weil ready to go as soon as it gets dark. And what is the Amsterdam address where Mrs. Weil is visiting?" He sighed, as if reluctant to draw his fifty-year-old Aunt Corrie into the fray.

Corrie rode the train back to Haarlem. That night, Kik came for Mr. Weil and they disappeared into the dark alley.

When Corrie saw him two weeks later she whispered, "How are the Weils?"

"If you are going to work in the underground you must not ask questions. The less you know, the less the Gestapo can torture out of you." Kik was smiling apologetically, but Corrie shivered. Everyone in Holland now feared the Gestapo.

Some of the Dutch openly defied the Nazis, and once again it hit home at Beje. Nollie's son, Peter, played the organ at the church in Velsen. On May 12, 1942, after the sermon and hymns and the final prayer, the organ began blasting the Dutch national anthem, "Wilhelmus," which the Nazis had banned.

"Oh, Peter," groaned Corrie. "Such defiance."

Nollie and Flip were sheltering two Jews: a young blonde woman named Annaliese, who looked very Dutch and went about freely, and Katrien, an older woman who posed as their maid. What would happen to this house if the Gestapo came after Peter? Would his proud moment of defiance cost two Jews their freedom? And who else would be lost?

Wednesday morning it happened. The Gestapo

arrested Peter and hauled him off to a federal prison in Amsterdam. Corrie thanked God that the Gestapo agents had overlooked the two Jewish women.

Two weeks later, Corrie heard a desperate knock on the alley door. She didn't hesitate a moment when she saw the fear in the woman's eyes. "Come inside!" She rushed the woman up to the dining room.

"I'm Mrs. Kleermacher. I'm a Jew," said the woman. The Gestapo had ordered her to close her family clothing store and her husband had already been arrested.

"God's people are always welcome in this house," said Papa.

Two nights later, an elderly Jewish couple joined Mrs. Kleermacher in hiding. Corrie knew the situation was explosive. Jews were fleeing to Beje, but they had to move on to safer places. Once again she traveled to Hilversum on the train.

This time Willem was there. He said, "Most Jews work on farms. But that's getting more and more difficult. Even the farms must account for their food now. We can find places on farms if they bring food ration books with them. Otherwise—"

"But Jews aren't issued ration books!" cried Corrie. "What can we do, Willem?"

"We must steal the ration books." He sighed as he noticed Corrie waiting expectantly. "I can't do it, Corrie. They watch me now every moment."

Then Corrie said, "I know a man named—"

Willem gently put a finger on her lips. "Don't tell me his name, dear sister."

She fretted about it all the way home on the train. She knew a man who worked at the Food Office. Would he help? What if he were caught? What if he were a Nazi sympathizer? What would happen to her and Betsie and Papa? And why was she doing this at her age?

Oh please God, help me, she prayed.

When she met with the man that night, he said, "There is only one way to get any books for your purposes."

"Yes?" she asked hopefully.

"We must be robbed. It happens more and more these days with Dutch people so desperate for food. They wouldn't necessarily suspect me. How many books do you want?"

How many should she ask for? He was going to be robbed. He would be grilled by the Gestapo. That sacrifice should not come cheap. "I need one hundred ration books," she said stoutly, hardly believing her own ears.

A week later, she visited the man again to pick up the ration books. His face was hamburger. His friends had done it for him. He paid a heavy price for the books. Yet she knew the Gestapo probably would not have believed anything less than a bloody thrashing.

"God will bless you for this," she said.

The best news was that the last coupon in each book was presented to the Food Office for the next month's ration book. So Corrie had one hundred permanent food rations to dispense. One hundred lives saved!

One night, Kik surprised Corrie and took her out into the darkness of the night to a mansion in Aerdenhout, a wealthy suburb of Haarlem. Inside, she saw an old family friend.

"Pickwick!"

Waddling up to her, Pickwick confided, "We are the link between the Free Dutch and the British. We also get crews from downed British planes back to England. There's lot of sympathy here for your work too." He introduced her to the group. "Miss Corrie Smit is the head of an operation rescuing Jews here in Haarlem."

In a daze, she whispered, "Me? The head of an operation? And I'm certainly not Corrie Smit."

"We have no other last names in the underground, Corrie Smit," said Pickwick soberly.

A few days later, a frail man with a goatee came to Beje. Corrie had been told about him at the underground meeting. He was named Smit, of course.

Papa was unaware of his significance. "Mr. Smit? I knew some Smits in Amsterdam."

Mr. Smit was soon exploring the house. "This structure is a dream come true," he said. "Never have I seen such a hodgepodge of rooms."

The layout of the home was peculiar. The front part was an old house three stories high that ran deep off Barteljorisstraat, yet was only one room wide. Behind it was joined another old house three stories high and one room wide but just one room deep. The floors of the two houses missed each other by several feet, but the mismatch was obscured by stairs in the seam between the two houses.

When Mr. Smit walked into Corrie's small bedroom on the third floor, he said, "This is perfect. It's high. It gives people time to get up here and hide as the Gestapo sweep through the lower part of the house."

"But this is my bedroom. And it's so small."

One week later, Corrie's bedroom was even smaller. Mr. Smit and his helpers had built a fake brick wall. There was now a small room between the fake wall and the real, outer brick wall. The room was two and a half feet wide by about eight feet long. The new brick wall had been painted, yet looked a hundred years old. The paint was peeling and water stained. The original molding was put back. In front of the wall was a dilapidated wooden-backed bookcase. Under the lowest shelf was a sliding door.

"Keep a mattress in your secret room, along with water, hardtack, and vitamins," said Mr. Smit as he left.

Corrie felt very cold. Would the Gestapo ever be in

her room scratching the walls, sniffing about like great stinking rats? She must have faith in God. The Gestapo would never find the secret room. It was guarded by God's angels.

Living with Nazis among them was a never-ending nightmare. Corrie remembered the first motto of her girls' clubs: Seek your strength through prayer. She could find strength from God. And she needed it.

Good news crackled over the radio from Britain in January of 1943. The hearts of the Dutch soared. The Russians had stopped the German advance eastward and were even thought to be turning them back! The new year really seemed a turning point in Hitler's fortunes. The United States had joined the war at the end of 1941, and the British and Americans had routed the Germans from North Africa. Glory to God, there was hope for Holland at last.

That winter in Holland was long and severe. Poor old Christoffels froze to death in his bed in a rooming house, the water in his wash basin frozen solid as a rock. Food and fuel were in short supply. Meanwhile, a steady stream of Jews was passing through Beje on their way to safer havens in the Dutch countryside.

Dark Days

When the Gestapo captured nineteen Jews at the De Boer's house, only four blocks from Beje, Betsie was sad. "It could happen to us. We too have a good-sized operation."

Corrie shook her head. "And now we must get bigger."

The operation at Beje expanded and more Dutch joined Corrie. It seemed she always needed another messenger, or a doctor, or transportation, identification papers, or ration books for fugitives. Soon she had eighty people working directly in her operation.

The safe house for Jews got special treatment from the Dutch underground. Beje's phone connection was restored. A buzzer was installed which sounded at the top of the house to warn the fugitives to get to the secret room at once. Buttons to trigger the buzzer were hidden throughout the lower part of the house

"If the phone and alarm system are ever discovered by the Gestapo, they have concrete evidence against us," worried Corrie.

After a while, it became more difficult to distribute Jews to the farms. A Jew who looked too Semitic was referred to in the code of the underground as a "watch with a face that needs repair." Several of these Jews became long-term residents in hiding at Beje.

Meyer Mossel was the first "watch" to remain at the ten Booms', but not all the permanent residents were Jews. Young Dutchmen, like Papa's apprentice Jop, were often seized and sent to Germany for the war factories. Jop was soon joined in hiding by Henk, a young lawyer, and Leendert, a teacher.

Soon the number of permanent residents grew to seven. The most dangerous was seventy-six-year-old Mary. Her asthma made her wheeze and cough uncontrollably.

The fugitives regularly practiced for the unexpected. It was no game. If only one was caught by the Gestapo, they were all caught. So they drilled.

The first time they drilled at a mealtime, it took them four minutes to disappear into the secret room. But on the kitchen table were two unexplained spoons, on the stairs was a carrot, and in one of the bedrooms were ashes from Meyer's pipe. They would have to do much better.

They practiced and practiced until they cut the time to two minutes and left nothing incriminating behind. Then they practiced some more. Their goal was one minute, but the task was complicated by constant turnover in the household.

Papa, Toos, and Corrie polished techniques to stall the Gestapo downstairs in the watch shop. They must do everything they could to slow down a search.

But life in Beje was not all stress. At night they gathered in Aunt Jans's rooms. It was like old times. They sang. They studied the Bible. They played the pipe organ, the violin, and the piano. They performed plays. They gave each other language lessons.

They waited for deliverance from the Allies through the last half of 1940, all of 1941, all of 1942, and half of 1943, hoping the British and Americans would come. How long could the secret of Beje last?

Their fear was not unfounded. One day Corrie looked out the dining room window. Cowering in the alley was a woman, confusion and terror written all over her.

"Katrien, of all people!" Corrie rushed down and pulled her inside.

Katrien was babbling. "Your sister has gone crazy. The Gestapo came to the house. And Nollie told them that Annaliese is a Jew. I ran out the back door."

Corrie grabbed her bicycle and careened frantically across town. Within ten minutes she was waiting near a lamppost on Bos en Hoven Straat.

It was true! Out of Nollie's house came Nollie escorted by a strange man in a suit. Behind them with a second man was Annaliese, almost limp.

The ten Booms soon learned that Nollie was jailed only a short distance away on Smedestraat. By all reports, she was in high spirits, singing hymns. Poor Annaliese was in the old Jewish theater in Amsterdam, awaiting transport to Germany. Were there really death camps there in Germany? That's what people were saying now.

How could Nollie have betrayed sweet Annaliese? How could Corrie ever forgive her?

Six days later, Pickwick phoned and in code urged Corrie to rush to his house in Aerdenhout. There he told her, "We freed forty Jews from the old theater in Amsterdam last night. One of them was very anxious that Nollie know about it."

Annaliese was free! So the only harm done was to Nollie, who had been transferred to federal prison in Amsterdam. Poor sweet Nollie. But Corrie knew no prison could defeat Nollie's spirit. She was much too near to God.

One night during supper at Beje, the doorbell to the front door of the shop rang. "It's after curfew!" gasped Meyer. "No one I would want to meet would be on Barteljorisstraat!"

Corrie hurried to the front door. "Otto!" she gasped with real surprise.

"Yes, it's me." Otto was the German apprentice whom Papa had fired for his viciousness to Christoffels. He was now a soldier in the German army and had come back to gloat.

Corrie screamed, "I can't believe it. It really is you, Otto!"

"You needn't yell like that." He barged in and began to strut to the back of the shop.

"Just one moment. I need to lock the door." Corrie hit the alarm button.

"What was that?" snapped Otto. "It sounded like a buzzer."

"One of the clocks. A buzzer went off accidentally."

Otto rushed to the back of the shop and into the workroom. Corrie hurried behind him. When she came into the kitchen right behind Otto, her heart started beating again. All the "watches" were gone. Only Papa and Betsie were at the table, which was set for three. The residents of Beje had dodged a bullet, but Otto was suspicious. Corrie was not acting herself.

Finally Otto tired of his juvenile game and left.

The ten Booms got an early Christmas present. Nollie was released from prison. Apparently the prison doctor thought her blood pressure was dangerously low. Nollie shrugged. She never doubted that God would take care of her.

In January of 1944, Jop was captured. He was bicycling on an errand for Corrie. It had to happen sooner or later. But unfortunately Jop was not caught en route. He was caught at an underground house. How would the seventeen-year-old hold up to torture by the Gestapo?

Each day now seemed more treacherous than the last. To compound the agony, in February 1944, Corrie came down with the flu. She lay under her vaporizer, aching with every breath. Oh, how she longed to hear the radio announce the British and Americans were storming the shores of France! The Nazis had infested Holland for almost four years! How much longer could the Dutch underground hold out? Corrie felt horrible.

What was that sound? Thumping feet? Was she dreaming or was this real? Were those frantic whispers she heard? Had she heard the buzzer? She struggled to rise.

"Is this finally the end?" she mumbled groggily.

Capture!

B odies were scrambling under her bookcase!
"Yes!" blurted Corrie. "This nightmare is real!"

How many had entered the secret room? Then Mary appeared, slumped in the doorway, gasping for air. She had to be the last one.

Corrie jumped from the bed and rudely shoved Mary under the bookcase. A man she had never seen before scrambled in after Mary and Corrie slammed the sliding door shut. She arose on wobbly legs and toppled back into bed.

Voices came from below: harsh, demanding. In German. *"Schnell!"* Thumps. *"Passen sie auf!"* The Gestapo!

In between the shrill barks below came a sound through the wall: Mary's wheezing! She was breathing like a freight train.

"Oh please, Jesus, heal Mary. Now! I know You can do it," cried Corrie.

"Was is das!" A man in a blue suit rushed into the bedroom. "Whom are you talking to?" he barked in Dutch.

"No one you would know," mumbled Corrie as she clutched the covers around her.

"What is your name?" he growled.

"Cornelia ten Boom."

"Prove it."

She opened the pouch she wore around her neck. She pulled out her identification folder. "Here."

He yanked it from her hand and checked a notebook. "So it is you!" He threw the folder back in her face.

"Why are you here?" She coughed at him with all her might.

"Cover your mouth! Have some decency." He backed up. "What is that smell? Menthol? Camphor? He backed out through the door. "Your room smells like a sewer." His pasty face sagged with revulsion. "Come downstairs at once." He held a handkerchief over his nose and mouth.

Corrie lurched to her feet. "Let me dress, please."

"Hurry up!"

She wanted to get out of the room as fast as possible herself. Mary might start wheezing at any moment. She tugged clothes over her pajamas. She struggled to put on two sweaters.

"No funny business!" he barked.

"I have the chills," she said. She grabbed her winter coat. Where was her precious prison bag?

Her prison bag was by the sliding door!

How could she have been so careless? She couldn't draw attention to it now. Corrie lurched out of the room and stumbled down the stairs.

In the dining room, a man in a brown suit sat at the table. Corrie cried, "Papa. Betsie. Toos." They were sitting on chairs against the wall. Beside them were three workers from the underground.

The pasty-faced man said in German, "I've got Cornelia ten Boom here." He paused for effect. "The ringleader," he sneered.

"Ringleader?" answered the man at the table in German. "That old frump?" He shrugged. "Take her downstairs and find out where the Jews are hidden."

The man in the blue suit prodded Corrie through the workroom into the front showroom. He slapped her hard. "Attention now!"

She held her stinging face. "What do you want?"

"Where are you hiding the Jews?"

"We have none."

He slapped her again. "Where are the stolen ration books?"

"We don't have any—"

He slapped her again. "Where are you hiding the Jews?"

Oh, please, Jesus, stop him. She was coughing. She tasted blood in her mouth.

He lowered his arm and backed up. "What do you have? It's not tuberculosis, is it?" He scowled at his notebook again. "Which one is Elizabeth?"

Soon Corrie sat in Betsie's chair in the dining room and Betsie was in the showroom taking the blows from the man in the blue suit.

Soon she was back, slender and limp, lips trembling and swollen. Corrie rose and helped sit her down. Betsie whispered, "I feel sorry for that man."

A woman blundered in the alley door. "They arrested Herman Sluring!"

"Quiet!" ordered Corrie.

She heard noises of splintering wood above them. Had they found the room?

So far the Gestapo had found the hidden silver, the radio, the telephone, even the alarm system. Only a fool would have not realized the ten Booms were in very deep trouble.

A man blundered in the alley door. He was arrested. Then another man. Finally, the traffic stopped. The word was out. Beje had been raided.

The man at the table stood up. "I guess we can leave now," he said in Dutch. He smirked at Corrie. "Aren't you happy? Your Jewish roaches are safe. Well, reflect on this. When you are rotting in prison, we will surround your house for as long as it takes. The Jewish roaches will turn into mummies. It will be a very long, very painful death!"

But Corrie was happy. The Gestapo had not found the secret room. There was still hope for the people in hiding. All the way down Smedestraat to the police station, Corrie thanked Jesus for helping them. Mary had not made any noise in all that time. The fugitives were still safe.

Inside the police station, soldiers herded them down a corridor into a gymnasium. Thirty-five people had been arrested at Beje. The Gestapo agents looked very proud. This was quite a roundup for them.

The next morning the prisoners were marched out of the police station and onto a long green bus. Corrie squeezed onto one double seat with Papa and Betsie. Farther back were Nollie, Willem, and Peter; behind them sat Pickwick and Toos. As the bus labored away, Corrie saw Willem's wife, Tine, in the stunned crowd along the sidewalk.

As they rumbled across the town square, Corrie remembered her vision the night of the Nazi invasion. They were being taken away against their will in a wagon drawn by enormous black horses. The bus headed south along the North Sea, and in two hours they were in The Hague.

Inside Gestapo headquarters was a grinding bureaucracy of clerks asking questions and typing answers.

There was a fuss when Papa reached the front of the line. "Was it necessary to arrest this old man?" boomed an official who seemed to be the head of the bureaucratic madness.

"He is one of the ringleaders," blinked the man in the brown suit.

"We don't want old codgers like him in our system,"

growled the head man in German. "Let someone else take care of him." He leaned over to Papa. He shouted in Dutch, "Listen up, old man. If I send you home will you behave yourself?"

"If I go home," said Papa, "I will open my door again to anyone who knocks."

The head man's face reddened. In German he barked, "Type this fool's papers!"

"It is an honor to go to prison for God's people," persisted Papa. "I pity you."

Many hours later, soldiers prodded them into the back of a canvas-topped army truck and drove them to the federal prison in Scheveningen.

Upon arrival, they scrambled down out of the truck and stood dazed in a courtyard surrounded by high brick walls. Soon they were led inside a long, low building, where the women prisoners were separated from the men.

"Good-bye, Papa. God be with you," cried Corrie.

"God be with you, Papa," echoed Betsie.

"And God goes with you, my daughters," Papa's voice was clear but thin with exhaustion.

Corrie held Betsie's hand and rushed ahead with the flow of prisoners. She saw Nollie just ahead.

A door banged behind them and the flow stopped. They waited their turn to surrender their valuables. Corrie gave up her Alpina wristwatch, a gold ring, and a few Dutch guilders. Her belongings disappeared into a large envelope.

Now they marched down a cold hallway scarred by narrow metal doors, stopping only long enough for a guard to roughly shove women into their cells. Betsie was the first sister to go. Nollie's cell was two doors down, but Corrie was prodded on, around several corners, until she was hopelessly disoriented. Finally, a guard shoved her inside a cell. Four women were already there, with one cot. Three thin mats were on the floor.

It didn't take long to learn prison routine. Once a day they got hot gruel, and later they got a piece of dark bread. Once a day they passed out the toilet bucket to be emptied. Once a day they passed out the grimy wash basin. It was returned with clean water.

Corrie thought about Papa. What a miserable place this was. He was eighty-four. How would he survive?

One day, after Corrie had been in prison for two weeks, she was taken from her cell and driven to a medical clinic in The Hague for treatment of her pleurisy. Her joy at being out of prison faded when she realized she was being returned.

Prison

Two days later, the matron entered again. "Get your hat and coat, ten Boom!"

This time she was led deeper into the prison and pushed into a solitary confinement cell that reeked of vomit. Corrie was so sick that she collapsed onto the soiled cot.

After a few days in the new cell, Corrie began to feel better, even though she was now in an outside cell, which was much colder than before. Corrie had been lucky. During the very coldest weather, she had been in an interior cell. If she had been in this cell the first week, she probably would have died.

"Praise God," she said to the blue sky through the barred window, "for fair weather."

Her birthday came and passed unobserved. But she did get a treat two days later: her first shower in six weeks. She was feeling much better. How had she survived? Praise God.

Then she received a package! Nothing but her name was written on it, but Corrie knew it was from Nollie's family. In it were sandwiches, a brown cake, a pan of porridge, a needle and thread, two bottles of vitamins, and a brilliant red towel!

The evening of April 20 was very unusual. For seven

weeks the prison had been like a tomb. But this evening she heard shouts.

"What is it?" shouted someone. "Where are the guards?"

"It's Hitler's birthday," answered a voice choked with bitterness. The guards are celebrating with the other miserable Nazis."

"Don't waste this time complaining," urged another voice. "We can exchange information."

What happened next was miraculous to Corrie. Somehow these poor lost souls organized and disciplined themselves to spread news all around the prison.

"I'm Corrie ten Boom in cell 384," yelled Corrie. "Where are the ten Booms: Betsie and Casper and Willem? Where are the van Woerdens: Nollie and Peter?"

Messages flew back and forth. It was a glorious time. Especially when news cycled back that Nollie was released! Nollie always landed on her feet like a cat! Young Peter was released. Praise God for that. Willem was released. Praise the Lord. Herman Sluring was released. Even Pickwick! And Toos! The news stunned Corrie. Had they all been released? Please God, let it be true. Then she heard that Betsie was still in cell 312.

That evening soothed much of the ache in her heart. But there still was no news of Papa. One week later another package was thrown into her cell. It was addressed by Nollie! Corrie recognized her handwriting. Inside were more vitamins. And cookies. And Nollie's favorite sweater: pale blue with flowers embroidered over the pocket. Rewrapping her treasures, Corrie noticed something odd about Nollie's handwriting. It seemed slanted toward the stamp. Quickly she worked the stamp loose with water. Yes! There was a message under the stamp!

Corrie whispered the words to herself, "All the watches in your closet are safe."

So the fugitives in Beje had escaped! Praise God!

A few days later, Corrie received a letter from Nollie telling her that Papa had died on the tenth of March. At first, she was saddened, but then she rejoiced to think of Papa in heaven with Mama.

The days dragged on. Of the thirty-five people arrested in February, only she and Betsie were still in prison. Poor sweet Betsie. She had only helped. She wasn't in the center of the storm like Corrie.

Eventually, Corrie was allowed to exercise in an open area inside the prison. Corrie could smell the North Sea beyond the wall. Her rubbery legs walked a rectangular path around a lawn. Shrubs by the path flowered red. Primroses were in bloom. The sun was warm. The sky was blue. Was this so bad? Surely she could endure this.

But then she saw a freshly dug trench, and there was a burning smell in the air, like nothing she had ever smelled before. Her soul wanted to cry out. Another inmate walked by her and whispered that the prison had a crematorium. No! That is too preposterous, thought Corrie. Not even Nazis are that evil. Suddenly her ears were pounded by noises beyond the walls. She was afraid to look at the other inmate.

"That was a machine gun," whispered the inmate, "I know. I was at Rotterdam."

One morning, the door opened and a woman guard stepped inside. "Come with me, ten Boom."

Corrie asked, "Do I need my coat and hat?"

"No!"

Reunion with Betsie

The guard led Corrie to a small hut in the middle of a courtyard. Inside, a tall thin man in a crisp gray and black uniform stood by a small potbellied stove. "I'm Lieutenant Rahm," he said in Dutch. "Sit down."

Lieutenant Rahm asked her many questions about a list of people and addresses the Gestapo must have found at Beje. He seemed unable to make sense of the list.

Corrie relaxed. "I don't know what you mean," she kept repeating.

She also enumerated her many activities before the occupation. Yes, she took teenage girls hiking and camping. Yes, she gave Sunday school lessons to retarded children.

"Retarded children?" For the first time, his face looked hard. "What a terrible waste."

"God values a retarded child as much as a watchmaker like me," she said.

"And just how do you know what God thinks?" he asked. His eyes were sorrowful.

"He gave us the Bible, so we would know what He thinks."

The lieutenant sighed. "I believe we have talked enough."

The next day, Corrie was summoned again to meet with the lieutenant. This time they met outside by the courtyard wall. After a long pause, the Nazi officer said, "I couldn't sleep last night. I kept thinking about the work I do. And I kept thinking about the work you were doing before the war."

"Are you worried?"

"My wife and children are in Bremen. Bremen is being bombed. The war is going very badly."

Corrie recognized the symptoms of someone truly crying out for God. "You are in darkness, lieutenant."

"A good person like you cannot know darkness like mine."

"Jesus is the light of the world. Whoever follows Jesus will never walk in darkness. There is always a second chance with Jesus. It's never too late."

She had four hearings with the lieutenant. At one session, he stoked up a fire in the small stove. Then he took Corrie's folder from his desk and fed the flames with the list of names of the people in the Dutch underground. Page after page went up in flames.

During the first week in June, Corrie was again escorted to the lieutenant's office. Inside was Nollie and Flip! Willem and Tine! And Betsie!

"We are being released!" cried Corrie and wildly hugged them.

"No," said Betsie, hanging tight to Corrie. "It's the reading of Papa's will."

Lieutenant Rahm excused himself and stepped outside. When the door closed, Nollie pressed a pouch into Corrie's hand. It contained a complete Bible! Corrie quickly put the string of the pouch over her head and slipped the treasure down inside her dress. Willem believed they might get Corrie transferred to a sanitarium because of her illness. The paperwork was being done.

When the lieutenant returned to read the will, Willem prayed, "Lord Jesus, we thank You for bringing us together for a while. Take this good man, Lieutenant Rahm, and his family into your constant care. Amen." The lieutenant's face shone with hope.

A few days later, the guards began screaming after the morning meal. "Inmates must throw their belongings into pillow slips and stand at attention in the hallways!" they yelled.

After a long wait, the guards shouted, "March this way!"

In the courtyard next to the outside gate were buses! Corrie searched desperately for Betsie, but she was nowhere to be seen. *Oh please, Jesus, let us be together again,* prayed Corrie.

When the buses unloaded them at the railway station, they stood at attention once again until their legs were shaky. Suddenly they were streaming onto railroad cars. Corrie tried to hang back. As she was jostled along, she saw Betsie behind her. Her prayer was answered! They were giddy as they found seats together on the train. Betsie could make any suffering joyous!

"Praise to God that we are not going east to Germany," whispered Betsie. "A while ago I thought I saw in the distance the cathedral in Delft."

"If you're right, we're going south." Corrie was so happy to be with Betsie she had not worried where they were headed.

They hugged each other and thanked God.

Sometime in the night they stopped. The prisoners were rudely prodded off the train. Soldiers brandishing rifles bordered a rough path through the woods. They slogged through puddles where it had rained. A soldier brutally kicked a woman who wandered off the path to avoid a puddle. Corrie and Betsie struggled on.

The next day, they learned they were still in Holland, near the village of Vught, in a concentration camp built by the Nazis for political prisoners.

The news filtered back down the line: Twenty women at a time were being herded into a shower. As the two sisters neared the head of the line, a male guard shouted, "Undress!" Soon they could see the guards laughing as they enjoyed the sight of naked women wiggling under the icy water. The showers were right out in the open!

Oh please, God, don't make us do this, prayed Corrie as she and Betsie waited their turn. *Poor, sweet, innocent Betsie. Don't let this happen to her, Lord.*

Moments before their group was to undress, a guard yelled, "We are out of uniforms. Send the cows back later." When the women's camp received a new supply of uniforms, the men were gone and Corrie and Betsie showered under the supervision of women guards. It was degrading, but still a small miracle.

"Praise the Lord," said Betsie.

One hundred-fifty women lived in their barracks. The inmates slept on real beds with two blankets. A young Jewish girl walked right up to Betsie like a baby chick. "I'm so scared." Betsie pulled her into her arms.

The Nazis were short of soldiers. Work was largely in the hands of prisoners. An *oberkapo,* a prisoner himself, examined the newcomers. Betsie was shunted aside into a group of the infirm who sewed prison uniforms. Corrie was marched to the "Phillips factory," a separate barracks where hundreds of men and women prisoners sat hunched over radio parts on long tables. The work was supervised by another *oberkapo,* a very soft-spoken, very shrewd Dutchman named Moorman.

With Corrie's background, she was soon assembling radios instead of sorting parts. The real art was to assemble the radio in such a way that it was hopelessly defective but not obviously defective. The radios were installed in German fighter planes.

The prisoners at Vught ate three times a day. And the food was better than at Scheveningen. There was plenty of time for chatter while they worked—if no guards were strolling the aisles.

Betsie greeted Corrie every evening at the barracks. She would say warm things to Corrie, such as, "I prayed with a woman from Hilversum today who knows Willem," or chilling things, such as, "A Belgian woman just got here who said the British and Americans are trapped at Cherbourg," or cheering things, such as, "The Russians are in Poland already!"

To survive, one listened to information, judged its credibility, and shared it with others. She and Betsie found out the name of their betrayer! He was a Dutchman from Ermelo. How Corrie hated him. And how she hated herself for hating him. Jesus commanded her to forgive enemies. But how could she ever forgive the wretch who caused Papa to die? And to think what suffering she and Betsie had been through! Betsie was weaker every day. And Willem had looked very unhealthy when she saw him in Lieutenant Rahm's office.

One night she argued about it with Betsie. Betsie had forgiven the traitor, even prayed for him!

"Pray for that devil? Never!" said Corrie.

"Think how much he must hate himself," answered Betsie. "Think how much he is suffering."

Corrie was skeptical but Betsie prevailed. Corrie forced herself to pray for him too, and for the first time since she learned the man's identity, Corrie slept without bitterness and anger.

They were allowed to exchange letters again with their family. Nollie's first letter to Corrie said that a letter had already been sent by Lieutenant Rahm to secure their release. Corrie could scarcely believe her eyes.

Hope of Freedom

Was it possible? Corrie and Betsie breathlessly motioned a gnarled camp veteran to meet them in the latrine, where all important business took place. A lookout was posted to watch out for the women guards.

In the latrine the woman told the sisters, "If you helped Jews, that gets you locked up for six months."

"Six months?" cried Corrie. "Let me see. We started our sentence the last day of February. March, April, May, June, July, August. We'll be free by September first!"

Corrie and Betsie rejoiced. Less than two months to go! They could serve that time easily. They gave Bible lessons to the others. They sang hymns. They gave evening devotions. As more time passed, they began to give sermons. Several dozen inmates, putting their bitterness on hold, listened to the ten Boom sisters deliver the Gospel.

Corrie had gained twenty pounds in the camp, but poor Betsie weighed less than one hundred pounds. Even packages from Nollie crammed with sausages and fudge couldn't seem to keep Betsie from wasting away.

Rumors began to circulate that the Allies had taken Paris! Their ground forces were knifing through France. They would soon cut Hitler's throat! Almost daily by the end of August, hundreds of silvery planes glimmered overhead, heading east into Germany.

Days later, explosions rocked the area.

"Bombs?" asked Corrie at the Phillips factory.

"No," said Moorman, "The Nazis are blowing up all the bridges. The question is: What are they going to do with us? Take us with them? Or leave us here? And if they do leave us here—"

"Surely they won't execute the whole camp?" said Betsie in horror.

Corrie was stunned. She could only say, "But our time is almost up."

As the magic date approached, conditions worsened in the camps. Executions in the men's camp were more frequent. Guards were extremely edgy in the women's camp.

Finally the day arrived: September 1!

Corrie could hardly wait through morning roll call to hear the list of prisoners to be released. But there was no list that day. She stumbled off to the Phillips factory, as depressed as she had been at any time since she arrived in the camp. How she had waited for this day! She prayed to Jesus for courage.

That night Betsie consoled her, "The notice of our release may be a day or two late. The Nazis seem to be distracted now."

Sweet Betsie. Who was more vulnerable than she was? And yet she had to console Corrie. Corrie was ashamed. But she did have a feeling of dread. They had to get their freedom now. If they didn't, two terrible choices awaited them: execution here or winter in Germany.

One morning there was no roll call.

Then a guard burst into the barracks. "Get your things together!" she screamed. The guard was frightened.

The women heard the dreaded pop-pop-pop of rifles from the men's camp. They marched out of the camp along the same wooded path they had walked three months before. They marched to the same railroad tracks. Soldiers lined them up along the track three deep. They waited, clutching their blankets and pillowcases stuffed with belongings. They whispered excitedly. Were they going back the same way? Would they ride that same train back to The Hague? Praise the Lord.

Betsie grabbed Corrie's arm. "There is no passenger train here. Only a freight train."

On top of the freight cars were German soldiers with machine guns. More soldiers were walking alongside the train, stopping at each car, throwing the bolt lock, then sliding the door open. After they opened the door to the car nearest Corrie, a red-faced soldier yelled, *"Schnell! Gehen sie weg!"* The women were being forced into the freight cars!

The soldiers kept adding women until they stood so close together Corrie had to wonder how they would ever rest. Suddenly they were plunged into blackness. The bolt slammed shut on the door. They were locked in!

Oh Jesus, save us, prayed Corrie.

"Thank God, Papa is in heaven," said Betsie.

The train lurched ahead—traveling east into Germany. Corrie couldn't bring herself to tell Betsie. They were already in hell.

Each day the car got hotter and hotter.

Finally, the door opened and a guard ordered them out.

They were too stiff to stand up and walk.

They crawled to the light and fell out the opening like blind crabs, clutching their blanket and pillowcase. They sprawled like fish on a bank gasping for air, praying for water.

Corrie began to look around. Their guards were young boys in baggy uniforms, standing far off, repelled by the stinking women.

"Where are we?" yelled a woman in German.

"Furstenburg," replied a scowling boy.

The boys marched them along the shore of the lake, then up a hill. When the women reached the crest of the hill, they saw their new camp down in the valley. The enclosure had concrete walls with strands of wire at the top. Inside the walls stretched dozens and dozens of cold gray barracks. A tall stack fouled the blue sky with smoke.

"I think this must be Ravensbruck."

Ravensbruck

Any woman imprisoned in Holland had heard of Ravensbruck. It was a camp for women who were considered incorrigible by the Nazis. It was a work camp, but the rumor was that the inmates were worked to death.

Oh Jesus, hold us tight, prayed Corrie.

After the women's hair was cut off to avoid an infestation of lice, Betsie looked so inconsequential with her tired shorn head wobbling on a thin goose neck. Never had she looked so frail, so wispy, so marginally alive.

They surrendered their names. Betsie was now Number 66729. Corrie was Number 66730. More of the reality of Ravensbruck soon hit them. They were asked to surrender all their belongings.

Oh please, Jesus, prayed Corrie, *please allow us to keep Your precious Word.*

Suddenly Betsie doubled over, seized by a severe cramp.

"Please, sir," Corrie implored the guard in German, "she has diarrhea."

The guard scowled in disgust. "Well, don't let her do it here! Get her in there." He jabbed his finger at the shower room.

Corrie rushed Betsie into the shower room. It was empty! Corrie quickly took the sweater from Betsie, wrapped the Bible and bottle of vitamins in the sweater and hid the bundle behind a wooden bench.

They returned to the line, shed their Vught overalls, and Corrie imagined to herself no one saw them as they walked past the guards. Inside the shower room, after the short icy blast, they dressed in their new camp garb—plus one sweater, one bottle of vitamins, and one Bible. But their problems were not over. The Bible in the pouch hanging from Corrie's neck was not well concealed under the flimsy dress. She prayed again. *Oh please, Jesus, protect me. Surround me with Your angels.*

They marched slowly past guards who made no effort to hide their disgust as they searched every woman from head to toe with groping hands. Rough hands covered the woman in front of Corrie. Rough hands covered Betsie behind Corrie. No hands touched Corrie. It was as if she were invisible. The Bible was safe.

Finally the guards marched them into the main camp and prodded them into the permanent barracks.

At four-thirty every morning, Corrie and Betsie marched outside the camp, with several thousand other women, into the woods toward the Siemens factory. The work was backbreaking. Corrie and Betsie had to push a handcart loaded with heavy metal plates along a dock to a boxcar. They tried to get their breath as they helped load the plates onto the train.

After a dinner of turnip soup, Betsie recovered enough for the most important moments of the day. They found a light bulb in the dormitory and read from the Bible. Betsie got stronger and stronger as they read. As the days passed the reading seemed to be enough to get her through the next work day as she weakened every minute during work and then strengthened every minute at night.

The nightly readings attracted more and more listeners. It was no longer enough to read the Bible in Dutch.

Corrie would translate the passage into German. Another woman would repeat it in Russian. Another in Danish. Another in French. And on and on went God's true Word in the world's stumbling tongues.

In November they were issued coats, and no more work details went to the Siemens factory. In the camp, Corrie and Betsie were put to work leveling rough ground close to the concrete wall. Betsie's health was failing. She could hardly lift her shovel. Would the guard notice how little Betsie was doing?

Suddenly the guard was staring at Betsie!

Made Perfect in Weakness

Why are you not working harder?" screamed the guard at Betsie. "That's nothing but a spoonful of dirt on your shovel."

"I'm sorry," Betsie answered good-naturedly, "but even spoonfuls add up."

If the other prisoners hadn't laughed, Betsie probably would have been all right. But the guard angrily struck Betsie with a leather crop. Betsie was bleeding. Her precious blood was streaming into the void. Corrie wanted to kill the guard. Betsie grabbed her hand. She saw the hatred in Corrie's face.

Rain and cold worsened Betsie's health. She now coughed blood. After Betsie had been in the infirmary two days, Corrie simply walked away from roll call to disappear into the morning fog.

Mien had shown her a way to sneak into the hospital. She wandered the hallways peeking into wards until she found Betsie sitting on a cot.

Betsie returned to Barracks 28 three days later. No doctor had ever seen her. She still had a fever. But the visit was not in vain. She was rested. And somehow she had been transferred to the knitting room.

As blessed as Betsie's life was in the dormitory, she

could not escape the dreaded roll calls twice a day. In December, the air iced their bones and all too frequently they were kept at roll call until prisoners started keeling over. Betsie was getting weaker. December 9th came and passed. They still hoped to be released.

Betsie began to speak about a mission after the war. She envisioned a mansion in Haarlem, with inlaid wood floors, a gallery around a central hall, manicured gardens, and bas-relief sculptures, where she and Corrie would help poor people who were warped by the war find Jesus. Her vision seemed prophetic.

One week before Christmas, Betsie could not move off the platform for morning roll call. Another prisoner helped Corrie carry Betsie to roll call. In a few minutes, orderlies miraculously appeared with a stretcher and Betsie was carried away to the infirmary. It was as if God had intervened. Betsie had suffered enough.

One dreary day at noon, Corrie slipped away from her work detail and crept around the infirmary until she found the window looking in on Betsie's ward. There was her dear Betsie on a cot. Corrie tapped on the pane. Praise the Lord, Betsie was resting, out of the cold.

The next day, Corrie sneaked back. Where was Betsie? On a cot was the corpse of an old woman, completely naked. She was pitifully thin. Yellow skin stretched over bone. Hair was matted. It was so sad. But where was Betsie?

Then she saw Nollie's sweater next to the cot, and the truth hammered her. The dead woman was Betsie!

Corrie now faced roll call alone. How many more could her aging body withstand? She was a bag of bones. How much punishment could one undernourished body take?

Jesus, help me, she prayed. *I must not give up hope.*

One morning at roll call the guard called out, "Corrie ten Boom. Fall out!"

Not Number 66730! But Corrie ten Boom. What did it mean?

Her heart was in her mouth as they marched her and several other older inmates away from the infirmary to a shed near the outskirts of the camp.

A guard sneered. "Step inside the dressing shed."

Was this to be her last moment on earth?

The Nightmare Ends

Corrie once again put her trust in God and stepped into the unknown. Inside the shed a guard issued Corrie some underwear, a wool skirt, a silk blouse, and shoes. She was given papers to sign stating she had never been mistreated at Ravensbruck. She signed. Freedom was too close.

Remarkably, the guards produced an envelope with her Alpina watch, gold ring, and Dutch guilders.

Outside once again, she watched the massive gates swing open. She and the others marched numbly back up the hill toward the railroad tracks where she and Betsie had arrived four months earlier. When she reached the crest she didn't look back. Ravensbruck was a nightmare.

"The nightmare is over," she said hopefully.

The group of inmates followed the tracks into the village of Furstenburg. Every moment seemed like a dream to Corrie. She waited numbly in the small train station. She was numb all the way on the boxcar into the sprawling rail yards of Berlin. Were they really free?

Corrie and another Dutch woman, named Claire, clambered into another boxcar, this one on a freight train bound west toward Holland. The boxcars were icy cold. They had no food coupons. The Nazis weren't going to waste food on foreigners.

Magically, one night a man spoke to them in Dutch! She and Claire discovered they were in Nieuweschans in Holland. Not long after that they were rolling into Groningen, where they had to leave the train. The rest of Holland's rail system was destroyed.

She limped with Claire to a Christian hospital called the Deaconess Home. The young nurse helping her asked, "Where are you from?"

"Haarlem."

"Oh, do you know Corrie ten Boom?"

Corrie blinked. "Are you one of my girls?"

"One of your girls? I'm Truus Benes."

"Truus! I'm Corrie."

Truus stared hard. Her face paled. "Of course it's you. I can see that now." She tried to hide her shock. Tears welled in her eyes.

Corrie knew now she was just a shadow of her former self. "Jesus will restore me," she assured Truus.

One February day, almost one year after the Gestapo hauled her away from Beje, she was back in Haarlem.

She tried to occupy herself with the watch shop. But Betsie's vision swelled up inside her. Now was the time. Corrie was back in Haarlem. What was her excuse? Betsie's vision could not be neglected. But where would Corrie find the mansion of Betsie's vision? Even Pickwick did not have a house that grand. And whom would she talk to? And who would want to listen? The Nazis were still here.

She began speaking to clubs, to people in their homes, to anyone who would listen. Often her contact at a garden club or Bible class would be reluctant, even frightened. But she felt that God had told her exactly what to say. No pit was too deep for someone who was safe in Jesus. She described every degrading detail of imprisonment, so people would know how deep the pit was. She described Betsie's vision. The Dutch must care for these poor people who were scarred by prisons and camps. The Dutch must give them a chance to find Jesus. The Lord would take care of their recovery.

One day, a woman dressed in such finery that she appeared untouched by the war, approached Corrie after a talk.

"I'm Mrs. Bierens de Haan. I live in a very large house in Bloemendaal. I am a widow and my sons are grown. My son Jan was taken to Germany. A lightning bolt suddenly struck me that if God would return Jan to me I would give my house for your sister's vision."

Corrie was leery. One does not bargain with God. "Are you sure?"

"It was a revelation, right out of the blue."

Corrie sighed. She didn't want to spurn an offer but what this woman was doing seemed wrong. Corrie said, "My sister had a very specific place in mind." This house of Betsie's has a golden floor of inlaid wood, manicured gardens surrounding it, a gallery around a central hall, and bas-relief sculptures—"

The woman's mouth was gaping. "That's my house!" she said.

Corrie was stunned. God was using the woman in His plan, just as He had used Betsie and Corrie in His plan.

Corrie was not surprised when Mrs. de Haan later sent her a note: "Jan came home!"

"The home is ours, Betsie," cried Corrie.

Corrie opened a home for unfortunate souls whose minds had been mangled by the prisons and concentration camps. Holland's liberation seemed almost anticlimactic. Oh, she knew in her head it was a great day for Holland, but in her heart she knew really great days were when people found the Light.

Corrie now operated on a new level. She became part of Betsie's vision and trusted God to tell her what to do next. She now studied the Bible as never before. She didn't want to make any mistakes. One of the first insights she had was that she had to forgive. Everyone. Even the Nazis. And the Dutch traitors who had helped the Nazis.

In June 1945, she wrote a painful letter to a Dutchman from Ermelo:

". . .I heard that most probably you are the one who betrayed me. I went through ten months of concentration camp. My father died. . .and my sister died in prison.

"The harm you planned was turned into good for me by God. I came nearer to Him. I have prayed for you, that the Lord may accept you if you will repent. I have forgiven you everything. God will also forgive you everything, if you ask Him."

Writing the letter was so painful she was nauseated. Would she meet others who turned her stomach? What if she met a guard who had beaten her? How could she ever forgive a guard for beating sweet Betsie when she was so weak? Could she still forgive? God said yes. You must.

She soon discovered that her mind was free of the man who betrayed her family. The hatred, the urge to kill was gone.

One of the first arrivals at the fifty-six-room mansion in Bloemendaal was Mrs. Kan, the wife of the watchmaker in Barteljorisstraat. Mr. Kan had died while in hiding, and Mrs. Kan was very old and infirm. Soon the great mansion was full of patients and volunteers. Corrie still went out speaking her message, organizing volunteers, and raising money for the rehabilitation center.

Then she surprised Nollie with her next plans.

Tramp for the Lord

"I'm going to America," said Corrie.

"But what about the watch shop?" asked Nollie.

"I'm giving the business to my helpers. I tried to get back into the business. I really did. I even traveled to Switzerland for watches, which are very hard to get right now. But I know Betsie would be sad if she knew I was using up my precious time for such things when I could be delivering her message about the victory of Jesus in the concentration camps."

"And Beje?" asked Nollie.

"I'm turning it into a home for victims of the war. The rehabilitation center in Bloemendaal is overflowing."

"But it is impossible to get to America. Everyone wants to go. The waiting list for a passenger ship is a year at least. And you need a lot of money to go to America, Corrie."

"If God does not want me to go, the gate will be closed for me. But if He does want me to go, the gate will open."

Nollie laughed. "Few people pound harder on the gate or more persistently than you do, Corrie. Be sure to write me from America."

Against all odds, Corrie found herself on a freighter just a few days later steaming for America! She didn't worry about her lack of money. She trusted God completely. In

New York City, she got a room at the YWCA and every morning she bought her one meal of the day: coffee, orange juice, and a donut, then trudged all day long through Manhattan knocking on every church door. She had to move out of the YWCA and drifted from room to room. She didn't quit but prayed harder. God would provide for her somehow. But she might have to suffer first.

She struggled. She was operating on nickels and dimes. Some Americans treated her like a beggar. Some told her no one wanted to talk about the war any more. When Corrie began to get a few invitations to speak, her audiences seemed riveted, especially the Americans who remained at home as civilians. They envisioned the war as battling soldiers, not fifty-year-old ladies. How would they have survived an occupation?

"But my survival is not my personal miracle," she insisted, "but the reality of Jesus!"

Word came from Nollie that Willem had died from tuberculosis of the spine, and that Kik had died in a work camp in Germany. More of Corrie's beautiful family had succumbed to the Nazis!

By year's end her first foray into America was complete. She had met some movers and shakers in the American churches. She had met a few publishers of Christian books and magazines and told them she had hundreds of stories to tell. Now it was time to move on.

She knew her next move would confound Nollie again. Corrie was going to go to Germany. She and Betsie had talked about it, huddled together in the deadening cold of the barracks. Betsie said they had to go back to Germany and paint the prison barracks bright colors and plant flowers. And they had to help the poor sick guards to find new lives through Jesus. Their rehabilitation was important. Any dream of Betsie's was reality to Corrie.

Corrie went to Darmstadt to help a church organization

renovate a concentration camp. It was a small but vibrant start. The brightly painted barracks now held one hundred-sixty Germans. Many were women with children.

Corrie found out that Lieutenant Rahm and his family were still alive. Rahm admitted he still suffered enormous guilt. And Corrie knew millions of surviving Germans carried that guilt. No one needed Jesus more. Once after Corrie talked in a church the people got up silently, as they always did in Germany, and filed out. But working against the flow was a man coming toward Corrie. He looked familiar.

No! she wanted to scream.

The man stopped in front of her, smiling. "What a fine message, Fräulein ten Boom. I'm so glad to hear our sins are forgiven." This man had been a guard at Ravensbruck! He had watched coldly as Corrie and Betsie had filed past, naked and degraded. She remembered him distinctly. Corrie could not speak. The man went on confidently, "After the war I became a Christian. God forgave me. Will you forgive me?" He extended his weathered hand. It was as repulsive as a snake.

Corrie had a thousand reasons to hate this man. Poor sweet Betsie. But Betsie would have been the first to forgive him. Corrie had to forgive him, or God would not forgive her. It was perfectly clear in the Bible. She looked at the man's repulsive hand. Forgiveness was not an emotion one indulged. It was the will of God.

She extended her hand. "I forgive you."

Warmth flooded over her. It was intense. She felt herself glow with love. But it was not her love. She was powerless. It was God's love.

After a while, Corrie saw her mission in Germany not completed but well under way. There were other places to go to deliver her message about Jesus. She left Germany to continue her odyssey.

She no longer accepted money. Corrie became like Paul. She arrived, she worked, she preached the Gospel, and she accepted whatever anyone wanted to give her. A bed. A meal. But not money. She proudly called herself a "tramp for the Lord."

For years she traveled alone, brazenly intruding on lives, preaching the Gospel in Cuba, South Africa, Japan, Bermuda, New Zealand, Australia, Spain, England, Denmark, Taiwan, and Israel. She returned to America and Germany.

She wrote books. Her anecdotes were becoming very popular. The royalties from the books were pumped into her work. She bought another house in the Bloemendaal district of Haarlem, which became another center for rehabilitation. She went there only to rest occasionally.

Nollie's death in 1953 stunned her. Nollie was only 63. Now Corrie's generation of the family was dead except for herself.

"Why do I remain?" she asked God.

By 1957, after twelve years of unrelenting activity, Corrie was being crushed under her own popularity. Her books were known far and wide, and she was in demand. Corrie needed help and she found a perfect companion: Conny van Hoogstraten, a tall, attractive Dutch woman. Conny became Corrie's buffer, making traveling arrangements, filtering invitations for speaking engagements, making guests welcome, but protecting Corrie.

In 1964, when Corrie was seventy, she was brought down by hepatitis. Her doctor ordered her to rest one year, so she went to Lweza, a missionary home on the shore of Lake Victoria in Uganda. It was very peaceful. Corrie slept in the same bed every night. Her clothes hung in a closet. She strolled into nearby Kampala two or three times a week to teach people about Jesus. Rest was paradise. At the end of the year she did not want to leave.

"Do You Know Him?"

Then she had a visitor, a minister from Rwanda, who invited her to come to minister to Rwandans who had been imprisoned during that country's civil war.

Once again Corrie packed her bags. God surely did not intend for her to slow down yet. After Conny left her in 1967 to get married, Corrie traveled alone again. She was still going strong, even though she was seventy-five years old.

When she was not in Holland, her travels took her to many very dangerous places. Who could believe this old lady was in the midst of civil wars in Africa? Who could believe she was so close to the fighting in Vietnam she heard bullets whizzing through the foliage? But there she was, crawling creakily out of a jeep to deliver the Gospel to startled soldiers. She worked with "Brother Andrew," known widely for smuggling Bibles into Communist countries, who was teaching the Gospel and ransoming Vietnamese children sold into slavery.

Traveling was harder for Corrie and she was often tempted to quit. Didn't she deserve to rest at her age? And how would she ever replace Conny? Then one day she met Ellen de Kroon, a tall, blonde Dutch woman in her late twenties. She too had scars from World War II.

"We were starving in Rotterdam," she told Corrie. "My father was taken to a work camp in Germany. So mother took us to a farm."

"God bless those wonderful Dutch farmers," interrupted Corrie. "What would we have done without them?"

"My family would have starved. Every time the Nazis came, we all rushed into the woods to hide."

"Did your father come back after the war ended?" Corrie asked.

"Why, yes."

"Praise the Lord. I'm looking for a companion, Ellen. And you seem just perfect," enthused Corrie.

"Me? But you don't know me well enough. I can't type. I can't drive a car. I don't speak German or English."

Corrie was beaming. "You cannot do it yourself, Ellen. But God can do it through you."

Ellen agreed to try.

Not long after they teamed up, Corrie was in a car accident. She broke her shoulder, and her right arm in five places. "It's a good thing you are a nurse," she told Ellen.

Corrie could not write with her shattered arm, so she practiced until she could write with her left hand! Later she worked with sandbags to build the strength back in her right arm.

"Not bad for an old lady of seventy-five," bragged Corrie.

The temptation to quit was still strong. Traveling tired her. Every speech tired her. Then she got news that Conny had died of cancer. How could Corrie quit when Conny had spent so much of her youth to help her spread the Gospel?

Years of speaking in public taught Corrie how to assemble a talk in seconds. All she needed to know was how much time her hosts were going to allow her. She had hundreds of stories she had polished over many years.

Betsie had taught her how to enchant listeners in the beginning. But now Corrie had a powerful story of the concentration camps too. "No pit is too deep when Jesus is in your heart," she said.

One day Corrie asked Ellen, "Do you remember this passage from chapter 15 of First Corinthians: 'Be ye steadfast, unmoveable, always abounding in the work of the Lord'?"

"I remember it well," said Ellen agreeably.

"And do you also remember chapter 1 of Second Timothy: 'For God hath not given us the spirit of fear; but of power, and of love, and of sound mind. Be not thou therefore ashamed of the testimony of our Lord'?"

"I remember it as well," answered Ellen suspiciously.

"Good, because you are going to have to start speaking to the public."

"What!" Ellen was terrified, but soon she was giving speeches when Corrie was simply too exhausted. The message was too important to cancel an engagement. For a while, Ellen felt like a fraud, until Corrie reminded her that she had truly suffered under the Nazis.

The Celebrity

A writing team praised Corrie for her book about Ravensbruck called *A Prisoner and Yet.* But they were sure there was a bigger story to be told. Soon Corrie was collaborating on a book emphasizing her war experiences from 1939 to 1944. The book was called *The Hiding Place,* referring both to the secret room where the ten Booms hid refugees from the Nazis, and Jesus, in whom Corrie hid when events were crushing her. Published in 1971, the book was a first-person cliff-hanger.

Billy Graham told Corrie that his motion picture company, World Wide Pictures, was interested in making *The Hiding Place* into a movie. Corrie shrugged off any credit for the film. "It's another way to let the world know Betsie's vision." She prayed that the movie would be filmed eventually, but she had too many other activities to think about it much.

By 1974, Corrie had collaborated with another writer on a sequel to *The Hiding Place* called *Tramp for the Lord.*

In 1975, Billy Graham's World Wide Pictures started filming *The Hiding Place,* at locations in England and Holland. That same year, Corrie finished collaborating on a third major book, *In My Father's House,* covering her early years. Billy Graham invited her to speak on his televised Crusades.

She still wanted to travel the globe and talk to groups. In Tel Aviv, she presented the two millionth copy of *The Hiding Place* to Golda Meir, the prime minister of Israel. How excited Papa would have been to see such a meeting.

Early in 1976, Ellen left Corrie to be married. An English woman named Pam Rosewell became her companion. She joined Corrie who was resting at her new house in a suburb of Haarlem. Imagine her surprise to learn that eighty-four-year-old Corrie had planned a seven-month, eighteen-city tour in America!

She told Pam she wanted to move to the Los Angeles area in California. Thirty-three years to the day after she was arrested by the Gestapo in 1944, she moved into a ranch-style home in Placentia. She dubbed it Shalom House, and celebrated her eighty-fifth birthday there.

She soon started a neighborhood group praying weekly for prisoners. And when she got an invitation to the prison at San Quentin, she went. And when people showed up at Shalom House saying God sent them there, how could Corrie refuse to see them? Pam watched helplessly.

She celebrated her eighty-sixth birthday while making a film with Christian Indians in Arizona. In the summer of 1978 she made a third film, *Jesus Is Victor,* and was honored in Denver on an episode of "This Is Your Life."

Following an unrelenting schedule, Corrie reached her goal of five books and five movie shorts in less than two years. But one morning in August, when she woke up she couldn't move. Was she only dreaming? In her heart she knew she was awake. All her memories of Mama's paralysis flooded back. Her troubling dream of being locked in a room had come true.

From Everlasting to Everlasting

S oon after she was rushed to the hospital, she lost con- sciousness. How long she drifted in the void she couldn't tell. Gradually she realized she was awake again. When she tried to speak, Pam just looked at her blankly. Soon she realized she was saying a few words like "yes" and "Conny."

Weeks later, back at the Shalom House, Corrie now played the guessing game with Pam, just as Mama had played it with her. Corrie would gesture yes or no to question after question until the answer she sought finally came.

But Corrie's life now was mostly a pleasant indul- gence. An old friend of Corrie's, Lotte Reimeringer, came to help Pam. The two helpers walked Corrie in the gar- den behind the house. She watched birds at the bird feeder. She did needlework. She listened to Bach. She prayed with Pam and Lotte, and the women read the Bible to her several times a day. She received only a few visitors. She was able to put together another devotional book with Lotte by indicating her choices of many clip- pings she had saved over the years. Sometimes she wept in frustration. *Why keep me here so long, God? Why?*

She was struck down again in May 1979. The doctors

no longer liked to make predictions about eighty-eight-year-old Corrie ten Boom. She returned home again, completely bedridden, her speech almost nonexistent, her arms and hands rags.

She lay immobile as Lotte and Pam entertained her. They played Bach for her. They read the Bible. They prayed with her. They read her own books to her. They even let a few visitors see her. In the evenings they gave her slide shows of the sixty-six countries and hundreds of dear friends she had visited. She had seven thousand slides! How fortunate she had been.

In the fall of 1980, she suffered a third stroke. She became even less responsive. This had happened to Mama. She must not forget the glory that awaited.

Corrie lived on and on. She experienced visions. She experienced despair. Eventually, she could not open her eyes. She had nothing left but her hearing. She heard Pam reading Psalm 103, a Dutch tradition for birthdays: ". . .who redeemeth thy life from destruction; who crowneth thee with lovingkindness and tender mercies." That verse seemed written for Corrie. And it was as if Betsie was reading it to her.

Then Corrie ten Boom slipped from this life into the arms of the Savior on April 15, 1983—her ninety-first birthday.

MARTIN
LUTHER

Iron Mines

On the morning of November 11, 1483, St. Martin's Day, the parish priest of the Church of St. Peter in Eisleben, Thuringia, baptized the day-old son of Hans and Margaret Luther. As devout Catholics, the Luthers chose the name Martin for their firstborn. Father Rennebrecher took the baby in his arms, touched his fingertips in the holy water and laid them gently on the boy's head. He marked the sign of the cross on little Martin's forehead to ward off the devil and all his works. When the baptism was completed, the proud parents carried their baby home.

Hans Luther worked in the mines of Eisleben. The son and grandson of peasants, he had been reared on the land in Mohra. Sturdy and fearless, Hans honored the church and was devout in his religious practices.

Hans had courted Margaret Ziegler, the daughter of burghers in Eisenach. The Zieglers would have preferred her to marry into an established Eisenach family, but Margaret and Hans had made plans for how they would work their way up in life.

The Luthers lived in a common house on a narrow, unpretentious street near the great St. Peter's Church. After the mines opened, Eisleben had grown rapidly from a village of five hundred to a town of about four thousand inhabitants, but the Luthers had no relatives there and few friends.

The summer after Martin was born the family moved to Mansfeld, a happy and lively town in the center of one of the mining districts. After a difficult start, Hans began to enjoy steady success in the mines, and the future held the promise of more.

Early in Martin's life, the Luthers instituted a rigorous but fair discipline. Obedience was exacted, and Martin learned that neither parent would let offenses go unpunished. Martin and his siblings certainly feared their father and mother, but the atmosphere in the home carried a sense of protection and affection into the lives of the children, and love was never absent.

Long afterward, Martin Luther would say that his boyhood fear drove him into the monastery. This fear was the great and strangely lovely experience in human life where a father and mother throw their earnestness into the corrective rearing of their child. Hans Luther's love would follow Martin through difficult experiences, and it would never falter.

From his mother, Martin learned to recite the Lord's Prayer and the Apostles' Creed. He waited for the years to give them meaning. He slowly mastered the Ten Commandments, and his parents taught him that breaking of any of them would earn a terrible, eternal punishment. They told him about the God who creates and governs, who watches, rewards, and punishes. They told him of the Christ who came for his salvation.

Through song and picture, he learned of the little Christ of love and the supreme Christ of judgment. Each week at church, Martin looked upon a sword-holding, thunder-visaged Christ on a rainbow in the great stained-glass window. His parents told him about the saints who would intercede for him with the great Judge, and who in tender mercy would help him if he would only call upon them. As he grew, these teachings became fixed in his mind.

Hans Luther was friendly with the priest at the church, and maintained an ever-increasing connection with the affairs of the parish. When Martin was eight, Hans was elected to the town council, where he continued to serve with distinction until his death. When Hans began to lease mines and smelting furnaces to operate for himself, the family prospered. Martin entered the common school in Mansfeld as the son of an independent and respected family.

The teaching methods in the Latin school were strict and brutal, and the instructors were unsympathetic. Martin did well in his early schooling, but while he sat in class, the world into which he had been born was passing away.

In 1492, while Martin ran from school to play, Columbus and his sailors looked at endless miles of water in terror mingled with hope; Lorenzo the Magnificent lay dying in Florence, the city-state which had been the glory of the Renaissance; and Rodrigo Borgia ascended St. Peter's throne, bringing to a climax the deadly secularization of the church.

While Martin played at warfare with the boys of Mansfeld, the knights of Ferdinand and Isabella drove the Moors from Spain and set the Christian flag above Granada, Henry VII nationalized England, and Maximilian became the new emperor of the Holy Roman Empire. Though the world was still fixed and stable in Mansfeld, Copernicus was busily poring over his books at the University of Cracow.

Ancestral Music

When Martin turned thirteen, it was time to abandon school and go to work or continue his education in a larger town. Hans wanted Martin to one day work in a profession, possibly law, so he decided to send him to the neighboring town of Magdeburg to continue his studies.

Martin said good-bye to his family, picked up his pack and his walking stick and embarked with his friend John Reinicke along the narrow winding road to Magdeburg. Some money was available to send with the boys, but not much. They would need to supplement their finances by begging and street-singing, which were normal activities of "wandering students."

Martin was strong and well-disciplined. Though he possessed a quick and powerful temper, he was also naive and spontaneous, and he laughed heartily. He enjoyed life. Religious in the way of his family, he relied on the Word of his parents and priests for Christian truth. Sensitive to beauty, he loved the fields and forests near Mansfeld.

In Magdeburg, Martin and John found shelter in Paul Mosshauer's home and sang on the streets for their bread. Martin's voice and his feeling for music were exceptional and would bring him enjoyment throughout his life, but it was not easy to secure a good living, and in Magdeburg he learned from experience about poverty and hunger.

Magdeburg had a fine, large cathedral, and the citizens were proud of its exceptional architecture. Magdeburg was the seat of the archbishop and was prominent in the affairs of church and state.

Attached to the cathedral was a well-known and popular school. In addition to an advanced Latin school curriculum, courses were taught in logic, rhetoric, dialectic, doctrine, and theology.

Martin became a regular scholar of the cathedral and took his place in the cathedral choir, where he absorbed the mighty liturgy of the church. In contrast to the harshness of the municipal grammar school teachers in Mansfeld, in Magdeburg he was taught by the well-loved Brethren of the Common Life, who were intent on the growth of their pupils in Christian character.

The Brethren taught Martin the pure Catholic faith. They were not heretical, and they did not lay in Luther's mind the foundations for any subsequent rebellion against doctrine. Instead, by example and precept, they taught the precious essence of the church's historic piety: to live in sincere simplicity, avoid sin, take duty seriously, serve fearlessly the commands of conscience, refuse wealth and position, scorn sin in high places, and feel the mystic satisfaction available to the Christian in prayer. Simple and obedient in doctrine, in life they were quiet, controlled, and sincere.

After Martin's year at Magdeburg, his mother suggested that he continue his education in her hometown of Eisenach, where her family could keep an eye on him and he could roam the streets she loved so well.

Eisenach had three fine churches and many monasteries. John Trebonius was headmaster at the school attached to the Church of St. George. Trebonius taught in the late medieval style, with lecture and question, textbook and recitation, but he also possessed the gift to inspire his students. Under Trebonius, Luther found new life and enthusiasm in the grand old studies of the medieval Latin school; he would come to owe his teacher a lifelong debt of gratitude.

As he had in Magdeburg, Luther sang on the streets in Eisenach and accepted bread in return. But with his relatives nearby, he did not have to depend on singing and begging for a living.

We do not know where he lived during his first year in Eisenach, but two prominent families soon took him under wing. The wealthy Schalbes were greatly interested in religious activity and supported a foundation, called the Kollegium, for one of the monastic orders. Luther spent a great deal of time with the monks of the Kollegium.

Another family, the Cottas, also captured his heart. Ursula Cotta took a fancy to Martin and invited him to her home, where he learned the graceful side of Thuringian custom. Here he sang traditional folk songs, laughed and drank and danced, and enjoyed the open freedom of a beloved circle of friends. Frau Cotta had a genius for friendship and for the gentility that makes an evening pass in harmony and happiness. The coarser habits he had picked up in Mansfeld and Magdeburg were softened considerably during his three years in Eisenach.

Saint Elizabeth was especially revered by the people of Eisenach. Born with rank and wealth, she had donned the robe of the Third Order of St. Francis and spent her life in service to the sick and needy. Hospitals, monastic houses, and churches bore witness to her lasting fame.

In youthful, idealistic fashion, Martin Luther was captivated by the otherworldly beauty of St. Elizabeth. He thought often of the superior quality of the consecrated life and the inferior quality of the normal life, but the warmhearted Frau Cotta often reminded him of the equally lovely value in a life of love and marriage.

Another friend who touched Martin's life was John Braun, the vicar of St. Mary's Church. Many years older than Luther, Braun befriended the students at Eisenach and would gather them for long evenings of conversation and music. Braun was a fine musician and taught Luther much. They played various instruments and sang far into the night.

John Braun was a man of deep religious experience. Luther found himself taking for granted the supreme desirability of the religious calling. Braun must have told him many times of the struggles that preceded and the deep peace that followed his own decision to take Holy Orders.

Would he, too, become a priest? Luther must have turned over in his mind the all-important question, but he put off the day of decision. His father had his heart set on the law, and that was enough for Martin.

In Luther's day, Eisenach was home to some strange ideas. A splinter of wood from a bed in which St. Elizabeth had slept was said to heal a toothache. Cripples were reputedly made whole by the power of the saint's relics. Indulgences were granted by visiting the grave of Heinrich Raspe, a man of unusual holiness. At the Dominican cloister an image of the Virgin Mary and Child was said to turn toward suppliants or away, depending on whether they brought a sufficiently large gift.

Luther's mind was solid and terrifically honest. He remained a child of the light and darkness of his Eisenach world. Though his mind and heart grew steadily under instruction, superstitions of the countryside were set deep in his nature.

When his days in Eisenach came to an end, it was hard to part with the Schalbes, the Cottas, John Braun, and other friends. But Erfurt, the greatest of late medieval German universities, lay ahead, and the eighteen-year-old Martin was ready to go.

Monastery Gates

As he neared Erfurt, Martin watched eagerly for his first glimpse of the great cathedral towers. With more than one hundred major buildings devoted to professional religion, Erfurt had earned the title "Little Rome." Luther stepped jubilantly into this new world.

In the early sixteenth century, Erfurt was Germany's greatest university. The combination of the old scholastic interests and the newer humanistic studies, as well as schools of law and theology, had brought renown.

Hans Luther had prospered in the mines and was now able to pay Martin's full expenses. Martin lived at the student dormitory called the "Burse of St. George," where most of the boys from Thuringia lived. His name appears on the university books as "Martinus Ludher ex Mansfeld." He paid his tuition in cash and settled down to his new life.

His studies now introduced him to philosophy, including Aristotelian thought. To the normal lectures in rhetoric and its kindred arts were added courses in arithmetic, the natural sciences, ethics, and metaphysics.

He met another world in the poets and humanists who were bringing renown to Erfurt. Though he was never able to spend the time he wanted in these studies, he became familiar with the mood of the humanists and with Renaissance-style poetry. He heard the exaltation of humanism, but his training in dialectics had been precise, and he remained somewhat of a master in that art.

Luther was an excellent student. At his promotion to the bachelor's degree in 1502, he held a respectable ranking; two years later, at his master's graduation, he was second in a class of seventeen.

Life in Erfurt was what Martin had anticipated, but other, deeper currents were moving in his soul. His father's strong will had directed his path and had furnished the incentive and the money for his privileged attendance at the university, but he had been away from the direct influence of his home since he was fourteen. Although Hans Luther had destined him for the law, young Martin was now seeing things differently. His native religious sensitivity began to assert itself as he thought again and again about John Braun's devotion to his sacred calling at Eisenach.

Slowly, throughout his student days at Erfurt, the vision of the eternal calling grew. Luther was happy, carefree, and enjoying student fellowship as always, but he was thinking deeply of the horrors of sin and its punishment.

As his months of study drew to a close, he faced the possibility of entering professional school. It seemed to Hans that the climax of long planning was almost at hand, but to Martin the air was charged with uncertain terror. He clearly felt a religious calling, but he had always followed his father's will, and these two things were warring in his mind.

The day came for him to be awarded the master's degree. Hans was proud of his boy and addressed him formally. His commencement gift to his son was a copy of the expensive but necessary *Corpus Juris*. Despite his apprehension and his dislike for law, Martin followed the wishes of Hans and entered the faculty in May 1505. He was under obligation to teach two years in the faculty of arts, but this did not preclude his own studies.

In June, Martin left school to visit his home. We do not know why—possibly because of the plague that was ravaging Erfurt in 1505, or perhaps because he wanted to talk with Hans about his distaste for the law—but on his return trip, as he came near the village of Stotterheim he was caught in a thunderstorm and knocked from his horse by lightning. Fearing instant death, he vowed his life to the monastic calling if St. Anna would save him.

Luther continued his journey, evidently at peace with his decision, although there were later indications that he regretted the vow. Upon his arrival in Erfurt, he immediately ended his studies and sought admittance to the Augustinian monastery. He could not have moved forward as rapidly as he did, defying the pressure of home and friends, unless he had won peace within himself.

The vicar-general of the Saxon province was John von Staupitz, a man known for his gentle piety and ordered life. The strict Augustinian order had a highly regarded theological school. To Luther, studying theology in the peace of the monastic life was a vision of paradise, but when his friends heard his plans, they pleaded in tears against his decision. But Luther's heart was set.

On July 17, he walked down the familiar streets of Erfurt to the long, high wall that enclosed the monastery. He quietly knocked on the wooden gate, bade his companions farewell, and entered the haven of his dreams.

When Martin wrote to inform his father of his change in plans, Hans refused to give his permission. For many months it seemed that the break between them would be severe and permanent. But the plague intervened.

When the disease again swept through Erfurt, rumor drifted up to Mansfeld that Martin Luther had died. Poor

Hans could not believe it. His two younger sons had already succumbed to the disease, and the prospect of also losing Martin was crushing. It brought him some relief when the report from Erfurt proved false.

In the Erfurt monastery, Martin submitted himself willingly to the disciplines of the order. He was taught how to walk, how to sit at table, how to rise, how to understand the sign language of the daily routine, how to wear his clothes, and how to do all the other little things that make the monastic day an ordered existence. In accordance with the ritual of the order, he vowed his life to the service of God in the monastic calling.

Hans Luther hoped that the call of God had been real and that the devil had not tricked Martin into a vow he would regret.

The Warfare of Christ

Luther's thoughts turned to the problems of religion. He and his comrades fought persistently against the encroachment of worldly thought. He examined his conscience with the relentless honesty that was one of his most outstanding characteristics. Day after day, in prayer and work, he concentrated on the cleansing of his mind. But the mind does not cleanse easily.

Luther drove himself still harder. He fasted until the hours seemed unreal and his strength was so far gone that he could hardly move. He locked himself into his unheated cell and remained there to pray until exhaustion overcame him and his brethren had to break in the door. He spent long hours in prayer, to the point of slipping unconscious to the cold floor.

Luther was not being abused by the order. His superiors were attentive to him, kind, and gently concerned. The deep trouble was not between Luther and his superiors, but within his own mind.

This inner strife increased as the day approached for his ordination and the saying of his first mass. Luther approached these events with mingled terror and exultation. He had moved step by step in the custom of the church, becoming subdeacon and deacon, and now was to be made a priest.

In April 1507, when he was twenty-three, Luther knelt at the feet of his superiors to be made a priest in the Catholic Church. He was deeply conscious of his high calling and fervent in accepting all the church's major doctrines.

He sang his first mass on May 2, 1507. The date was set for the convenience of Hans Luther and some of Martin's friends. On the appointed day, Hans Luther, now prosperous, rode into Erfurt at the head of twenty horsemen. He presented himself at the monastery, was well-received by the monks, and gave them a gift of money large enough to pay for all expenses. They visited until the hour for service, then silently took their places in the church.

Luther had been preparing for this hour for many months, yet it seemed now that his will would fail. With every nerve trembling, he stood at the altar of the medieval church while the mightiest words known to man came slowly and with difficulty from his lips. Hans Luther bowed his heart in prayer in the cool, silent church and heard the voice of his boy fill the house with the presence of God.

Later, at the table in the refectory, Hans and Martin, who had not seen each other since July 1505, discussed the affairs of life in Mansfeld and the deaths by plague of Martin's brothers. Then the talk turned to Martin. Hans was still unhappy about Martin's "religious" calling. Martin argued that it was the will of God and described again the divine call that had come to him on the road near Stotterheim.

Martin was disturbed by his father's suggestion that the call had been an illusion, but he suggested that his happiness in the cloister was sufficient justification for his action. Hans called Martin sharply on his disobedience, saying, "Have you not read in Scripture that one shall honor one's father and mother?"

So the conversation ended. Martin never forgot his father's appeal to Scripture, and he felt himself tempted more than once by Hans's suggestion that the vision at Stotterheim could have come from the devil as well as from God.

Hans rode out from the monastery courtyard at the head of his party and started home. Martin returned contentedly to his study and prayer.

Luther's personal religious development paralleled his theological and biblical study in the Erfurt monastery. He studied under highly regarded teachers, but he tested every theory of theology in his personal experience. By the intensity of that experience, he became a religious pragmatist.

The foundation of his philosophic thought was influenced by Gabriel Biel, who taught in the tradition of William of Occam, a Franciscan who had carried to logical completion the implied distrust of the papacy that the Franciscan order had always known. Occam was openly convinced that popes and councils could err. Biel, Occam's follower, did not admit this, so it may have been from Occam that Luther learned to distrust the papacy.

The most important influence of these teachers was the conviction that man could attain righteousness by his own will and action. They taught Luther that stern, rigorous thinking and decisive, ordered action could produce a sense of assurance in his life. Luther went from study to prayer to action, striving to find the peace of God. Yet all the while, he knew the immovable righteousness of God which he, in his humble human life, was utterly unable to gain.

He found a hopeful, happy counterbalance in biblical studies. He read his Bible so steadily and thoroughly that he could quote whole passages by heart. Biblical content became the major unit in his thinking, and he used it as a criterion for all judgments.

One of his teachers, Dr. Usingen, disturbed by Luther's constant intellectual activity, advised him to let the Bible alone. "What is the Bible?" Usingen asked. "It is better to read the old doctors who have drawn the truth from the Bible. The Bible is the cause of all sedition." History bears witness to the exceptional strength of Scripture to make men think and act along independent lines.

Luther immersed himself in the Bible at Erfurt. What later came to public expression in his lectures at the University of Wittenberg had its beginnings here. The Christ in the Gospels and the Christ in the letters of Paul slowly supplanted in Luther's mind the Christ of stern, severe judgment.

He found his mind in constant upheaval, turning from philosophy to Scripture and back again. One taught him to counter his sense of insufficiency with more strident efforts of the will and action; the other taught the open acceptance of the free love of God, unearned and undeserved, but real and historic in Christ.

His study broadened, and in the fathers of the church he found the central stream of piety. The great insatiable desire of Christianity for the perfect life was upon him. The stark reality of Jesus' requirement that the mind be pure terrified him. In the sacrament of penance he hoped to find relief, but the beauty of this sacrament lies in the heart's belief in God's forgiving goodness. Thus, the sacrament becomes an expression, not a contributing cause.

He argued it out with his confessor, who finally told Luther point-blank, "It is not God who is angry with you. It is you who are angry with God."

Luther's confessor told him to read the works of Bernard of Clairvaux, who had found the grace of God to be the source of peace. Bernard had felt a strong sense of sin, and he, too, had fled the world to make the mighty effort for redemption in the monastic life. In the historic work of Christ, he found the proof of God's everlasting affection. He wove his hope around Christ and the crucifixion, and all the operations of the visible, established church became avenues of the grace of God. In Bernard, Luther discovered a vision of the crucifixion from which the riches of the love of God could be understood.

Luther was confronting issues of personal religion, but he sought solutions in systematic thought. The combination of these two realms is most apparent in St. Augustine, who was the product of his own religious experience to a greater degree than any of the great church fathers. Only grace could have rescued him from the depths of his depravity. Sin was central in his teachings because he knew it personally. Grace was irresistible because he himself could not resist it. He taught that the human will is impotent, because his was impotent.

With growing satisfaction, Luther read the pages of St. Augustine. The difficulties of his speculative thought began to disappear in the presence of Augustine's piety. A strong and new concept of Christ began slowly to establish itself in his heart.

Luther was greatly troubled by the specter of eternal damnation involved in the doctrine of predestination. In Augustine, he had the chance to study the master of that doctrine, who at the same time was the master of the doctrine of God's free grace in Christ. As a result, predestination lost its terror and passed into the larger doctrine of human dependence on the will of God. Augustine was indeed a rock in a weary land, and Luther temporarily rested.

The ritual of the church also began to yield up to Luther its hidden spirit. In service after service of the appointed monastic rounds, he heard the historic affirmations of the reliance of the church on Christ's mercies. He chanted the great liturgical praises to Jesus as the hope and salvation of the world.

When the great religious experiences are encased in a beautiful form and become daily liturgy, they invariably lose their power. Nevertheless, the liturgical service of the church and monastery brought into Luther's mind many of the ideas about Jesus that finally came to fruition in an adjusted theological structure and a transformed faith.

The man most influential in Luther's development was John von Staupitz. He had entered the university at Leipzig in 1485, received his M.A. at Tubingen, and lectured there in theology. He joined the Augustinian order and was chosen vicar of the Saxon province in 1503, two years before Luther entered. When the elector Frederick established the University of Wittenberg, Staupitz was made dean of the theological faculty.

Staupitz watched Luther, who had entered the monastery as a strong, enthusiastic young man, gradually grow thin, tired, and nervous from his inner spiritual struggle. Eager to help this brilliant new member of the order, Staupitz befriended him.

In Staupitz, Luther began to feel that he had a sympathetic, understanding superior. Time after time, he unburdened his soul, revealing how he feared eternal damnation, how the doctrine of predestination worried him, and how he was unconvinced he had won the mercy of Christ. With keen insight, Staupitz tried to make Luther see the introspective quality of his meditation and to direct him to historic and actual things.

One day Staupitz said, "Look not on your own imaginary sins, but look at Christ crucified, where your real sins are forgiven, and hold with deep courage to God." Luther never forgot this. Throughout his life he acknowledged his indebtedness to Staupitz for teaching him to center the concept of forgiveness around the crucifixion of Christ.

In 1508, Staupitz moved Luther from Erfurt to the monastery at Wittenberg, with hardly an opportunity to bid good-bye to his old friends.

At Wittenberg, he was committed to biblical studies, and he chafed under the philosophical emphasis. Although the desire of his life focused more and more around the Bible, he could not teach it until he earned his doctorate. Staupitz said to him one day, half-seriously, "You should take the degree of doctor so as to have something to do."

Luther protested that his strength was already used up in his regular duties and he was certain he could not survive the duties of a professorship.

Staupitz answered, "Do you not know that the Lord has a great deal of business to attend to in which He needs the assistance of clever people? If you should die you might be His counselor."

Luther laughed and agreed to follow Staupitz's advice, taking up his doctoral studies.

In preparation for lecturing on the Bible, the university required each candidate to teach three semesters on the *Sentences* of Peter Lombard. For this work, Luther returned to Erfurt. He began his work under Staupitz's supervision, and they kept in close touch.

Luther was not unfriendly to Lombard's thinking, but he did perceive a deficiency. "He would have been a great man," Luther said years later, "if he had read more in the Bible and incorporated it in his writings."

Luther continually emphasized faith against reason, tradition against speculation, theology against philosophy. He evidenced a keen consciousness of the power of sin, and tended to bring every problem around the person of Jesus.

Hail, Holy Rome

It is a tribute to the position Luther had attained within the order that, when a dispute necessitated representation at Rome, he was chosen to accompany the messenger to the Papal See.

In October 1510, John von Mecheln and Luther left Erfurt for Rome. Down through the lovely valleys of central Germany, Luther and Mecheln walked. As a boy, Luther had roamed the hills of Mansfeld. Now, in the black robes of the Augustinian order, he was out on the high road again.

Descending through the rich plains of northern Italy, the brothers came to Florence. Though twenty-five years past the height of its Renaissance, its rich treasures were still unsurpassed in the world of art.

But Luther's attention was elsewhere. Oblivious to Florence's beauty in stone and on canvas, he visited the hospitals and churches of the city.

The brothers continued their journey toward Rome, through the lovely fields and under the quiet skies of Umbria. The night before they arrived in sight of the holy city, Luther's religious devotion rose to almost ecstatic heights. The next day, when he saw the central city of western Christendom spread out before him, he fell on his knees, overcome with joy.

They lodged in a monastery, where they were shocked at the indifference and ease with which the monks went through their routine services.

Pope Julius was away from Rome on a campaign against Bologna. The future Pope Leo X, now Cardinal Medici, was at the head of a papal army attacking his native city, Florence. So John von Mecheln carried his papers to the cardinal secretary of state.

Luther was a real pilgrim. He anxiously and joyously sought the great church shrines. He visited the catacombs and felt the strange influence that comes from the memories of the martyrs buried there.

As was the custom with Roman pilgrims, he climbed the great sacred stairs up near the Lateran Church. Roman tradition held that these steps were those that Jesus had walked the night He appeared before Pilate. For centuries, devout Catholics climbed these steps, reciting the proper prayers. Luther had walked the great pathway of penitence for five years now, and this was a kind of climax.

Preaching in Wittenberg the year before his death, Luther told of his experiences in Rome and related how, as he had reached the top of the stairs, a doubt regarding the power of the penitent practice had come into his mind.

Luther did not come down from these steps a rebel against his church. He did not orient his thinking from this moment around the text, "The just shall live by faith." He did not forsake the great comforts and assurances of his church's sacraments and "works." The "Holy Steps" were only one movement in the experience. He was a child of Rome when he came, and a child of Rome when he left.

But the ideal Rome of Luther's dreams was forever broken. The Rome of the apostles, once so precious in his mind, became the Rome of reality. The Renaissance papacy, which had controlled Rome since 1447, had steadily centered its policy around the secularization of the church. Rome had become a place of notorious anti-Christian life.

Luther found Rome utterly abandoned to money, luxury, and kindred evils. He was stunned, but he did not stay in Rome long enough to rebel against it.

In January 1511, the weary Luther, his mind filled with conflicting thoughts, started home with John von Mecheln. In Milan, where Leonardo da Vinci was at work painting *The Last Supper,* Luther found to his amazement a group of priests refusing allegiance to Rome.

Upon his arrival in Erfurt, Luther was glad to return to his books and the routine of his study, but his life was not the same. He had been to Rome. Soon Rome would hear from him.

The Rising Tide

In the autumn of 1511, Staupitz again called Luther to Wittenberg, a small, humble town on the Elbe River. The townspeople were uneducated, coarse, and generally uncultured.

The town had two churches: the cathedral church attached to the university, and a smaller, less conspicuous parish church, which served the inhabitants of the town. Luther came to the Augustinian cloister, known as the "Black Cloister" because of the black robes worn by the priests.

His first year at Wittenberg was devoted to personal study, following the plans for his doctorate, but he was deeply interested in the affairs of his order. In May 1512, Luther was elected subprior of the Wittenberg monastery and he assumed many administrative functions.

On October 18, 1512, he received the doctor of theology degree. He wrote to invite his friends from Erfurt to come up for his promotion, but relations now were strained because his former colleagues resented his transfer to Wittenberg. The Erfurt men did not attend the commencement, and from this day an increasing difference grew between Luther, who stressed the biblical aspect of theology, and the philosophical bias of the Erfurt teaching tradition.

When Luther joined Wittenberg's staff of professors, he brought intellectual leadership and a moral vigor that led to the development of what became known as "the Wittenberg theology."

Sometime during this year, Luther focused his conflicting thoughts and for the first time saw them with such clarity and harmony that he called this experience the "birthday" of his faith. In the tower of the Black Cloister, where he often studied, he meditated on the great text in Romans 1:17: "The just shall live by faith."

He had always felt so thoroughly his own sinfulness, in contrast to the perfect righteousness and perfect justice of God, that he could not understand how anyone could be justified in the sight of God.

The Apostle Paul, above all other men, had pointed out the sinfulness of the human race. What, then, had he meant when he wrote, "The just shall live by faith"?

Luther reviewed the positions of Bernard and Augustine, and he remembered the consistent advice of Staupitz to look upon the crucifixion. He recalled how Paul had centered his whole thought around the crucifixion. Paul must have meant by "faith" the acceptance of the work of Christ! By faith in the crucifixion, could Luther find release from the burden of sin? By the sheer act of acceptance, could he find the mighty gulf between himself and God bridged? Was it true that God's righteousness was not the righteousness of condemnation but the righteousness transferred from Christ to him?

He began to feel the mighty rhythm of Pauline thought. It was no longer a battle with God to force God's recognition of his good deeds, because God was on his side. He could now stand steadfast by faith in Christ and know that the tremendous pressure of his sin was offset by the endless mercy made possible in Christ.

This was the hour of his freedom, the hour of his

great "illumination." His entire theology was not yet clearly wrought, but its basis was fixed. From this day forth there was a new note in his message. All his teachings began, centered, and ended in the history of redemption. Not that faith moved without works, but life came by faith, and works were the result.

From 1513 to 1515, he lectured on the Psalms. Though he lectured in Latin, he would break into German if it better served his point, and he created new and striking illustrations. The students knew they were listening to one who spoke with authority, and they flocked to his classroom.

In 1515 and 1516, he lectured on Paul's Epistle to the Romans. As he set forth the mind of Paul through chapter after chapter of this book, his students saw the whole drama of heavenly redemption unveiled.

In his lectures on Psalms and Romans, Luther's concept of theology was formulated systematically. Though his interest was always in practical piety, never in the system, these lectures brought his thoughts into ordered shape.

As he lectured on Romans, he brought the society of his day before the judgment bar of this mighty book. He bitterly attacked Julius II and the frightful immorality of Rome. He denounced the church hierarchy for their widespread corruption and vileness. In severe language he arraigned the clergy for thinking that their task was to defend the church instead of to preach the Gospel.

Luther's elevation to the doctor's degree included preaching to his brother monks. At first, he objected steadfastly to this requirement, but his distinctive sermons attracted such attention that the town council soon petitioned him to preach in the parish church.

Added to the burdens of professorship and preaching was Luther's election, in May 1515, as district vicar of the monasteries in Meissen and Thuringia. Once a year, he was required to visit each of the ten monasteries in the district (later eleven with the addition of his birth town of Eisleben). He ceased to be the introspective, troubled monk of his Erfurt days, becoming a strong, assured, confident leader who enjoyed the respect and confidence of his entire circle.

The plague came to Wittenberg in the fall of 1516. Many citizens left immediately, and many of the monks were transferred temporarily to other cloisters. But Luther stayed in Wittenberg. Neither plague nor emperor nor pope would move him from his chosen course.

The elector of Saxony, Luther's own civil lord, had assembled hundreds of so-called religious relics in the Wittenberg cathedral. The veneration of relics—the belief that they carried spiritual power—disturbed Luther greatly. Many of the claims for the relics were preposterous. Into early 1517, a note of protest was sounded again and again in his sermons and lectures. A devout son of the church, Luther was by no means a rebel. He labored in his chosen field, but increasingly he protested against abuse.

Meanwhile, Europe's disaffection with Rome was growing. John Colet, Sir Thomas More, and others in England steadfastly called for a higher, cleaner administration throughout the church. Erasmus insisted that the church reform itself. Leaders of the church in Italy had banded into a society dedicated to reform. Throughout western Christendom, the cry of scandal had been heard steadily for fifty years. The oncoming tide of reform was gathering momentum.

Luther pleaded in lecture and sermon for the commoner, whose blood was his own. The strong claim of the people, rising steadily for half a century, now found a voice. He championed the peasant, challenging the right of the nobility to enact and enforce tyrannical laws. He called the great civil lords "robbers" or "sons of robbers."

The oppression of the under classes by civil and ecclesiastical overlords moved him to fury, and he spoke openly against it. He became a gloriously eloquent spokesman in the name of religion for all the mighty causes that uplift mankind.

The Freedom of a Christian Man

In 1517, in defiance of canon law, Archbishop Albert—a prince in the house of Brandenburg—secured election to the archbishopric of Mayence by bribing Pope Leo X for confirmation. To finance his ambitious endeavor, Albert had borrowed money from the House of Fugger, Augsburg bankers.

Albert and Leo compromised on a fee of ten thousand ducats, and in order to ensure payment, the pope granted Albert the privilege of selling an indulgence. Half the proceeds of this sale were to go to Albert, to pay his debts to the bankers, and the other half would go to Leo, supposedly to be used to rebuild St. Peter's Church.

Before long, parishioners began to come to Luther with letters of indulgence they had purchased, which promised release from all punishment imposed by church law and release from the penance they must do in purgatory for their sins.

Luther was unaware of the inner workings of this scandalous operation, but he knew that the clear and expressed intention of Christian piety had been brutally and inexcusably broken.

He argued with himself for months while the sale went on. He believed that Christ had stored up great benefits for the human race by means of His passion, and he believed that the heroic Christian activity of the saints benefited the common Christian. He agreed with the church that the Bishop of Rome held the "power of the Keys," but this sale was different.

The Black Cloister became the scene of a furious battle in Luther's heart and mind. How could the heads of the church act like this? Did they not understand the limits of papal power? Did they not know that the mercy of Christ was not for sale? Finally, Luther could no longer hold his peace.

What followed were ninety-five distinct propositions challenging the power of the pope and attacking greed and the abuse of indulgences in the church.

On October 31, 1517, when Wittenberg was crowded for the anniversary of the consecration of the Cathedral Church, Luther posted his ninety-five theses with a brief preamble on the wooden doors of the Cathedral Church, which were used as the school's bulletin board.

It was not as though Luther took a hammer—symbolic of revolution—and struck at the portals of the cathedral—symbolic of the whole church. Rather, here was a theology professor and village preacher in correct academic fashion calling his colleagues to dispute the fundamental questions of their generation.

Martin posted his handwritten original, but the Wittenberg printers quickly published both Latin and Greek texts for broadcast throughout Germany. Luther was unprepared for how his words swept through Europe. They appeared in every language and every place in Christendom "as though carried by angelic messengers."

Luther now found himself the rallying leader for the disaffection of half a century, and he was forced to direct a campaign for the clarification of the Gospel and the reform of the church.

A movement opposing Luther was initiated by Albert, who brought the matter to the attention of Rome. But the pope was in no mood to give serious consideration to a question of piety. Completely immersed in secular affairs, Leo X could not understand the religious issue of this northern quarrel.

Luther wrote to the pope in May 1518. He told him he had always accepted papal authority and in no way desired to appear heretical, but the recent papal indulgence had spread grave scandal and mockery, driving him to protest the abuse. Luther now desired only that the pope should understand his position and carefully consider the matters at issue.

Careful consideration was not something Leo X was prepared to give. He instructed the general of the Augustinian Order to quench these fires of rebellion. Accordingly, the matter was brought up at the meeting of the order at Heidelberg in May 1518, where Luther explained and defended his theses. Because Luther did not want to involve his order, he resigned as district vicar.

On August 25, 1518, twenty-two-year-old Philip Melanchthon entered Wittenberg as the first professor of Greek to be invited to teach.

Luther had preferred another candidate, but his reservations vanished four days later when Melanchthon delivered his installation address to the university faculty. Melanchthon made impassioned pleas for an orientation of the curriculum around the humanities and the New Testament. As Melanchthon argued for a union of classical and Pauline studies, Luther's heart rejoiced. A steadfast friendship sprang up between the two men, never to be broken until death.

The ability and devotion of Melanchthon became more important each day to Luther. The fine, sensitive, accurate, grammatical scholarship of Melanchthon, the finest humanist Germany had yet produced, was joined to Luther's powerful, emotional dynamic.

Rome, meanwhile, did not let the case rest. Luther was called to defend his action before a representative of the pope in Augsburg, but Cardinal Cajetan, a zealous defender of papal rights, was unwilling even to let Luther speak.

The conference ended in thorough misunderstanding. The cardinal insisted that Luther recant, but Luther insisted on discussing the issue. The cardinal charged Luther with heresy, but when Luther challenged him to prove any statement of the theses to be heretical, the cardinal was unable to do so.

After three unsuccessful meetings, Luther withdrew from the audience and waited a few days in Augsburg before leaving the city quietly by night to avoid a rumored trap.

The next attempt at reconciliation was conducted by Charles von Miltitz, a papal ambassador to the elector Frederick. Miltitz failed to conciliate the parties, but in January 1519, he won from Luther a promise to write the pope a letter of apology for the whole business. Luther promised to support indulgences in their proper sense and to urge steady reverence for the Holy See. But the mission of Miltitz was disowned by his superiors and came to naught.

The next stage in the controversy was far more dramatic. John Eck, a professor of theology at the University of Ingolstadt, a Dominican monk, and a man of considerable ability in debating, challenged Luther and his Wittenberg colleague Andrew Bodenstein to a public discussion in Leipzig.

Considerably disturbed, Luther set forth from Wittenberg, but the faculty and students of the university would not let him go alone. Philip Melanchthon, Justus Jonas, Nicholas Amsdorf, Andrew Bodenstein, and Duke

Barnim, the rector of the university, rode with Luther in two country carts, while 200 students, thoroughly armed, walked beside and behind them. In Leipzig, they faced the constant threat of rioting.

In debate, Eck continually shifted from the present considerations to past records. He wanted to drive Luther into admitting a position similar to that held by past heretics. After several unsuccessful attempts, Eck brought up the work of Jan Hus. Luther interrupted him. "But good Dr. Eck, every Hussite opinion is not wrong."

Eck was jubilant. He countered Luther with the challenge that the church had denounced the Hussite opinions, that the Council of Constance had condemned them, and that the pope had declared them heretical. Luther was driven finally to the damning admission that popes and councils could err. The days of indecision were over. Now he was out in the open.

The Leipzig debates ended and Eck journeyed triumphantly to Rome. Luther left Leipzig branded a "heretic, rebel, a thing to flout."

On June 15, 1520, Leo signed the bull *Exurge Domine,* a solemn papal letter calling upon Luther to recant within sixty days or be excommunicated. In many of the northern provinces, however, the people were so thoroughly on Luther's side that they refused to allow the letter to be published.

When the bull came to Wittenberg, Luther headed a march of the students and faculty outside the city to a nearby field. There a huge bonfire was prepared and, with quiet dignity, Martin Luther himself placed the books of the canon law on the fire, in token of his refusal to be bound by them. Then, taking the papal bull, he placed it on the fire and said, "Because thou hast brought down the truth of God, He also brings thee down to this fire today. Amen."

In the summer of 1520, Luther presented three pamphlets that outlined his offensive and defensive positions. He attacked the sole, arbitrary authority of the papacy. In the spirit of growing nationalism, he appealed to the German people to free themselves from the tyranny of papal power. He contradicted the famous Roman positions that the clergy are superior to the laity in controlling the church, that only the pope may interpret Scripture authoritatively, and that only the pope may call a church council. These, he said, were the three walls behind which the power of Rome had hidden itself. All of them, he maintained, are invalid in light of the great essential doctrine of the priesthood of all believers.

Hardly had Europe caught its breath when Luther published a work examining the sacramental system of the Roman church. Luther maintained that no sacrament was valid if it could not find justification in the New Testament. Apart from the Eucharist and baptism, and possibly penance, Luther found no scriptural justification for declaring Christian customs to be sacraments.

In November 1520, Luther followed these aggressive documents with a sensitive, lovely presentation of the center of his own belief. Here he stated the paradox: A Christian man is the most free lord of all, subject to no one. A Christian man is the dutiful servant of all, subject to everyone. From this he wrung a glorious presentation of the free spiritual life of the Christian believer. Because he is free, the Christian is bound by the great law of Christian love and by the indwelling spirit of Christ to serve all mankind in perfect charity. The freedom that belongs to a Christian is the freedom created by the indwelling spirit of Christ, and it leads to constant Christian service.

The Epic Hour

Through the winter of 1520–1521, Luther was active in all his regular work. He preached daily, taught his regular classes in the university, and wrote commentaries on Genesis and the Psalms. He answered the criticism of his enemies with insults and biting sarcasm of his own.

On January 3, 1521, Pope Leo X signed the final bull demanding complete excommunication for Luther. To many, this decree meant that Luther should be executed as a heretic.

On January 25, 1521, Charles V, newly elected head of the Holy Roman Empire, convened his first diet, at the German town of Worms, to consider all the affairs of the empire.

Jerome Aleander, a representative from Rome, spoke to the diet for three hours on February 13, demanding that Luther be delivered up bound and condemned without a hearing, and that all Luther's work be burned.

Frederick the Elector intervened on Luther's behalf, and Charles promised that Luther would be accorded protection to answer a summons, and that he would be treated lawfully and would receive a fair trial.

In Wittenberg, on March 26, Luther received the summons from Charles V, and on April 2 he left for

Worms. On April 16, Luther rode his humble wagon triumphantly into Worms and lodged at the house of the Knights of St. John. A crowd gathered rapidly and kept him busy with visitors late into the night.

The next day, Luther was ushered into the meeting of the diet, with Charles V presiding, and was instructed that he was to say nothing except in answer to questions. Immediately, the representative of the archbishop's court pointed to a group of books on a central table and asked Luther whether these books were his and whether he would recant the positions set forth in them.

This call to recant was too sudden for Luther. Charles's summons had promised a hearing, not a recision demand. Luther seemed powerless to answer. Jerome Schurf, his friend and lawyer, stepped to his rescue, crying out, "Let the titles of the books be read."

By the time the reading was over, Luther had recovered his presence, and he asked for more time to consider his proper response.

Confusion followed for a moment while Charles conferred with his counselors. Finally, Luther was granted a one-day delay in the proceedings, whereupon he withdrew from the hall and returned to his rooms. Now he knew the question—and he would be ready.

He was in prayer much of the night, his mind fastened rigidly to its one great task. A strange mingling of faith, fear, strength, and exultation possessed him.

When he appeared again before the diet, Luther spoke calmly, in complete command of himself, but his deep intensity stilled every noise in the hall. He acknowledged authorship of each of his books, but held that each should be considered on its own merits. Much of what he had written was held above reproach by even his enemies, and to recant those writings would be to deny the truth.

The second class of his works were those that inveighed against the papacy. To recant from these, Luther said, would "add strength to tyranny" and turn Luther into "the tool of iniquity."

Luther then confessed that "a third sort of book I have written against some private individuals who tried to defend the Roman tyranny and tear down my pious doctrine" were perhaps "more bitter than is becoming to a minister of religion," but he refused to retract these writings again on the basis of not wanting to give license to tyranny.

Luther paused a moment, then picked up a triumphant strain, moving in prophetic humility from rebuke to proof, and calling on all present to rise and answer him, to give proof to their charges of error or heresy. The archbishop's representative rose, amazed that Luther would dare to speak this way, and asked for a simple, unsophisticated answer: "Will you recant or not?"

Luther answered briefly and exactly: "My conscience is captive to the Word of God. I neither can nor will recant anything, since it is neither right nor safe to act against conscience. God help me. Amen."

Again came the call for recantation, and again Luther declined. The tumult increased and Charles V rose abruptly and left the room, signifying an end of the audience. The marshal took Luther quickly from the hall. Fearing an attempt on Luther's life, friends gathered in a marching circle around him and escorted him through the crowds.

The counselors of Frederick and the emperor tried to arrive at a compromise. They called on Luther several times during the succeeding few days, but he was adamant that compromise was impossible. In despair, the intermediaries gave up.

High above Eisenach

Luther slipped out of town on the morning of April 26 to return to Wittenberg. The journey home was leisurely and absent of anxiety. He visited his relatives in Mohra and preached the next day in the village. Back in the field and forest of his family, Luther visited many friends and relatives in and around Eisenach.

Resuming his journey on May 4, he was surprised by a company of armed horsemen, who forced his carriage to stop along a narrow road through the forest. The men whispered something to Luther, who turned to his friends and told them he had to leave, but that all was well and he would write to them soon. Then Luther mounted a horse, and off the men galloped through the forest.

After a hard ride through the day and well into the night, they arrived at the castle of Wartburg, where Luther was turned over to the commandant. Word spread rapidly that Luther had been kidnapped, but no one knew who the kidnappers were or why they had grabbed Luther.

The secret of his disappearance was guarded rigidly. To reassure some of his most intimate friends, Luther wrote to them after a few weeks, reporting on his health and safety, but he did not divulge his hiding place.

Luther himself had been taken by surprise, but he was

quickly reassured at Wartburg, where he was treated as an honored guest. In his room, undisturbed by the routine duties of professorship and parish, he set about translating his beloved New Testament into German. Many German translations were available, but each was in a dialect. He would set forth the blessed stories so they could be understood generally.

There also came from his pen tract after tract on all the major issues of the controversy. He wrote sermons on the Gospels and Epistles to be used in the regular cycle of the church year. He wrote on the Mass and on monastic vows.

He treated the problem of vows as he did everything else, asking only one question: "What does Scripture say?" From Scripture he argued that vows were hostile to the good of Christianity. He strongly cut away the basis for the great monastic emphasis on celibacy. The Bible encourages marriage, does not place a greater premium on virginity, and destroys the distinction between clergy and laity.

Impatient, restless to return to leadership, Luther finally was permitted by Frederick to come out of his seclusion by the course of events at Wittenberg. There, in his absence, colleagues like Andrew Bodenstein wanted to overthrow the entire ancient organization and faith. Luther, by nature and training, was thoroughly conservative. He had been driven by life's severest experiences to open up the abuses in his church, but he devoutly loved the church itself, and he would keep all its ancient customs. Not so the more radical men who had welcomed his leadership. Wittenberg needed him badly.

He had corresponded with his friends all winter and knew the situation exactly. Melanchthon pleaded with him to return. Finally, in the spring of 1522, he quietly slipped away from Wartburg. Dressed as a knight and with a sword by his side, he journeyed incognito through the territory of Duke George of Saxony—who willingly would have turned him over to the authorities, had he caught him. When he arrived safely at Wittenberg, he talked with Melanchthon and his other friends and analyzed the situation. Then for eight successive days he preached in the village church against the fanatical activities that had resulted in the destruction of pictures and images and in the breakdown of organizational morale.

At the close of the week, he was once again the leader of the Wittenberg movement. The radical wing of the Reformation would locate its center elsewhere. Luther turned his attention to explaining and defending his cause. With Melanchthon's help, he now concentrated on a clear formulation of the Wittenberg position. Throughout 1520 and 1521, Melanchthon had worked on an outline of theology constructed from Paul's letter to the Romans. Now, with Luther's approval, he published it in Wittenberg. Such a logical, systematic presentation was needed, and Melanchthon's skill was equal to the task. The proofs of argument were all scriptural, and the book marked a tremendous advance for the Luther forces.

The Whirlwind

The severest test Luther ever faced came in 1524–1525, during the Peasants' Revolt. For centuries in central Europe, the peasant class had been ruled strictly by both civil and ecclesiastical nobles. The long story of uprisings to gain their birthright is told throughout history.

In Germany, these uprisings had become increasingly severe and frequent during the 150 years preceding 1525. Long before Luther, the streams of rebellion and the Gospel had met in the forests of central Germany. The peasants would gather strength for a century and break into rebellion, only to be beaten back by superior technique and equipment. Then they would nurse their wrath for generations until, sorely pressed, they would again storm the princes' castles.

In the volatile days of the late fifteenth and early sixteenth centuries, a groundswell of rebellion erupted throughout central Europe. As the movement spread violently northward into Saxony, it became increasingly clear that Luther had to speak.

Luther's mind was clear. He was thoroughly conservative in civil affairs. Never in his life had he sanctioned force, except by the civil magistrate. Had they led him to the stake, he would have died unresisting at Worms. He would never have approved an armed defense by the Elector Frederick and Saxon warriors on his behalf.

Nevertheless, his heart was a peasant's heart. The blood in his veins, he boasted, was peasant blood. No one in Europe had spoken more directly against the abuses of the ruling class than he, and now he faced the strange, terrible conflict between his native, idealistic sympathy for the peasants and his strong belief in the divine order of civil government.

He preached against violence in town after town and in the camps of peasants who were gathered for war. He pleaded for peace, and he hoped for arbitration. But it was too late for arbitration. Not even Luther's powerful spirit could check the rising fury of the struggle. It was a frightful, bitter hour.

The decisive battle of the revolution was fought near Frankenhausen on May 15. The peasants were equipped with rude weapons—pitchforks, wood axes, scythes, spears, and bows. Across a long, open field they barricaded themselves behind overturned farm wagons and whatever other impediments they could find.

The landholders' assault came under the able leadership of Philip of Hesse. Well-armed knights on armored horses, with stout lances and sharp swords, swept across the plain. No peasant was alive when the sun went down, except those who had hidden or fled.

Social darkness settled over Germany. The peasants were bitter that the lion of Wittenberg had not fought with them. All over Europe, the conservative class—men who rationalized their own desires—blamed Luther for the rebellion.

Catharine von Bora

Luther's boyhood in Mansfeld had given him a deep and affectionate appreciation of a Christian home. But any thoughts of a wife and family had been forced to the background when he had taken the monastic vows in 1505.

Back in Wittenberg after his Wartburg seclusion, he found that, as a result of his attack on monastic vows, men and women were leaving the monasteries and convents.

Luther defended marriage of the clergy on the grounds that it was the first picture of humanity presented in the opening chapters of Genesis. God had created man and woman and had called for their life together. All through the Scriptures, marriage appears as the ideal life. Nowhere in Luther's reading of the Old Testament could he find justification for suspending this relationship. By the laws of nature and the laws of God, the married life is justified.

Luther found cause for joy when his friends in Wittenberg and other northern German towns, released from their vows by allegiance to the Reformation, began to marry. Philip Melanchthon, Justus Jonas, and other leaders in the movement were established in homes of their own by 1525.

The issue took on serious consequences, however,

when a group of nine nuns sought refuge in Wittenberg in April 1523. One after another, the nuns in this group were cared for by friends or married to suitors. All except Catharine von Bora.

Catharine had been born in a little village twenty miles south of Leipzig in January 1499. Her mother's early death and her father's remarriage had placed her in a convent school at age five. She had received the veil when she was sixteen.

In the general exodus from the monasteries, Catharine succeeded in making her escape on the night of April 4, 1523, when she was twenty-four. Arriving in Wittenberg, she settled in the home of a wealthy citizen, where for two years she helped with the housework. Toward the end of 1523 she fell in love and was engaged, but her suitor left Wittenberg and neglected her.

Not long afterward, a friend of Luther's courted Catharine and decided to marry her, but she refused and laughingly said she would marry only Dr. Amsdorf or Dr. Luther.

For a long time, Luther's father had been urging him to marry and Martin finally agreed. He wrote to a friend that he would marry to "please his father, tease the pope, and spite the devil."

Catharine von Bora held for him no youthful charms; he was forty-two, she was twenty-six. His mind and heart, exposed for years to public life, were somewhat toughened. The long years of monastic discipline had given him complete control over himself. This decision was a choice, not an emotion.

Catharine came from a good family and she was capable of the duties that would fall on the wife of Martin Luther. She was strong, rugged, healthy, with vitality and good humor.

In the spring, he spoke to her of his hopes. It was not

easy. They both had known the monastic life. He knew what would be said of them, but his heart was gentle and his honor unassailable. They were immediately in harmony, and when once the gentle words were said, the differences in age and temperament dissolved.

On the evening of June 13, 1525, they were married in Luther's home by John Bugenhagen, a faculty colleague. After the quiet wedding, Luther sent invitations for a public announcement and festivities. On June 27, Hans and Margaret Luther and many friends gathered in Wittenberg to celebrate the marriage.

Europe went into turmoil at the report of the wedding. Luther's more violent Catholic opponents lashed out at him. Rumors spread that it was a marriage of necessity—but this was too much even for Erasmus, who came to Luther's defense.

Luther married with a clear expectation of the difficulties to follow, but he was not prepared for the strange, quiet happiness that slowly came into his life as their home settled into a normal routine. Catharine brought to him a strong and willing service, a loyal and sympathetic heart, and a keen and delightful sense of humor. She was a source of joy and peace to him for the rest of his life.

The Mills of God

In 1526, as Luther carried on his epic battle with the papacy and the state, he was forced to remain in seclusion. Under the provisions of the Edict of Worms, any German citizen was obligated to deliver Luther alive or dead to the authorities. His friends were careful not to allow strangers around, and Luther was unable to attend meetings to try to heal the schism.

The first important diet after Worms was held in the German town of Speyer in 1526. Charles V was unable to attend because of the constant turmoil in European politics. The diet met at Speyer under the presidency of Charles's brother Ferdinand.

After a long debate, the Catholic party, headed by Ferdinand, insisted on the execution of the Edict of Worms. The Protestant party, headed by the Saxon elector, steadfastly refused to carry it out. The reformers were permitted to return to their states and continue their evangelical work.

To counter French influence on Pope Clement VII, the nephew of Leo X, Charles felt compelled to invade Italy and march on the holy city with his army of Spanish and German soldiers. Men who had hissed and cheered Luther at the diet of Worms now found themselves marching together under a German general to attack Rome.

As the northern army approached, the papal party took refuge in the impregnable castle of St. Angelo. The Germans and Spaniards thoroughly sacked the city.

At home in Wittenberg, Catharine gave birth to a son and Martin proudly named his firstborn Hans, after his father. Luther continued to preach and teach daily, though his health began to show signs of weakening under the long strain. On July 6, 1527, rising from the dinner table, he fainted before he could reach his room. For days he was seriously ill.

Before his recovery was complete, the plague came again to Wittenberg. The university was moved to Jena— but Luther never fled the plague. While Catharine was carrying their second child, little Hans, now more than a year old, fell desperately ill and for eleven days could neither eat nor drink.

It was a time of deep misery and uncertainty. Death was all around him. The great authorities of his childhood, church and state, were battling each other. Yet Luther found strength through his faith in God. During his hour of deep distress, Luther penned his song of triumph, "A Mighty Fortress Is Our God."

Hans recovered and Catharine weathered the plague to complete her pregnancy in fair health. A daughter, Elizabeth, was born December 10, but she died before her first birthday.

Luther now turned his attention to the condition of the newly reformed parishes in Saxony. With Melanchthon and others, he visited town after town, examining each one's educational system and church practices. In response to the miserable state of instruction he found, Luther set himself to writing a catechism, which he completed within two years. The Smaller Catechism, designed for family and school use, set in gentle, quiet form all the familiar doctrines of historic Christianity. His gift for practical application was put to great advantage in explaining the doctrines of the church to little children.

In 1529, Charles V called for a second diet to meet at Speyer. He forced the delegates to annul the action of 1526 and succeeded in obtaining a majority vote to prohibit reformed worship.

In response, the delegates from the Lutheran areas of Saxony, Brandenburg, Brunswick, Hesse, Anhalt, and fourteen of the free cities presented a formal protest, challenging the legality of the recision of the previous diet's actions.

From this point on, the party of non-Catholic adherents was called Protestant. Some of the signers of the protest were not supporters of Luther, so the term Protestant carried a broad connotation.

Almost a year after her little sister had died, Magdalene Luther was born. She was named for Magdalene von Bora, Catharine's aunt, who had been a companion in the Nimbschen convent and who was now a well-loved member of the Wittenberg home.

The division in the Protestant party was caused by the rapid growth of a reform movement in Switzerland headed by Ulrich Zwingli. In his early days of preaching, Zwingli had violently opposed the abuses of popular Catholic life. His protests steadily grew into a reform movement in Zurich, where he was a pastor from 1519 until his death.

The center of the Zwinglian movement was intellectual and humane. Zwingli was not deeply concerned over the problem of sin—Luther's central issue. Zwingli spoke the language of the Christian humanist, Luther that of the old Catholic, and they could not understand each other.

Those signing the protest at Speyer—who were more Zwinglian than Lutheran—desired greatly to unite the two forces of the reform movement. Philip of Hesse was the strongest and most capable of the reform princes, and he urged a meeting between Zwingli and Luther.

At first, Luther did not want to go, because he distrusted the Zwinglians, but for political reasons, the elector John bade him to go.

Outside the meetings, Luther and Zwingli enjoyed friendship and came to appreciate and admire each other. But in the conference sessions it was a different story. With all the arguments of the humanists, Zwingli attacked Luther's orthodox position on the Lord's Supper. Luther adamantly defended the doctrine of the Real Presence. Many times the two men came to harsh words, but at the end of the conference they offered mutual apologies for the outbursts.

Philip asked them to draw up a statement of belief that all could sign. Luther wrote out a definition of fifteen cardinal doctrines, showing their agreement in all but the last, which concerned the Lord's Supper. The delegates signed the document.

The Lutheran and Swiss reforms thereafter went their separate ways. Zwingli returned to Zurich to continue his plans for organizing a political Protestant party around the northern Swiss states. He died heroically four years later when Switzerland was torn by religious civil war.

In an effort to reconcile the differences in Germany, Charles V convened a diet at Augsburg in 1530. Luther, however, was denied safe passage to the assembly and took refuge for five months in the great castle overlooking the town of Coburg.

These were bitter days for him. He was sick and discouraged, but he kept himself busy translating Jeremiah and all the lesser prophets and beginning Ezekiel. He published some of Aesop's fables in German and completed twelve other works. There are 123 letters preserved from these months in the Coburg castle.

He received messages from Augsburg, where his friends were steadfastly maintaining the faith. But Luther grew anxious when he heard that Melanchthon was drawing up the great confession, because he feared that the younger man would concede too much to the papists. The fear was well-grounded, because Melanchthon was eager, above all else, to heal the break.

In Augsburg, Melanchthon's confession was read in the diet on July 25. It was a clear, concise, theologically conservative statement setting forth the religious views of the Lutherans and listing abuses which must be corrected. Charles asked a group of papal theologians, headed by Eck of Ingolstadt, to prepare an answer.

Eck was a bitter man. Five times his report was returned to the committee for softening and revision. The final version was still too harsh for the Lutherans. John, the elector of Saxony, refused to remain at the diet under such conditions and departed after a difficult scene with the emperor.

Meanwhile, as Luther waited anxiously, John Reinicke brought news from Mansfeld that old Hans Luther was dead. Luther rose, took his psalter and entered the study, where he stayed for almost two days in unnerved sorrowing. Near the close of the second day, he regained control and picked up the routine of life.

The diet of Augsburg closed unhappily for the Protestants. Luther returned to Wittenberg in the fall, knowing that imperial pressure would be more severe than ever. From now on it would be a battle of political alliances, with Luther more and more in the background.

He journeyed in 1537 to Schmaldkalden, where he struggled to draw up a confession of faith emphasizing the differences between Protestants and Catholics more strongly than the "Augsburg Confession."

He returned to Wittenberg to continue his labors, but life was increasingly painful. The severity of his headaches, severe rheumatism, recurring digestive disturbances, neuritis in his chest, and a dizzying disease in the middle ear all plagued him.

Then Philip of Hesse came to Luther for advice regarding his unhappy marriage. At nineteen, Philip had married the daughter of Duke George, but they repelled each other and had not lived together for years. At first, Philip had kept a mistress, but his conscience troubled him greatly. Long after he dismissed his mistress, Philip fell in love with a young lady of the Leipzig court. Her mother refused to let them marry unless Philip was divorced or obtained permission from the great Protestant preachers for a second marriage.

Luther talked it over with Melanchthon and Bucer. In European thought, the question of a man having two wives was open. Luther firmly believed that the church had the right to authorize it in special cases for the protection of morals and character. The ancient church had argued that when a man's wife was stricken with leprosy or insanity it was quite within the realm of moral law that, without deserting her, he could marry a second wife.

Arguing from the Old Testament that they were no better than Abraham, Isaac, and other patriarchs who had enjoyed this privilege, Luther, Melanchthon, and Bucer granted Philip of Hesse permission to marry under what they called the seal of the confessional, requiring secrecy from all parties.

Unfortunately, it was impossible to keep this secret. Within months, Luther was once again the center of a storm of protest. He had sanctioned the breaking of a moral law, defying the accepted canons of Christianity.

Meanwhile, the inner life of the Lutheran Church developed steadily. A man of deep historic piety, Luther constantly struggled to impart this feeling to his people. His translation of the Bible finally was completed in 1534.

Luther succeeded beyond his fondest dreams to create a version understandable to all Germans. So powerful was his work that it practically created a new

German language. The Bible was read by hundreds of thousands of Germans and the imprint of Luther's style and phrasing was permanent.

He also translated into German the great Catholic services in which he had been raised. The Mass, the central point in Lutheran worship, was set in German under Luther's personal editorship. He produced a series of noble hymns for public worship.

Steadily, Luther added hymn after hymn to his church's worship. They were bold, martial, triumphant expressions, addressing the doctrine of redemption and revolving around the blood and sacrifice of Jesus. He sensitively furnished both music and words for the rhythm of his movement.

Luther was thoroughly unsystematic in the use of money. He never sold a book or manuscript in his life, steadfastly refusing, although printers offered him hundreds of dollars a year for his written works. These, he said, were the gifts of God and were not for sale. Nor did he receive a salary for teaching. He was supported after the break from the monastic order by an annual gift from the elector. But even with this, there was no money to be had.

But underneath the stress of this visible life was a very quiet, gentle current. Catharine and Martin loved each other more dearly as the years passed. She never lost her high respect for him—but neither did she surrender her independent will. Luther often said laughingly that he had merely exchanged one authority for another when he married.

Luther was particularly happy with the smallest children in the house, but when his second daughter, Magdalene, died in September 1542, he entered the depths of human sorrow.

Dear Genesis

On November 10, 1545, old friends came to celebrate the sixty-second birthday of the man they loved; but Luther's heart did not rejoice. The infirmities of age weighed heavily on him. Like a stranger in a foreign land, he longed for the sweetness of death. He wanted peace and quiet, but the world would not permit it.

The next day, he lectured on the Book of Genesis. He closed his notebook, looked up gently, and quietly told his students, "This is dear Genesis. God grant that others do better with it after me. I am weak. Pray God to grant me a good, blessed hour."

Still, his race was not yet run. In Mansfeld, Counts Albert and Gebhardt were in bitter dispute, and only Luther could solve the difficulty. He left for Mansfeld in a cold December storm, but returned home in January with the dispute unsettled.

On January 23, he left home again. Catharine begged him not to go because of his health and the bitter weather. But Luther had known only duty for too long. He could not spare himself.

When at last the counts signed an agreement settling the dispute, Luther's work was done. Preparations for the homeward journey were made, but Luther was sick. He felt a tightness in the chest. Hot towels and brandy helped, and he tried to sleep.

The agony increased. Terrific pain seized him—but he was accustomed to pain. He called on Jonas and Colius to pray for the great battle within the church.

The pain would not subside. Jonas asked, "Dear Father, will you stand by Christ and the doctrine you have preached?"

Luther's mighty will held off the coming stroke, and he answered, "Yes."

In the final moment, his halting voice whispered the glorious message, "Who hath my word shall not see death." Then darkness.

On February 22, they buried him in the cathedral church at Wittenberg. Philip Melanchthon preached.

The Living Spirit

Charles V continued to strive to bring his domains under control. At the head of a victorious army he entered Wittenberg in 1547, one year after Luther's death. Catharine, fleeing the emperor's approach, was thrown from her cart on the rough roads. She never recovered from her injuries and shock.

A pitiful attempt at peace in Augsburg in 1555, brought only a breathing period. The warring parties agreed that the prince of any given political unit should decide the form of religion his subjects should adopt. If they disapproved the prince's choice, the subjects could move to another province. This freedom to move was an advance over the Roman Catholic policy, where one could move only to the next world—via the stake—if he or she disagreed with Roman dogma.

The world would not let Luther rest. He had set a mighty force in motion, and long before his physical death that power had transcended his limitations to make its way in the land.

Men with Luther's vision carried on the battle for freedom. John Calvin, the leader in France, moved into the evangelical faith under direct Lutheran influence while being taught New Testament Greek by a German of

Wittenberg sympathies. Calvin then combined his gifts of clarity, precision, indomitable will, and rich humility with the Lutherans' scriptural authority to construct the powerful Puritan theology.

At the feet of Calvin, the Scottish leader John Knox learned the inner strength of the independent evangelical faith. In Edinburgh, he built the foundations of the stern and lovely piety of the Presbyterians.

But all these movements, as well as Lutheranism, soon moved far from the basic strength of Martin Luther. They defined faith and doctrinal standards so strictly that the ancient freedom of Christians again was denied.

And what of his great enemy? The Roman church, whose historic Catholicism was the center and soul of Luther's life, should number him among the saints. The present Roman church is built in large measure on the results of his magnificent, lifelong campaign.

Luther was a man of his own day. Rough, strong, boisterous, he knew that he and his Germans were often viewed as unlettered and uncultured. But in terms of the external, Luther was free, transcending all things constricted by time and custom.

Were Martin Luther to speak to us again, we would hear the old plea of the believing heart to hold by faith to the truth of the historic life of Jesus, to move by faith from this to its high implications for the character of God, and to live by faith in the eternal, blessed communion of the timeless City of God.

SOJOURNER TRUTH

Born into Slavery

Colonel Johannes Hardenbergh visited the slave quarters on his farm near the Hudson River in upstate New York. Few families in Ulster County held slaves, but the Hardenberghs were wealthier than most and owned seven. A daughter had been born to his slaves Baumfree and Mau Mau Brett. They named her Isabella, but they called her Belle.

Belle's parents had served the Hardenberghs faithfully for many years, and Belle was their eleventh child. She was born around 1797, but the exact date is unknown because slave births weren't recorded.

Belle's father, Baumfree, was a tall, strong man who was proud of his ability to do hard work. But years of hard labor had taken their toll. Mau Mau Brett was a big, stocky woman with large hands. She was much younger than Baumfree, but they loved each other and had a good marriage.

Slave parents had no control over their families. All of Baumfree's and Mau Mau's other children had died or been sold into slavery. They worried that Belle might be sold as well. The best they could do for her was to teach her how to handle her life.

Because slaves were often punished harshly, Belle was taught obedience at an early age. Her parents instilled in her the importance of hard work, honesty, loyalty, and suffering in silence. "Never make a fuss in front of the white folk," her mother told Belle. "When you've got to cry, cry alone."

When Belle was about three years old, Colonel Hardenbergh died. His son Charles moved his inheritance of livestock and slaves, including Belle and her parents, to his new limestone house in the nearby hills. The new property had no slave quarters, so Charles housed his slaves in the damp cellar of the stone house.

At night, the slaves slept on hard wooden pallets. During the winter, they huddled around a fire to escape the bitter cold and wrapped worn-out blankets around themselves. In the summer, the cellar was hot, humid, and smelly, so most of the time, the slaves slept outside.

In spite of the harsh living conditions, Belle's parents remained obedient to their new master and worked hard at plowing his fields and harvesting the crops. Charles developed some affection for the couple and eventually gave them their own land, where Baumfree and Mau Mau could raise corn, tobacco, and other crops to trade for additional food and clothing.

Soon after the move to the new farm, Belle's brother Peter was born. One night when both children were still very young, their mother took them outside under a tree. "My children," she said, "there is a God who hears and sees you."

"Where does God live?" Belle asked.

"He lives in the sky," her mother answered, "and when you are beaten or cruelly treated or fall into any trouble, you must ask His help, and He will always hear and help you." Clinging to her mother's promise, Belle faced her difficult life with confidence. One night, Belle heard her mother crying.

"What's wrong?" she asked.

"I'm groaning to think of my poor children," Mau

Mau Brett said. "They don't know where I be, and I don't know where they be. They look up at the stars, and I look up at the stars, but I can't tell where they be."

Despite Mau Mau's fears, the family remained together until Charles Hardenbergh suddenly died when Belle was about eleven years old. His heirs decided to auction off his horses, cattle, and slaves, but they freed Belle's parents. The couple was allowed to live in the dark cellar as long as Mau Mau worked for the family. They had no choice but to accept the offer, because they couldn't speak English. The Hardenberghs had taught their slaves only Dutch to prevent them from communicating outside the farm.

The day of the auction, the Stone Ridge farm was crowded with people. Belle stood trembling beside her mother. "I don't want to leave you, Mau Mau! What if they beat me? Why can't I go free like you and Baumfree?"

With tears in her eyes, Mau Mau told Belle, "Child, you can't stay with us. All our other children were sold. Now it's your turn."

"Just remember what we've taught you, Belle," Baumfree said. "Obey your master and work hard."

"And if you pray to God, He'll see that you're treated right," Mau Mau added.

A white man motioned for Belle. It was time for her to be auctioned. "Good-bye, Mau Mau. Good-bye, Baumfree."

Belle stood with Peter in the auction arena until he was sold to a man from another area. Although Belle felt like crying, she stood in stony silence, repeating the Lord's Prayer to herself.

Belle's turn was next, but at first no one offered a bid. Belle thought maybe she would be allowed to stay on the farm with her parents. The auctioneer cajoled the crowd, but without success until he threw in a flock of sheep to sweeten the deal.

John Neely, a shopkeeper from Kingston Landing, recognized a bargain. He offered one hundred dollars and, with a crack from the auctioneer's gavel, Belle had a new master.

Neely thought he had struck a good deal, but his wife was not impressed. "This girl can't speak English," she yelled. "What good is she?" When Belle couldn't understand Mrs. Neely's instructions, Mrs. Neely beat her.

One Sunday morning, Mrs. Neely's frustrations overflowed. She sent Belle out to the barn where Mr. Neely was heating metal rods over red-hot coals. Without explanation, Mr. Neely grabbed Belle's hands and tied them together. He tore her shirt off her back and began to beat her with the rods. Belle begged him to stop and called out to God for help. Finally she fainted and lay in the straw, soaked with her own blood.

Afterward, Belle crept off into the woods and cried out to God. "Was it right for them to beat me? You've got to get me a new master. You have to help me, God."

Her prayers were not instantly answered, but Belle learned how to cope. She scrubbed the floors so clean that Mrs. Neely had no cause to complain. Slowly, she learned to speak some English.

One winter evening, when Belle had almost lost hope of ever seeing her family again, Baumfree arrived at the Neely's, looking old and very sick. He and Mau Mau still lived in the cellar of the big house, but they barely had enough money to buy food or clothing. Belle didn't mention her own struggles.

When Baumfree hugged Belle as he prepared to leave, she drew back in pain. Out of sight of the house, she showed him her scarred back. Baumfree was filled with rage and sadness that he hadn't been able to protect his daughter. Though old and crippled, he vowed to use his freedom to help her.

Two years later, God answered Belle's "desperate

prayer." Baumfree persuaded a fisherman named Martin Schryver to purchase Belle from the Neelys. He didn't own any other slaves, but he had a farm and a tavern about five miles from the Neely's farm.

Belle worked hard for her new owner, tilling cornfields, hauling fish, and gathering roots and herbs for the homemade beer sold in the tavern. She had a great deal of freedom to roam outdoors. The Schryvers were coarse and uneducated, but they weren't cruel. They spoke both English and Dutch, so Belle could easily talk with them. Gradually, Belle's English became more fluent. With the Schryvers, Belle had plenty to eat and grew to six feet tall before she turned fourteen.

Unfortunately, Belle's parents did poorly as freed slaves and soon fell ill. Mau Mau Brett eventually died. Belle and Peter were able to attend their mother's funeral and visit their father. Poor Baumfree was grief-stricken. He cried out, "I am so old and helpless. What will happen to me?"

Despite her concern, Belle couldn't do anything for Baumfree. She had to return to the Schryvers. She prayed that God would give her a means to help her father.

Working in the tavern, Belle overheard many conversations about slavery. Her ears perked up at any talk about abolition, a new English word she had learned. Belle vowed to go straight to Baumfree if she were freed. She prayed that God would bless the abolitionists.

Soon afterward, Belle received word that her father had starved to death alone in the cellar. When the Hardenbergh family learned of the old man's death, they donated a pine box and a jug of whiskey for the mourners—a final tribute to a man who had been a faithful, kind, and honest servant.

God seemed distant to Belle, but she remembered Mau Mau's words, "God is always with you," and she continued to pray for her freedom.

Sold Again

One day, a short, ruddy-faced man came into the tavern and began a conversation with Martin Schryver.

"That slave girl yours?" the man inquired.

"Yes," Schryver replied.

"I need her on my farm in New Paltz," the man said. "I'll buy her for three hundred dollars."

The offer price was three times what the Schryvers had paid. Martin accepted the offer, and John Dumont became Belle's new master.

When Belle came to the Dumonts' farm, the ten other slaves welcomed her and told her about her new master. Mr. Dumont was a decent man, they said, who didn't deal out excessive punishment. "If you do your work and don't make trouble, you'll get along fine."

"But watch your step around Mrs. Dumont," they said. "She's got a spiteful tongue and a sour temperament. Keep away from her or it will only get you into trouble."

Belle worked part-time in the main house, so keeping away from Mrs. Dumont was impossible, and Mrs. Dumont took an instant dislike to her. Despite the harsh treatment, Belle remembered her mother's lessons on obedience and tried hard to please her owners. Belle had been taught to repay evil with good, and she deeply believed that her hard work would eventually be rewarded. The other slaves chided her saying, "Girl, you're too obedient."

When Belle became a teenager, she had the mind of a young girl in the body of a woman. She decided that Master Dumont was a god. She reasoned that if God knew everything, He must know about slavery. And if God knew about slavery and didn't—or couldn't—stop it, then her master must be very powerful—almost a god himself.

Because Belle believed that John Dumont was all-seeing and all-knowing, she was driven by fear. To gain favor with her master, she often worked herself to exhaustion. Convinced that he knew her thoughts, Belle told Dumont everything—even reporting the actions of her fellow slaves.

Dumont often bragged about the hardworking Belle. "Why, she could do a good family's washing in the night and be ready in the morning to go to the field and still do as much raking and binding as my best hands," he told his neighbors.

The other slaves grew impatient and drove Belle out of their circle of friends.

One day, Cato, the Dumonts' driver, took Belle aside and said, "Can't you see you only hurtin' the rest of us when you work yourself to death like you doin'? Next thing we know, the master'll be expectin' us all to work like that. Workin' hard ain't gonna free any of us. Just kill us sooner, that's all."

Cato also served as the slaves' preacher, and he taught Belle that God didn't always answer prayers immediately or stop evil in its tracks. "He studies on the situation, hoping the evildoers will make a change of heart and correct themselves," Cato said.

Fifty days after Easter, the slaves got a break from their grueling farm work to celebrate Pentecost, which the Dutch called Pinxter. For a full week, the slaves were given a holiday from labor, or were paid if they chose to work.

The slaves went to a nearby clearing, where the men competed in contests of strength and endurance. After the games, feasting began, followed by endless dancing to the beat of drums. The slaves clapped and sang far into the night. At dawn they rested, but at sunset the activities began again.

During one Pinxter celebration, a handsome young slave named Robert from a nearby estate introduced himself to Belle. For Belle, it was love at first sight. The young couple shared lunch, talked, and enjoyed the dancing. After the holidays, they continued to meet whenever they could break away from work.

Robert's owner, a man named Catlin, opposed the relationship. He was only interested in building up his estate, and he wanted his female slaves to bear lots of children that he could either sell or put to work in his fields. Catlin ordered Robert to stop meeting with Belle and to take a wife from his own estate.

Nevertheless, Robert continued to sneak off to see Belle until Catlin became suspicious and set a trap for his disobedient slave. He sent word to Robert that Belle was sick and needed his help, even though she was in perfect health and hard at work in the Dumonts' kitchen. When Robert ran to see Belle, Catlin and his son pounced on him outside the Dumonts' house.

Belle heard loud screams outside the kitchen window and looked out in horror to see Catlin and his son beating Robert with heavy sticks. John Dumont also heard the commotion and came running. When Belle pleaded with her master to help Robert, Dumont broke the gentleman's agreement that slaveholders usually accorded one another and stopped Catlin from reprimanding his slave. "I won't tolerate that kind of beating on this farm," he yelled angrily.

The Catlins yanked Robert to his feet, bound his hands, and marched him away. Dumont followed them home to make sure that Robert wasn't killed along the way, but the Catlins seemed satisfied that the beating had changed his attitude.

As Belle watched Robert being beaten, she felt each lash in her heart. The only way she could cope was to shut down her emotions. She slipped away from the Dumonts' house to a secluded spot near a creek. In the quietness, Belle prayed and sang the songs her African grandmother had taught Mau Mau Brett. Alone, Belle cried long and hard. Then, just as she had been taught from childhood, she dried her tears, put away her pain, and returned to work. She never saw Robert again.

One day John Dumont decided it was time for Belle to get married and have children. He chose a slave named Tom to be her husband. It made no difference that Belle and Tom did not love each other. They were just two slaves.

When Belle learned of her master's decision, she insisted that a real preacher marry them. Dumont agreed to her request and a black preacher married the couple.

At one time, Tom had been a good-looking man, but when Belle married him, he was stooped and worn from years of hard field labor. Years earlier, his wife had been sold to a family in New York City. Enraged and hurt, Tom had run away on foot to find her. With the help of freed slaves, he had stayed away from the Dumonts' farm for a month until slave-trackers caught him. He never located his wife.

In their own way, Tom and Belle loved each other. Belle was considerate and cared for her husband, and Tom was quiet and agreeable. After a year of marriage, the couple had a daughter named Diana. Over the next twelve years, Belle gave birth to four more children: Elizabeth, Hannah, Peter, and Sophia. Belle taught each child the lessons she had learned from her mother: never steal, never lie, and always obey your master.

Although her life was increasingly complicated with nursing and caring for her children, Belle continued her hard work for the Dumonts. Year after year, she chopped wood, planted corn, and hauled water, but she never gave up hope that one day she would be free.

In 1824, she finally heard good news. Pressured by abolitionist groups, the New York state legislature passed an emancipation law that required all slaves born before July 4, 1799, to be freed on July 4, 1827. Male slaves born after that date would gain their freedom when they turned twenty-eight, and female slaves would be freed after their twenty-fifth birthday.

Belle wasn't certain of her exact birthday, but the Dumonts agreed that she would be eligible for freedom in 1827. The mere idea put a bounce in Belle's step. She sang while she worked and set her sights on Freedom Day.

One day in 1825, Dumont came to Belle with an offer. He complimented her for her fifteen years of hard work in the past, then added, "I'll let you go a year earlier than the law says if you promise to work extra hard for me. And as a bonus, I'll let Tom go free with you and you can live in the cabin I own down the road."

Belle accepted the offer. Over the next several months, she put in extra-long hours of planting, washing, cooking, and cleaning. In the spring, she cut her hand on a scythe blade, but she never missed a day's work. The thought of freedom kept her going. When the year ended, Belle had fulfilled her promise to Dumont.

She waited for her master to free her, but he didn't say a word about the agreement. Finally, she could stand it no longer and she burst into the house and confronted

Dumont. With arrogance in his voice and a wave of his hand, Dumont sneered, "Our deal is off. Go back to work."

Belle was furious at the curt dismissal. "Why won't you honor your word?"

Dumont searched for an excuse. Noticing her bandaged hand, he said, "You can't expect me to free you. With a hurt hand, how could you put in extra work?"

Belle touched her injured hand, now stiff and twisted from hard work and neglect. Her anger exploded like steam roaring from a kettle on a hot stove. Without bothering to argue, Belle stormed away. In her mind, she was now a free woman, regardless of what her small-minded master said. Her days of slavery were over!

She wanted to run away, but she knew that she wouldn't be able to take her children with her. In order to leave on somewhat good terms with Dumont, she decided she would first finish spinning the annual harvest of wool. That year, the Dumonts' sheep yielded more wool than usual and, by the time Belle finished her spinning, it was late autumn.

Free at Last!

E arly one morning, Belle summoned Tom and their five children, who ranged in age from twelve to less than a year. "Mr. Dumont has cheated me out of my freedom," she said, "and I'll not let him get away with it. I've got to run away and I can't take you with me, but I'll be back for you. Someday we'll be together again."

Tom objected. "Belle, calm down. It's not worth trying to escape. We'll be free anyway in another year." But Tom couldn't dissuade her. Belle was determined to escape.

Night seemed the best time to run away, but Belle was afraid of the dark. Escaping during the day was much too dangerous. Belle prayed for guidance, and the Lord showed her a solution—escape at dawn when there would be just enough light to calm her fears, yet the Dumonts and their neighbors would still be asleep. Belle told no one her exact plans—not even Tom.

On the morning of her escape, Belle arose before dawn and wrapped some food and clothing in a large piece of cloth. Next, she bundled up Sophia, whom she had decided to take with her. Belle knew that the other slaves would take good care of the rest of the children. When full daylight arrived, she would be far from her master's house, but she had no idea where to go. Once again, she turned to God for direction.

While Belle was praying, a memory flickered into her mind. Long ago, a stranger had stopped her along the road. "It's not right that you should be a slave," he'd said. "God does not want it." Belle remembered the man, a Quaker who lived down the road from the Dumont estate. In the early morning light, she knocked on his door.

Levi Rowe patiently listened as the frightened runaway slave poured out her story. He was old and too ill to help Belle, but he directed her to the home of Isaac and Maria Van Wagener, a Quaker couple whom Belle had known since her childhood. "Maybe they will hide you," he said. Belle thanked him and continued her journey with fresh hope.

When the Van Wageners heard Belle's story, they offered her a job and place to stay. A short time later, John Dumont arrived, searching for his slave. He suspected that the Quakers had offered her shelter. When Belle stepped forward, Dumont threatened her with harsh punishment.

When Belle refused to return, Dumont tried another tactic. "When you are not looking, I'll steal Sophia, and then you'll come back."

"Your threats don't frighten me," Belle said firmly. "I'm not coming back!"

Just then, Isaac Van Wagener offered to buy Belle for twenty dollars and her baby for five dollars. Realizing that Belle wouldn't return to his farm, Dumont accepted Van Wagener's offer and left in a huff.

"Thank you, Master Van Wagener," Belle said to her new owner.

"Belle, you and Sophia are free," Isaac said. "There is but one Master, and He is also my Master."

Belle worked through the winter for the Van Wageners. The couple lived simply, often praying and meditating silently for hours on the Bible—a sharp contrast to the constant chatter in the Dumonts' slave quarters.

Although content to stay with the Van Wageners, Belle was tempted to return to her children at the Dumont estate. Years later, she told friends that a powerful force turned her around whenever she tried to leave. "Jesus stopped me," she explained simply.

Freedom Day was getting closer every day, but it didn't arrive soon enough. One day, Belle learned that Dumont had sold her only son, Peter, to a doctor who planned to take the boy with him to England. When the doctor discovered that Peter was too young to serve him properly, he left the boy with his brother, who in turn sold Peter to a wealthy Alabama planter.

Belle was furious. She hurried to the Dumonts' farm and confronted her old master with anger and determination. "Alabama is a slave-for-life state," she said. There's no way Peter will ever be free. If you hadn't sold him, he wouldn't be there."

Belle pleaded with Mr. Dumont for help, but to no avail. Mrs. Dumont chastised her with stinging words that infuriated Belle. "Haven't you got as many children left as you can take care of? It's a shame you aren't all back in Africa!"

Belle burned with anger, but her response was slow and deliberate. "I'll have my child again."

Belle walked along the road and prayed, "Show those around me that You are my helper!" She turned once again to the Quaker abolitionists for help. They met at the Van Wageners' home to discuss what they could do to help.

A New York state law forbade selling slaves out of state. The seller could face a fourteen-year jail sentence and a stiff fine, and Peter would immediately be freed.

The Van Wageners recommended that Belle seek help from friends of theirs to file suit against Solomon Gedney, the man who had sold Peter to the Alabama planter.

Belle walked for the better part of a day to reach the home of the Van Wageners' friends near Kingston, New York. The hostess graciously offered Belle supper and a clean bed for the night.

The next morning, the family took Belle to the courthouse. Determined to get her son back, she gathered her courage and walked inside to file a complaint.

The grand jury heard Belle's case and decided in her favor. A lawyer, Esquire Chipp, helped Belle make out a writ, which she took to the constable of New Paltz. The document ordered Solomon Gedney to appear before the court with Peter.

Unfortunately, the constable served the document on the wrong man, and Solomon Gedney slipped away to Mobile, Alabama, before the constable realized his mistake. For months, all Belle could do was wait.

When Gedney returned in the spring, Belle went to his home to claim her son. Gedney slammed the door in her face.

Belle refused to back down. She visited Esquire Chipp again. This time the writ was properly served and Gedney appeared in court. He paid a six-hundred-dollar bond, promising to appear to face the charges. Unfortunately for Belle, the case was postponed for several months until court was in session.

"I cannot wait. I must have Peter now!" Belle cried.

While walking back to the Van Wageners' home, Belle met a man who greeted her and asked, "Have they returned your son yet?" When Belle shook her head, the man pointed to a stone house. "The lawyer Demain lives there. Tell him your case with Peter and don't give him a moment's peace until he helps you."

When Demain heard the details of Belle's case, he promised to return Peter within twenty-four hours for a fee of five dollars. Belle's Quaker friends gave her the money, and Demain went to the courthouse. He quickly returned with bad news. Peter didn't want to return to his mother.

"She's not my mother!" Peter explained the next morning when the case was heard in the judge's chambers. But one look into the boy's eyes made it clear that he was simply terrified of his master. The judge awarded Peter his freedom and released him to his mother.

Belle didn't know that she was one of the first black women in the United States to win a court case. She was simply happy to have her son back. That evening as she prepared Peter for bed, Belle noticed that his back was streaked with old and fresh wounds. "Peter," Belle whispered gently to her son. "What kind of monster would do this to a six-year-old?"

Peter finally told the truth. "Master Gedney told me to say that I didn't know you," he explained as tears ran down his cheeks. "He said if I didn't, I would get the worst whipping I ever had."

"Now, now child," Belle said as she held her son in her arms. "You're free now and safe with me." Belle was certain that the man who had pointed her to Demain was an angel from heaven. She thanked God for His answer and for Peter's freedom.

"God," she prayed, "if You will, no child of mine will be sold away from me again!"

The Work for the Kingdom

On July 4, 1827, Tom was freed, but he died before the end of the year. Belle and Peter returned to the Van Wageners, who welcomed them back and provided work for Belle. She clung to her dream of having all her children under one roof but, for the time being, all she could do was be nearby. She settled her differences with the Dumonts, and they allowed her to visit her daughters regularly.

Belle became so comfortable that she nearly forgot about God. As the holiday of Pinxter approached, she thought about giving up her freedom and returning to the Dumont estate, where she could sing, drink, smoke, and dance with her slave friends. But as her 1850 narrative reports, "God revealed Himself to me with all of the suddenness of lightning." Overwhelmed with the presence of God's greatness, Belle fell on her hands and knees, trying to crawl away from the Almighty, but she could find no place to hide. Years later, Belle described this moment as her conversion to Christ.

She admitted that she had urged God to kill "all the white people and not leave enough for seed," but after her conversion she said, "Yeah, God, I love everyone, and the white people too."

Belle's time with the Van Wageners were some of the

happiest months of her life. When the day's work was finished, Mr. Van Wagener read his Bible aloud to Belle and the others. These lessons from God's Word gave Belle a better understanding of the relationship between God and humanity.

A new Methodist church opened in New Paltz, and one Sunday morning, Belle put on her good black dress and dressed Peter for church. Neither one had shoes, but Belle decided that shoes didn't matter to God.

The Methodist meeting was held in a private house, and it was not customary for blacks to attend white meetings unless they sat in a separate "Negro pew." But when Belle and Peter finally mustered the courage to enter, the congregation welcomed them.

The Methodists taught Belle to tell all her troubles to Jesus. At one meeting, when she said a devil was after her, a Methodist brother advised her to call on Jesus and the devil would leave. Belle later said, in her droll style, "I told him I knowed that all the time, but I didn't happen to think of it before."

Many Methodist churches were open to blacks and Kingston Methodist established a Sunday school for them as early as 1811. Belle took her children with her to church as often as possible.

At one of these meetings, Belle met Miss Geer, a vacationing schoolteacher from New York City. Miss Geer was struck by Peter's inquisitive nature and bright mind. She told Belle, "There are many jobs available in New York City and a world of educational opportunities for Peter. You should consider moving."

The idea opened Belle's mind to all kinds of possibilities. In New York City she might find a better paying job and be able to save money for a home. Then, as her children came of age and were freed by Dumont, they would have a place to live.

Belle felt liberated by making such a decision without needing to get permission from a master.

In 1829, Belle and Peter said good-bye to New Paltz and boarded a boat down the Hudson River. When they arrived in New York City, Miss Geer met them at the docks with her carriage. The busy streets and masses of people amazed Belle, who had only known small town life. The clutter and the noise bombarded her senses and confused her. Miss Geer arranged work for Belle and enrolled Peter in a navigation school, which piqued his interest in ships and sailing.

Before long, Belle discovered the long-standing free black community in New York and proudly joined their growing ranks. She visited the Mother Zion African Methodist Episcopal (AME) Church. The AME church was the oldest African-American organization in the United States. Belle became known for her spirit-filled prayers and original hymns. According to a white Methodist leader at the time, "the influence of her speaking was miraculous."

One Sunday, a man and a woman approached Belle after the service. The woman told her, "I am your sister Sophia, and this is your brother Michael. We are also the children of Mau Mau Brett and Baumfree. Some of our friends told us that you worshiped in this church, so we came here to find you." The three siblings spent the entire day talking and catching up on their lives.

Miss Geer continued to encourage Belle and Peter as they adjusted to life in New York City. She invited Belle to join a small group of Christians who went into the Five Points area of New York to tell people about the changing power of Jesus Christ. They greeted people and sang hymns on the street corners. Belle went a few times into this poor section of the city, but she wondered why. The people who lived in Five Points needed food, decent houses, and clothing, she thought. There must be another way to show Christ's love.

When Belle heard about the Magdalene Asylum, a shelter for homeless women, she volunteered to help. Elijah Pierson ran the shelter at a large gray house on Bowery Hill. Several years earlier, Pierson had been a merchant, but after an intensely spiritual experience, he had sold his home and started the homeless shelter. He claimed to run the Magdalene Asylum with instructions directly from God. Such a claim wasn't hard for Belle to believe because she felt God directly guided her decisions and life. Belle liked Pierson and agreed to work part-time, often participating in his religious services.

After a prolonged fast in 1830, Pierson's wife, Sara, died. Her husband was so convinced that God had given him supernatural powers that he called his followers together and attempted to bring Sara back to life. After their attempts failed, Elijah Pierson again claimed that he had been given divine powers and that God had chosen him to start a Kingdom of God on earth. In June 1830, he began to call himself a prophet and claimed that "God has called me Elijah the Tishbite and said, 'Gather to Me all the members of Israel at the foot of Mount Carmel,'" which Pierson understood to mean the Magdalene Asylum on Bowery Hill.

When Belle answered the front door of the asylum one Sunday morning, she was startled to see a long-bearded figure in a flowing robe. The man asked to see Elijah the Tishbite and told Belle, "I am Matthias. I am God the Father and have the power to do all things." His eyes were piercing, and Belle thought the man might be an angel. Matthias wore his beard long because he believed that no man who shaved could be a true Christian. In actuality, Matthias was a middle-aged hustler named Robert Matthews who had arrived in the city with a new scheme to steal money from people.

Within months, Elijah Pierson and Matthias became partners in a wicked plan of deceit. Pierson said he was John the Baptist and Matthias claimed to be God on earth. Matthias preached, "Ours is the mustard seed kingdom which is to spread throughout the entire earth. Our creed is truth, but no one can discover truth unless he comes clean into the church." Belle listened to these men, and their smooth talk convinced her that they were telling the truth.

Pierson and Matthias founded their community, "the Kingdom," on a farm owned by Benjamin and Ann Folger. The men accepted Belle into the group on the understanding that she would do the washing, ironing, cooking, and cleaning. For her hard work, Belle gained the privilege of worshipping with the others in the Kingdom.

The family of one of the Kingdom's followers soon brought charges against Matthias for lunacy. The police came to the house and arrested him. They stripped him, took his money, and cut off his beard. Matthias submitted to the police as they hauled him to Bellevue prison and put him in the section for the insane. Supported by Belle, Pierson later arranged for Matthias's release.

For a while, the members of the community lived in peace and harmony. Then Matthias's unusual teaching began to exert control over the community. Belle began to tire of the constant bickering and the strange religious rituals. She decided that Matthias and Pierson didn't deserve her trust and confidence. She had no proof of their dishonesty, but she didn't want any part of deceiving others.

In August 1834, Belle returned to her old job with the Whiting family in New York City. When she arrived she learned that Peter had dropped out of school and had hired out as a coachman for one of Miss Geer's friends. He was also running around with a rough crowd. This disturbing turn of events gave her further incentive to break her relationship with the Kingdom. Belle made a brief trip to the farm to gather her possessions and tell the leaders that she was leaving. While she was there, Elijah Pierson, who had been ailing for some time, collapsed suddenly and died.

Pierson's relatives and friends raised questions about his death. Suspecting murder, the local coroner asked doctors to examine Pierson's body. A jury investigated and the trial turned into a media circus. Every day the newspapers featured stories about the strange religious group and the two leaders who had used money for their own greedy desires. Belle felt betrayed and hurt. These articles told about cheating, lying, and other evils, such as adultery. To Belle's dismay, the public didn't believe that she knew nothing about the strange practices.

In the aftermath of the trial, the Kingdom began to fall apart. Westchester County seized the Folgers' farm, forcing all of the members to move. Belle, along with Matthias and his children, moved in with the Folgers, although they were not welcome. Hoping to fend him off, the Folgers gave Matthias $530 to carry out his dream of buying a farm. By September 1834, Matthias had gone to Albany to prepare to move west.

Belle expected to go west with Matthias, even if it meant leaving her children behind. Traveling north, Belle visited her children who were still at the Dumont estate, then took a steamboat up the Hudson River to Albany. Belle was surprised to learn that the Folgers had brought charges against Matthias for stealing the $530. Confused and upset, Belle returned to New York City.

The Folgers also charged that Matthias, with Belle's help, had murdered Pierson by serving him poisoned blackberries. The Folgers also claimed that Matthias and Belle had tried to serve them poisoned coffee.

Benjamin and Ann Folger wrote a novel, which was

thinly based on fact. In their story, a "black witch" maid introduced evil into a holy community and murdered the leader of the organization. The book detailed how the murder was accomplished. When the public read the novel, they believed the story was about Belle. Newspapers published excerpts and continued to spread the false account.

Perez Whiting, Belle's employer, was convinced she was incapable of the crimes the Folgers described. He persuaded his fellow journalist Gilbert Vale to take up Belle's cause. In 1835, Vale published a pamphlet called, "Fanaticism: Its Source and Influence, Illustrated by the Simple Narrative of Isabella," which gave Belle a chance to tell her story. Vale also advised Belle to sue for defamation.

When Matthias's murder trial came to court, doctors testified that they had not clearly found poison in Pierson's stomach. Matthias's lawyer argued that Pierson had died of epilepsy. When the prosecution could offer no substantial evidence that Pierson had been murdered, the judge advised that Matthias be acquitted. The jury promptly agreed.

Belle believed that justice had triumphed, but she was disappointed that she had not been called to testify. She wanted a chance to tell her story.

Her suit against Benjamin Folger soon came to trial. Perez Whiting testified that Folger had admitted that his charge was not true. When Folger offered no defense, Belle won, but again without having an opportunity to testify in court. The court awarded her $125 in damages plus costs.

Belle found little joy in her victory. Instead, she felt she had wasted three years of her life. In God's economy, however, these years were not wasted. Her painful lessons equipped her to face what life was soon to bring.

Disappeared Forever

B elle won the fight to preserve her reputation, but at home a new battle was already brewing. Her son Peter had "gone to seed." For a while, she had been able to keep him under control, but when she had moved to the Kingdom and left Peter in the city, he had dropped out of navigation school and had gotten in trouble with the police. After repeated offenses, Peter ended up in the Tombs, New York's dreaded jailhouse. Together with a local pastor, Belle convinced the judge that Peter needed discipline—and that the best place for discipline was at sea. The judge sentenced Peter to work as a sailor and, in August 1839, he shipped out aboard the *Zone of Nantucket*.

Belle received occasional letters from her son, which he signed Peter Van Wagener or Peter Williams, but a few years later when the ship again made port in New York Harbor, there was no record of a sailor by either name on board. Belle never heard from her son again.

Nine years passed, and Belle continued to live and work in New York City for Mrs. Whiting. Often during the pitch black of the night, she would look at the night sky and wonder if her children were seeing the same beautiful stars. By 1843, all of Belle's daughters had grown up, married, and started their own families. Belle was sad that she had not spent more time with her daughters when they were young, but she could do little to change the past.

Belle began to realize that New York City was a dangerous place for blacks. Slave catchers roamed the streets, and sometimes free slaves were captured along with runaway slaves. Some blacks competing for jobs faced severe discrimination and became victims of racial violence.

Belle believed that everything she had undertaken in New York had failed. She had tried to preach, but the blacks had rejected her. Matthias's community had blown up into a scandal and damaged her good name. She had failed to save enough money for her own home. At age forty-six, Belle decided to leave the city, but she was afraid that her children and friends would object.

She decided to become a traveling evangelist, following the example of several other black women in the Northeast, such as Rebecca Jackson, Jarena Lee, and Julia Foote. She embarked without the promise of support from any church or denomination, and with no one advising her.

Belle understood that her perspective as a freed slave, a mother, and a devout Christian gave her a unique view of human rights and spiritual well-being. She wanted to tell others about her experiences. As Belle prayed, a powerful voice told her, "You have a mission to the needy and the oppressed."

During another time of prayer, Belle thought she received a message from God: "Go east." The words troubled her, but when they came again, "Go east," Belle made a decision to follow the Lord wherever He took her.

To Belle, the name she had been given as a slave now seemed inappropriate for a person beginning a new life as God's pilgrim. Calling on God for help, Belle remembered Psalm 39:12: "Hear my prayer, O Lord, and give ear unto my cry, . . .for I am a stranger with thee, and a sojourner, as all my fathers were." "Sojourner" sounded like a good name for someone called to travel the land. The name reminded Belle of the holy people described in the Bible who traveled to foreign countries and preached the Word of God.

Before first light on June 1, 1843, Belle awoke and packed her few dresses into an old pillowcase. She informed the Whitings that she was quitting.

"You're crazy, Belle," Mrs. Whiting said. "We need you here and this is your home. Why travel to the east?"

"The Spirit calls me and I must go. The Lord is going to give me a new home," she said. With those words, Belle flung her pillowcase across her shoulder and walked to the Brooklyn ferry. Belle left New York City and never looked back.

By evening, she had walked well out of the city. At a Quaker farm, she asked for a drink of water. The woman gave it to her and asked her name.

"My name is Sojourner," she replied firmly.

"Sojourner what?" the woman asked. The former slave had no answer.

As Sojourner continued her trip, the woman's question nagged at her. *Only slaves don't have a last name,* she thought. In prayer, Sojourner remembered another Bible verse, John 8:32: "And ye shall know the truth, and the truth shall make you free."

I've only got one master now—and His name is Truth. My name is Sojourner Truth, she said to herself. It seemed a perfect name for one of God's pilgrims.

A New Direction

Sojourner continued walking east across Long Island preaching at farms and villages. White farmers stopped their work to listen, enthralled by her powerful speaking voice and manners. She seemed to know every word in the Bible even though she was illiterate. Word soon spread about the fiery preacher.

One afternoon, Sojourner approached a large outdoor religious meeting and asked to speak. Hundreds of families gathered to listen. Sojourner stood tall and proud in the late afternoon sunshine, talking about God's love, glory, and protection in her deep melodious voice. A murmur spread throughout the crowd. She concluded her message with a hymn, "In my trials—Lord, walk with me. In my trials—Lord, walk with me. When my heart is almost breaking, Lord, walk with me. . . ."

After this introduction, Sojourner traveled and spoke from meeting to meeting. People whispered, "It must be Sojourner Truth," whenever she appeared in a new neighborhood.

When someone asked Sojourner to speak about her life as a slave, she said to the attentive audience, "Children, slavery is a evil thing. They sell children away from their mothers, and then dare the mothers to cry about their loss. What kind of men can do such an evil thing?"

A murmur of agreement went through the crowd. Sojourner saw heads nodding with respect. "Some of my brothers and sisters were sold off before I was born, but my poor mother never stopped crying for them."

Word soon spread throughout the region that Sojourner Truth was an inspirational speaker with a stirring message. Whenever she arrived at a camp meeting, people rushed to greet her. After people heard her speak, they were often so filled with emotion that they cried or cheered. Speaking against slavery became the central focus of her ministry.

Sojourner stayed with whoever offered her food and lodging. If she needed money, then she stopped and did domestic work for a while. As she later explained, "I found many true friends of Jesus with whom I could have communion."

The theme of her speeches during these days was, "God's mercy will be shown to those who show mercy." The crowds marveled at her speaking. She couldn't read, yet she could quote Scripture flawlessly and then appropriately apply it—the fruit of years of listening to others read the Bible. The sincerity of her message meshed with the simplicity of her language and the courage of her convictions. Many people began to seek her out to speak at their meetings.

Eventually, Sojourner decided to follow God's call and traveled to Connecticut and Massachusetts. Wherever she went, people flocked to hear her preach.

Arriving in Northampton, a town in the heart of Massachusetts, she "hushed every trifler into silence," and "whole audiences were melted into tears by her touching stories."

Sojourner visited the Northampton Association of Education and Industry, a cooperative community founded in 1842, that operated a silkworm farm and made silk. She was attracted to the group because of their spirit of fellowship and idealism. Northampton was a friendly haven for leading abolitionists and became the perfect training ground for Sojourner's work as an activist.

The Northampton Association was led by two advocates of abolition, Samuel L. Hill and George Benson. Benson's brother-in-law, a frequent visitor, was William Lloyd Garrison, editor of an abolitionist weekly newspaper in Boston and, to many, the leader of the antislavery movement.

Sam Hill and George Benson had heard about Sojourner Truth from friends and asked her to stay in their community at Northampton. After her experience with the Kingdom, Sojourner was cautious about the community's lifestyle, but she agreed to stay.

Sojourner met David Ruggles, who had been born free in Connecticut, but who had worked most of his life in New York for the abolitionist movement as a writer and editor. In private, along with his friend William Sil, Ruggles helped more than six hundred fugitive slaves along the Underground Railroad. To the delight of the children at Northampton, Ruggles told stories about the escape of slaves with great excitement and adventure.

Among the community's frequent visitors were Wendell Phillips, called "Abolition's Golden Trumpet" because of his powerful speaking abilities; Parker Pillsbury, an uncompromising abolitionist whose booming voice shook the chandeliers; and Frederick Douglass, a runaway slave who had gained a reputation for outstanding speaking. Douglass never forgot his old friend David Ruggles and his help in the Underground Railroad, and whenever Douglass was in the area, he stopped to visit.

Frederick Douglass was the only black representative

in the Anti-Slavery Society, but along with William Garrison he pushed the society to seek peaceful solutions and moral persuasion rather than violence to end slavery. As much as she despised slavery, Sojourner could not condone violence, so she supported Douglass and Garrison.

A few months after Sojourner joined the Northampton community, she attended a nearby camp meeting. As often happened, young rowdies invaded the meeting to amuse themselves. When the mob began to shake the tent where Sojourner was seated, she hid behind a trunk fearing that they would single her out as the only black person present, and kill her. As she hid, she began to wonder whether a servant of the living God should hide. *Have I not faith enough to go out and quell that mob?* she wondered. *After all, it is written, "One shall chase a thousand, and two put ten thousand to flight."*

Sojourner invited a few of the camp meeting leaders to go outside with her to try to calm the disturbance. When the leaders refused, she went out by herself. She walked to a small rise and started to sing one of her favorite hymns.

A few of the rioters gathered around her. During a pause in her singing, she asked them, "Why do you come about me with clubs and sticks? I am not doing harm to anyone." Sojourner believed that some of these youths would be open to the Gospel so she began to preach to them. They asked questions, and she answered them, and the group began to calm down.

Sojourner continued talking and singing. Finally the crowd agreed that if she would sing one more song, they would go away and leave the camp in peace.

After that incident, Sojourner decided never to run away again. She developed skill in handling rough crowds.

At Northampton, Sojourner heard lecturers who advocated that women should be given the same political and legal rights as men. Recognizing that she and the women's rights speakers were kindred spirits, Sojourner decided to join their ranks and take on this new battle for freedom.

In July 1848, Olive Gilbert, an early feminist and a member of the Northampton society, read Sojourner an article in the *Liberator* reporting on the first women's rights convention in Seneca Falls, New York, where Elizabeth Cady Stanton had submitted a resolution calling for women to have the right to vote.

Although white women had some rights, they couldn't serve on juries, hold public office, or manage their own finances. In a divorce, the husband was automatically given custody of the children. Women would never be able to change these practices in the United States without the legal power to vote.

Sojourner listened to the conversations around her. While it was true that white women had few political rights, free black women had even fewer rights, and a slave woman had no rights. She decided that the struggle of all women for freedom was a cause worth fighting for.

Olive Gilbert encouraged Sojourner to publish her own story. "You dictate it to me and I'll write it for you," Gilbert volunteered. William Lloyd Garrison offered to print the book and wrote the introduction. The book was printed in 1850, the same year that Congress passed a more rigid version of the Fugitive Slave Act as part of the Compromise of 1850.

Angered by the new law, antislavery sympathizers expanded the Underground Railroad network, which each year helped more than a thousand slaves to escape from the South. In some northern communities, slave catchers began to encounter armed resistance.

Not every Northerner supported abolition. Many maintained that the Fugitive Slave Law had to be obeyed so peace could be maintained between the North and the

South. They accused the abolitionists of trying to divide the nation.

In October, Sojourner traveled to Worcester, Massachusetts, to speak at the national women's rights convention. The local clergy took an active role in resisting the women's meeting, and the male-dominated press called the conference a "hen party." Nevertheless, more than a thousand people from eleven states participated in the conference. Sojourner noticed, however, that she was the only black woman.

It took all of the patience she could muster to listen to many of the speakers who discussed issues—such as a woman's right to keep her jewelry in a divorce or women's rights to wear bloomers—that Sojourner thought were irrelevant. She was more concerned about whether a divorced mother should be allowed to keep her children.

Toward the conclusion of the conference, Sojourner was asked to address the convention. She began, "Sisters, I am not clear on what you be after. If women want any rights more than they've got, why don't they just take them and not be talking about it?"

By the conclusion of the convention, the women's motto clearly stated their primary objective: "Equality before the law without distinction of sex or color." Sojourner left the conference feeling inspired and motivated. The problem of attaining equal rights for women was more complex than she was willing to admit at the convention, but her defiant message stirred the ranks of the nation's feminists and abolitionists. "Why not just take your rights?" she had asked, and many other Americans were beginning to ask the same question.

On the Move Again

After Sojourner Truth published her autobiography in 1850, she became well-known to both the antislavery and the women's rights movements. Soon she was traveling with other lecturers throughout New England. Though she was only fifty-three years old, her black hair had turned gray, her forehead was deeply lined with wrinkles, and she wore metal-rimmed glasses to help her fading eyesight. She usually wore a plain black dress with a long white shawl and a white handkerchief wrapped into a turban.

From her appearance, some people guessed that she was in her nineties, and they were astonished at the vigor with which she attacked the institution of slavery. She denounced slave owners as sinners who would some day feel God's wrath. Most speakers used formal and flowery speech, but Sojourner cast a spell over her listeners with the rough, uneducated manner and language of an unschooled slave girl who had never learned to read or write. Unlike some speakers who droned on for hours, Sojourner cut to the heart of a complex issue in just a few words.

She soon became known for her simple but moving antislavery speeches and her witty, biting attacks on people who continued to own slaves yet said they were Christians. She knew that many Northerners wanted to pretend that slavery was strictly a Southern problem. To these people, millions of black slaves were practically invisible. Sojourner believed it was her mission to force all Americans to confront the nationwide moral problem of slavery.

Throughout this period, Sojourner continued to travel and speak at different conventions. She felt that God was telling her to go west, and as always she obeyed. She went to Ohio, which was a free state and one of the main arteries on the Underground Railroad. Despite the strong abolitionist movement in Ohio, there were many who supported slavery, especially in the rural areas.

On a bright, cloudless day in 1852, hundreds of men and women packed an Akron, Ohio, church for a convention on women's rights. Suddenly the doors to the church swung open and a tall, proud figure stood framed in the doorway. "It's Sojourner Truth," someone whispered. Seeing no empty seats in the back, she walked slowly, proudly, almost defiantly past the lily-white crowd to the front of the church and sat on the steps leading to the pulpit. The people craned their necks to see her.

Throughout the morning, speakers both for and against women's rights stepped to the podium. Sojourner sat with her face in her hands, seeming distracted but listening to every word. During the midday intermission, she walked among the audience, selling copies of her book, while a group of women's rights advocates, afraid that she would damage their cause, were asking Frances Gage, the convention's moderator, to prevent Sojourner from speaking. Gage listened carefully, but made no promises. "When the time comes, we'll see," she said.

During the afternoon session and again the next morning, the former slave sat silently on the pulpit steps listening to the speakers. One minister told the convention that men deserved greater rights because they were more intelligent. Another preacher said, "Men should rule over women because Jesus Christ was a man." Yet another preacher asserted that women had a lower status because Eve had committed the original sin. Finally, another pastor said, "Women don't deserve the same rights as men, because they are so much weaker." Many women in the audience were visibly upset, but none was prepared to argue in public with a clergyman.

Then Sojourner Truth stood and walked to the pulpit. She removed her sun bonnet and turned toward the moderator for permission to speak. Frances Gage hesitated, then introduced the black woman to the audience.

Sojourner began to speak in a low, soft voice. "Well, children, where there is so much racket, there must be something out of kilter. It will be fixed pretty soon," she promised.

Sojourner addressed the concerns of the minister who had declared women too weak to have equal rights. As she spoke, she straightened her back, and her tall frame gave her words greater impact. Her voice sounded like rolling thunder. "Ain't I a woman? Look at me!" she proclaimed. "Look at my arm." She rolled up her sleeve to show an arm lean from years of hard labor. "I have plowed and planted and gathered," she declared. "And ain't I a woman?"

She turned to the minister who had argued that women were less intelligent. "What does intelligence have to do with rights?" she asked angrily. "And where did your Christ come from?" she asked the minister who had said men were superior because Jesus was a man." He came from God and a woman. Man had nothing to do with the birth of Jesus Christ."

Finally, she discussed Eve and the origin of sin. "If the first woman God ever made was strong enough to turn the world upside down, all alone, these together—" she motioned toward the women in the audience—"ought to be able to turn it back and get it right side up again." Most of the audience applauded.

"Now old Sojourner hasn't got nothing more to say."

Proclaim Liberty

In mid-1853, after her successful tour through the Midwest, Sojourner was tired of traveling and decided to take a period for rest. That winter, she stayed with Isaac and Amy Post, well-known Quaker abolitionists, in Rochester, New York. At the Posts' home, letters from her children finally caught up with her.

Her daughter Diana wrote that John Dumont had become a strong abolitionist who now said "slavery is an evil institution." Sojourner made a trip to visit her daughters in New York and New England. Her oldest grandchild was already nine years old. After enjoying a pleasant stay, Sojourner returned home to her house in Northampton, Massachusetts, with a brief stopover in Andover, where she visited the home of abolitionist writer Harriet Beecher Stowe.

After returning home, Sojourner decided to resume her speaking tours.

As she addressed her audiences, Sojourner blended tones of pride and modesty. She addressed her audience as "children" and individuals as "honey," showing affection for all sympathizers, which endeared her to many people. Her characteristic salty wit appeared on many occasions.

Not only did her humor and sharpness make Sojourner

an effective speaker against slavery, but her experience of having felt the whip's lash influenced her delivery. She explained, "As now, when I hear them tell of whipping women on the bare flesh, it makes my flesh crawl, and my very hair rise on my head." But more than this, she had the ability to appeal to white people by shaming them or encouraging them or even complimenting them.

Sojourner passionately continued to attack slavery as inhuman, unchristian, and intolerable. She was not always kind or moderate. Sometimes she gave vent to her anger when she thought about what slavery had done. On one occasion, she declared, "All the gold in California, all the wealth of this nation could not restore to me that which the white people have taken." Although Sojourner usually spoke to white audiences, she never diluted her criticism and opposition to those who had enslaved her and her fellow blacks.

When Sojourner was sixty years old, she decided it was time to retire and enjoy the life she'd dreamed of for years. In 1857, she sold her Northampton house for $750 and moved to Harmonia, Michigan, along with her daughter Elizabeth Banks and her grandson Sammy. Later they were joined by Diana and her husband, Jacob Corbin, and their son, Frank.

Sojourner was content to sit on the front porch, telling stories to her grandsons and singing hymns. But just as she was settling down into retirement, the Supreme Court ruled that Dred Scott, a slave who had sued for his freedom because he lived in a free state, was "property" and therefore not a citizen. They said that Scott didn't have the right to sue. This decision was a blow to the abolitionists, but it didn't affect Scott. His "owner" freed him immediately after the case was final.

When Sojourner learned about the Dred Scott decision, she became convinced that it was not time to retreat.

Against her daughter's wishes, Sojourner prepared for another speaking tour. Before she left, she had her autobiography updated by her friend and neighbor Frances Titus, who edited and expanded the narrative six times between 1853 and 1884. Then, taking Sammy with her, sixty-two-year-old Sojourner Truth returned to the lecture circuit. Sojourner's message was clear and uncompromising: "Slavery must be destroyed, root and branch."

In one town, protesters threatened to burn down the meeting hall where she was scheduled to speak. Without fear or hesitation, she replied, "I'll speak on the ashes."

The hard years began to catch up to Sojourner, and it was difficult for her to get started in the morning. "But once she gets up," Olive Gilbert said, "she can go as long as a woman half her age." Though Sojourner had aged, another observer noticed "both power and sweetness in that great warm soul and that vigorous frame." Sojourner was still able to keep the crowd on the edge of their seats.

A House Divided

Between 1800 and 1859, bold black leaders like Gabriel Prosser, Denmark Vesey, and Nat Turner led at least two hundred slave uprisings. White Southerners knew that blacks outnumbered them three to one, so they had reason to worry about rebellions.

Sojourner argued that slave masters had much more to fear than slave insurrections. "It is God the slave owner will answer to on the day of judgment," she declared.

Although Sojourner was illiterate, her grandson Sammy kept her well-informed about the political affairs of the day, including John Brown's ill-fated raid on the arsenal at Harper's Ferry, Virginia, and the upcoming presidential election. Sojourner was particularly interested in Abraham Lincoln and the new Republican party. Though convinced that Lincoln would be a good president, she hesitated to endorse him because he hadn't called for the immediate elimination of slavery.

When Lincoln won the presidency and the Civil War broke out, Sojourner gave her full support to the Union soldiers. She decided to tour the Midwest to rouse support for the war effort. As Sojourner traveled on this speaking tour, angry mobs and bands of supporters greeted her. The anti-war and anti-black feelings ran especially high in Indiana, where the state legislature had passed a law forbidding blacks from entering the state. Sojourner defied the law and campaigned throughout the state for the Union cause. She was arrested numerous times, but friendly crowds gathered to defend her each time. Eventually, the rigors of such conflict exhausted Sojourner, and she returned home to recover.

On January 1, 1863, President Lincoln signed the Emancipation Proclamation, ending slavery in the rebel states. The executive order was received across the North with cheers and tears. Thousands of churches rang their church bells and people danced in the streets. Sojourner gathered her friends in Battle Creek and celebrated with cheering, singing, and long speeches. No Pinxter festival could compare to the joy and enthusiasm now shared by people who had dedicated their lives to freedom.

Several days after the emancipation, Sojourner Truth suffered a stroke. Somehow the rumor spread that she had died. The *Anti-Slavery Standard* printed a story about her, and Harriet Beecher Stowe wrote a tribute to her life, which was published in the April 1863 issue of *Atlantic* magazine.

But the great lady wasn't dead. With the help of her friends and family, Sojourner recovered quickly and plunged back into her work. "There's a war going on," Sojourner said, "and I mean to be a part of it."

After the Emancipation Proclamation was issued, the North began to recruit blacks to serve in racially segregated units. These black soldiers weren't paid the same as whites, and sometimes their white officers mistreated them. Sojourner spoke out against this injustice, pointing out that if black soldiers were dying equally, why weren't they paid equally for living?

By Thanksgiving of 1863, Sojourner received news that her grandson, James Caldwell, was missing in action in South Carolina. Sojourner wondered whether he was lying in a common grave with other soldiers or had been captured and suffered a fate worse than death—slavery. After the war, James returned home after surviving months as a prisoner of war.

Sojourner traveled to Camp Ward, an army base near Detroit, where more than fifteen hundred black troops were stationed. She took food donated by the residents of Battle Creek so the soldiers could enjoy a proper Thanksgiving dinner. While the men ate, she sang a hymn she had composed especially for the Michigan Infantry, to the tune of "John Brown's Body."

During the spring of 1864, Sojourner decided to visit President Lincoln in Washington, D.C. Although many abolitionists believed that Lincoln was moving too slowly to bring about an end to slavery, Sojourner greatly respected him. "Have patience!" she told her friends. "It takes a great while to turn about this great ship of state."

Until the day of her departure, Sojourner didn't tell anyone about her plans. Then, accompanied by her grandson Sammy Banks, Sojourner boarded the train for the nation's capital, stopping in several towns along the route to give speeches.

When at last Sojourner reached the nation's capital, she saw the flag and whispered to Sammy, "No more scars and stripes, just stars and stripes for all God's children."

After Sojourner had been in Washington, D.C., several weeks, she still hadn't met President Lincoln. When she found that she was unable to make an appointment on her own, she asked Lucy Colman—a white, Massachusetts-born abolitionist—to arrange a meeting for her. After some time, Colman succeeded, using Mrs. Lincoln's black dressmaker, Elizabeth Keckley, as a go-between.

When Colman finally took Sojourner to the White House on October 29, 1864, the two women waited several hours for their turn to see the busy president.

Finally, Sojourner was ushered into the president's office. When she looked at Lincoln's weary face and his shoulders, which seemed to sag heavily with the burden they carried, Sojourner's heart was moved by the great sadness of this man who had freed her people.

President Lincoln showed her his office and pointed out a Bible that a group of Baltimore blacks had presented to him. Remembering one of her favorite Bible stories, Sojourner reminded President Lincoln that he was like Daniel in the lions' den; and with God on his side he'd win, just like Daniel.

In November, as Sojourner had predicted, Lincoln was swept back into office by an overwhelming margin. By that time, Sojourner had discovered she enjoyed the busy atmosphere in the nation's capital. Instead of returning to Battle Creek, she decided to stay in Washington, D.C., to assist the Union's war effort.

Toward the end of 1864, a public welfare organization called the National Freedman's Relief Association asked Sojourner to work as a counselor to former slaves who were living at a camp in Arlington Heights, Virginia. There she educated former slaves about the need to locate work and housing and about the other responsibilities which came with their newly won freedom. Sojourner was still working at the Freedman's Village when General Robert E. Lee surrendered to General Ulysses S. Grant at Appomattox on April 9, 1865.

Six days after the surrender, President Lincoln was assassinated. Sojourner was devastated by his sudden death.

On December 12, 1865, Sojourner and millions of other Americans celebrated as Congress ratified the Thirteenth Amendment to the Constitution, officially ending slavery in the United States. Sojourner's prayers were answered. She had lived to see the end of slavery.

The Final Effort

Illiteracy continued to handicap Sojourner, limiting her opportunities for leadership, and keeping her poor by limiting her job opportunities. But her overwhelming faith convinced Sojourner that her illiteracy was another God-given trait, like her blackness and womanhood, which fashioned her beautifully to carry out her mission.

For years, abolitionists and women's rights activists had worked together and supported each other's cause. In 1869, the Fifteenth Amendment to the Constitution was passed, giving black men the right to vote, but women were still excluded. Women abolitionists felt betrayed by black men who benefited from their efforts and then seemed to desert them. Even Frederick Douglass, who had been the first to back women's rights to vote, said, "This hour belongs to the Negro."

Sojourner felt strongly about the women's suffrage issue. She not only spoke about it, but she acted on her beliefs. Some report that Sojourner tried to vote for Ulysses S. Grant in 1868.

Sojourner Truth was absolutely firm in her conviction about her rights as a citizen—whether or not the authorities agreed with her. She could do no less than attempt to exercise her rights. Sojourner truly believed that she was doing the work of God and that somehow her person and her actions embodied God's will.

Although Sojourner Truth was over seventy years old, she took up one more cause—land rights, working for government-sponsored black homesteads out west. She argued that blacks had been forced to work with no profit from their own labor, yet no slave had ever been compensated. In her opinion, the government could pay its debt in full by setting aside land for each slave. Sojourner knew that the government owned vast lands in the West and was giving many acres to the large and rapidly expanding railroad companies. She wondered why some of these acres could not go to the women and men whose bondage had served to increase the nation's wealth.

On March 31, 1870, Sojourner visited the newly elected president, Ulysses S. Grant, hoping to gain support for her land-grant proposal. But when the help that Sojourner expected from Grant was not forthcoming, she took her request to Congress. Senator Charles Sumner of Massachusetts promised to sponsor a bill if she could show him that there was widespread support. Sojourner had a petition drafted and set out across the nation to collect signatures.

Sojourner never grew discouraged in her fight for freedom and women's rights. Not only did she make her own gestures toward exercising her rights, but she also encouraged others to exercise their rights. In 1871, she heard that her friend Nannette Gardner had actually succeeded in voting in Detroit. She asked for a written statement from Gardner to substantiate the story, and the letter of response she kept among her treasured autographs and papers until her death.

Despite attacks during this period, Sojourner refused to give up her fight to get land for indigent black people. Ignoring her advancing age, precarious health, and numerous threats against her, Sojourner continued to travel and preach. She passed through Massachusetts, western New York, Michigan, Kansas, Iowa, Illinois, Missouri, Wisconsin, Washington, Ohio, New Jersey, and Kentucky during the last ten years of her life.

A year after leaving Washington, Sojourner returned with a thousand signatures. She hurried to Sumner's office and was told by his secretary that the great senator had recently died. When no one else would help Sojourner with her cause, her hopes of getting a bill introduced into the Senate evaporated. The tide of black progress continued to be blocked by conservative whites. More and more, she began to realize that the battle for black freedom had only begun.

At last, Sojourner decided to return home to Michigan. She missed Battle Creek and her family, but more importantly, Sammy was ill. At first his condition didn't seem serious, but his fever grew worse along with his cough. Worried about her favorite grandson's illness and suffering with an ulcer on her leg, Sojourner grew depressed. When Sammy died at age twenty-four in February 1875, her condition worsened. She never stopped mourning his death.

Meanwhile, conflict throughout the nation continued. In the South, many whites rebelled against the Reconstruction laws by forming white-supremacist groups such as the Ku Klux Klan. Blacks armed themselves and fought back, and President Grant was forced to send federal troops to restore order.

The Supreme Court supported the anti-Reconstruction sentiment by issuing rulings that weakened the effects of the Fourteenth and Fifteenth Amendments.

In 1876, Rutherford B. Hayes became the nineteenth president of the United States. One of his first acts was to withdraw the federal troops that were helping to protect the civil rights of southern blacks. The action signaled that the Reconstruction era was over and the gains that blacks had won after the Civil War would be rolled back. Despite the significance of this action, Sojourner did not have the strength to go on a speaking tour to protest against the new attempts to deprive blacks of their rights.

Rumors began to circulate that she had died or that she had celebrated her one hundredth birthday and was too old to travel. Actually she was nearing eighty years old at her home in Battle Creek, and her hearing and sight had almost completely failed. The once tall and strong Sojourner Truth needed the support of a cane to walk.

In 1877, according to some accounts, Sojourner's health mysteriously improved, her hearing returned and her eyesight sharpened dramatically. That next year, Sojourner went on another speaking tour, covering thirty-six different towns in Michigan. Then at eighty-one years old, she was one of three Michigan delegates to the Woman's Rights Convention in Rochester. Later, after a grueling trip to Kansas, Sojourner returned home for good.

To observers, she seemed blessed with boundless energy. Despite her age, she never seemed to tire and would pick up new causes to champion with vigor. The general perception of Sojourner was wrong, however. She was very human and her health was steadily declining.

One morning early in November 1883, Olive Gilbert visited Sojourner and found her in extreme pain. Yet when Sojourner saw her old friend, she smiled and, with a faraway look in her eyes, began to sing her favorite hymn, which she had often used to gather crowds for her speeches.

Two weeks later, at her home in Battle Creek, Sojourner Truth sank into a deep coma. She died November 26, 1883. She did not fear death, she had said, for she was confident that she would be happy in heaven.

Two days after Sojourner Truth's death, nearly a thousand people gathered at her house and formed a procession behind a black-plumed hearse. Her coffin was decorated with the images of a cross, a sheaf of ripe grain, a sickle, and a crown. Many of her fellow activists in the women's rights and abolitionist movements spoke about her "rare qualities of head and heart." At her funeral, Sojourner was remembered as a dynamic woman with strength, integrity, poise, and wit.

The sun was setting in Battle Creek's Oakhill Cemetery as Sojourner Truth was lowered into her final resting place. Crimson and gold lit up the western horizon. Olive Gilbert later said that the sun seemed "unwilling to leave the earth in gloom." When the sun finally set, millions of stars lit up the heavens in which Sojourner had found assurance that God was watching over her. She was buried near her grandson Sammy.

When Belle became Sojourner Truth, she declared that her devotion to the truth would never die: "And the truth shall be my abiding name," she promised. Whenever people speak out against injustice and scorn oppression, they keep Sojourner Truth's ideals of justice and freedom alive.

WATCHMAN
NEE

Family Tree

For eighteen hundred years after Jesus died for the sins of the world, the most populated country in the world never really heard the Good News. Then in 1839, England declared war on China. After the three-year Opium War, China was defeated and forced to open diplomatic relations with the West. Along with the merchant ships that now sought trade with the coastal cities of the Far East came zealous Protestant missionaries from America and Great Britain.

The Congregationalists of the American Board chose the seaport of Foochow, an ancient city on the southeastern edge of China. There, in 1853, they started their first missionary school and taught the children about God's great love. A fourteen-year-old boy named Nee U-cheng believed the message and asked Jesus Christ into his heart that summer. When he was later baptized in the nearby Min River, the Nee family's centuries-old enslavement to pagan religion was broken.

U-cheng had a gift for evangelism, which the American missionaries encouraged him to develop. He was the first Chinese evangelist that Foochow, a city of half a million, had ever seen. A highly effective preacher, Nee U-cheng was also the first ordained pastor in that part of the world.

When U-cheng was old enough to marry, he had a dilemma. There were few local Christian girls (and none in whom he was interested!), and it was a social taboo to marry someone from outside your province. But U-cheng trusted Christ, and before long a marriage was arranged with a young Christian woman from Kwangtung, almost five hundred miles away.

U-cheng and his wife were blessed with nine sons. The fourth son, Nee Weng-shiu, was born in 1877. As a pastor's son, he was educated in Western-style Christian schools and eventually studied at the American Methodist College in Foochow. Weng-shiu was one of the brightest students in his class and was awarded the post of state customs officer.

In 1880, a little girl named Huo-ping was born to a large peasant family. Her name means "peace," but for many years she was the least "peaceful" person she knew. Huo-ping escaped the common fate of female babies last born into poor homes. Instead of being drowned or buried alive by her father, she was sold to a family who intended to make her a slave girl.

God intervened, however, through a wealthy merchant named Lin, who adopted her as his own. After his conversion to Christianity, Mr. Lin saw to it that his new daughter, now called Peace Lin, received a Christian education. She became one of the keenest students in her school. In fact, she was so capable that, at the age of sixteen, she was accepted into a program that would eventually take her to a medical school in the United States. But first she had to attend the Chinese Western Girls' School in Shanghai to refine her English skills.

Christian in name only, the school was not good for the young Peace Lin's faith. Daily her worldly ambitions grew as she focused on her appearance as much as her studies. Then she met the extraordinary Dora Yu.

Dora Yu was not much older than Peace Lin when she came to the Shanghai school as a guest speaker. She told a story that burned into the student's heart. A few years earlier, Dora had done so well in her studies that she was accepted by a medical school in England. She was sent off with great fanfare by her family and friends on a journey she would never complete.

Like Jonah and Paul before her, Dora Yu clearly heard the Lord's voice above the waves while aboard ship. Just past the Suez Canal, He instructed her to give up her career and return to her homeland to preach the Gospel of Jesus Christ. Now she stood in the school chapel, passionately testifying to her love for God and challenging the students to commit their lives to Him.

Peace Lin was deeply moved by the penetrating words and humble lifestyle of the visiting preacher, but before she could make a decision about what to do with her life, the choice was made for her. At the age of eighteen, Peace Lin received a letter from her mother stating that an October marriage had been arranged for her with the son of a pastor's widow, a certain Nee Weng-shiu of Foochow.

"Marriage! How I hated that word!" she later said. But Peace Lin would not be the first girl in her province to violate the ancient custom of arranged marriage. Just a few months before the dawn of the twentieth century, the strong-willed and driven Peace Lin married the gentle and quiet Nee Weng-shiu.

About that time, the Boxer Rebellion broke out in Northern China. Had the anti-foreign madness spread to the southern provinces, it is likely that both Weng-shiu and Peace would have died along with the hundreds of Chinese Christians murdered in the north. Instead, they set up house in the little coastal town of Swatow and began their family.

After the birth of two daughters, Peace Nee was beside

herself with anxiety and depression. Like Hannah in the Bible she vowed to God, "If I have a boy, I will present him to You." God heard her prayer, and on November 4, 1903, little Nee Shu-tsu was born. The Nees eventually added four more boys and two more girls to their family.

Humbling Experiences

By 1920, Peace Nee had drifted far from her Christian upbringing. She'd never forgotten her earlier poverty or how her arranged marriage had diverted her promising professional career. She became obsessed with political ambition and her social connections.

But she had not forgotten the ringing testimony of Dora Yu, the woman who had abandoned a lucrative career as a doctor to preach the simple Gospel of Christ. And now, Dora Yu's prophetic words cut through the layers of unbelief surrounding Peace Nee after years of self-serving pursuits. After listening to Dora Yu for four nights in a row at an evangelism meeting, Peace Lin became a true Christian. The change in her life was like new blossoms on a lotus plant.

She went to her eldest son, Shu-tsu, and asked him to forgive her for having beaten him unjustly and in anger. Instead, Shu-tsu said, "Yes, you did, honorable Mother, and I hated you for it." Then he turned and left the house.

That night, Shu-tsu couldn't sleep. His harsh words to his mother punished him all night. He later said, "I lay in bed thinking that if the power of Christ could move Mother to lose face so badly that she would humble herself to me, then Christianity must be more than another empty religion."

The next day, Shu-tsu went to hear Dora Yu for himself, and he was so overwhelmed by the love of God that he wept and confessed his sins. Recognizing that he now faced an all-or-nothing decision, Shu-tsu accepted Jesus Christ as his Savior and Lord.

It is customary for the Chinese to choose a new name at a turning point in their lives. When he committed his life to Christ after his family's return to Foochow, young Nee Shu-tsu changed his name to Nee To-sheng, or in English, Watchman Nee.

Watchman's friends now saw an abrupt change in him. At Trinity College he stopped cheating on exams, violating the school rules, and leading his friends in open ridicule of Christian classmates.

The die was cast. Watchman Nee set his hand to the plow and did not look back. As a seventeen-year-old boy, he vowed, "I will give Christ all of my life, my loyalty, and my love." He abandoned all his previous career goals of becoming wealthy and well-positioned and chose preaching for his lifetime career, the very profession he had once labeled as "the most despised and base of all occupations."

Godly Guidance

In the spring of 1920, the same season of Watchman Nee's conversion to Christianity, another young Chinese man was completing his conversion to the gospel of Karl Marx. Born into a peasant family, Mao Tse-tung had participated a few years earlier in the People's Revolution. He had done his part to sweep away the Imperial Dynasty that had controlled China for centuries.

As Mao sought out a mentor who could teach him Marxist ideology, the adolescent Watchman Nee was looking for a guide who would train him in godliness. Mao searched for a political connection that would prepare him to ascend one day to the leadership of China's Communist party. Watchman prayed for God to send a mature believer who would teach him the deep truths of God's Word.

Mao found the militant atheist Chen Tu-hsiu, who would later direct the persecution of Christians as secretary general of the Communist party. Watchman found Anglican missionary Margaret Barber, and together they laid the foundation for the Christian church in China.

Margaret Barber never did anything the easy way. As a vibrant, single woman in her twenties, she traveled alone from England to China in 1899. Laboring for Christ in obscurity, she threw herself into the work at the girls' middle school in Foochow. When she finally took a furlough after ten years, envious coworkers took the opportunity to slander her good name to her superior. He believed the fabricated charges and recalled Margaret from the mission field.

Margaret would not defend herself. Even after the truth was discovered and her bishop offered full restitution, she would not accept reinstatement. Instead, stripped of all financial support, she returned to China on her own.

It seemed impossible to stop her faith. Margaret Barber inspired Watchman with her radical devotion to the cross and her unflagging passion for God's Word. Margaret had prayed the year before that God would raise up young Chinese men and women to reach their country for Christ. She vowed to sharpen Watchman like iron sharpens iron.

"Stay broken," she would often say to him. "Don't believe all the good things that people say about you. His Word says that if your ways are pleasing to the Lord, He will make your enemies be at peace with you. He is most pleased with your brokenness. Remember the cross. You must stay broken."

After Watchman joined her in ministry, Margaret purposely put him under the charge of a supervisor who drove him to distraction. Watchman's temper flared up every time he disagreed with this man, and he would heatedly bring his grievances to Margaret.

Predictably, she would firmly reply, "The Scriptures say the younger should obey the elder. You have much to learn." Time and again, Watchman would walk away angry with her, the Bible, and life in general. But slowly the lesson began to take hold.

Like Margaret Barber before him, Watchman eventually became a "person of the Cross" and refused to defend himself when falsely accused. He also learned other important lessons from Margaret that would play key roles in his ministry. For example, Watchman came to believe, based on 1 Corinthians 1:10–13, that denominationalism was condemned by Scripture. He was later criticized for his conviction that there should be only one church in each locale. Under Margaret's tutelage, Watchman thrilled to the doctrine of Christ's imminent return and kept it at the forefront of his preaching.

Watchman took his lifelong motto from the example set by Margaret Barber: "I want nothing for myself; I want everything for the Lord."

Margaret Barber chose to live by faith in God alone, following the same principle that governed George Müller in England and Hudson Taylor in China. She refused support from any missionary organization, trusting that God would supply all her needs.

Watchman was so impressed by the unusual ways that God consistently would get the money to her, that he decided he would live by faith also in this matter. It was not an easy decision to make for a young man who had ample resources available to him for the asking. But it was a decision he would not regret.

Once, as a novice preacher, Watchman was meditating on three Scripture passages: the story of God's directing the ravens to feed Elijah by the brook Cherith, the story of God's filling the large jars borrowed by the widow of Zarephath with the little oil left in her tiny jar, and Jesus' promise in Luke 6:38 that if we give, it will be given back to us, full and overflowing.

Watchman was invited to preach in a city far to the north in his province. He had only fifteen dollars, about a third of what he needed for the trip. On the morning of his departure, he was praying for God's provision when he felt impressed to give five dollars of his meager funds to a coworker. "But Lord," he argued, "I must leave to do Your work tonight, and I'll never find a boat to take me for less than forty dollars." Nevertheless, with tears in his eyes he found his colleague and surprised him with the gift of five dollars, saying, "Don't ask me why; you will know later."

He set out to catch his boat, not even knowing how to pray except to say, "Lord, You know what You're doing." When he got to the wharf, a boatman approached him, saying, "I have one space left at the stern, and I don't care how much you pay me. Let's say seven dollars." The tears returned to the young preacher's eyes.

As the meetings drew to a close, he began praying for money for his return trip. On Sunday evening, a man offered to pay his travel expenses both ways. Watchman's heart leaped at the offer, but he heard his voice say, "No, my friend. That is very generous, but someone has already accepted this responsibility."

The next morning, with just a few dollars in his pocket, he walked to the boat, wondering if he had made a mistake yet excited to see how God was going to provide again. Even before he reached the wharf, someone ran up to him with a letter from the man whose help he had declined the night before. The letter asked Watchman to please accept a small donation toward his ministry even though his travel expenses were covered, and the man had included some money.

When Watchman arrived home in Foochow, he encountered the grateful wife of his coworker, who tearfully told him, "On Friday, we prayed all day because we had no money. Afterward, my husband felt that he should go for a walk, and then he met you, and you gave him five dollars. The five dollars lasted us through five days."

Watchman was overjoyed and he firmly learned the truth that if you freely give, it will be given to you. Later, he was able to teach with conviction: "As God sent the ravens to feed Elijah, He will do the same for you today."

Following the Scriptures

When he wasn't at White Teeth Rock learning from Margaret Barber, Watchman was finishing his courses at Trinity College in Foochow and evangelizing everyone he knew. He kept his vow to read through the entire New Testament at least once a week. Nothing could keep him from witnessing to all of his classmates, but after nearly a year of sharing his faith, not a single person had prayed to receive Christ.

One day, a coworker at the White Teeth Rock mission told him point-blank: "You are unable to lead people to the Lord because there is something between God and you. It may be some hidden sins not completely dealt with or something for which you are indebted to someone."

Watchman immediately took these honest words to heart. After making a list of every person he could possibly have offended, he went to each of them, confessing his wrongdoing and humbly asking their forgiveness. At the same time, he entered the names of seventy schoolmates into his notebook and systematically began to pray for them individually every day. Within months, all but one of them were born again!

These were exciting days when faith was fresh, ideals

were lofty, and the word "impossible" was not in Watchman's vocabulary. With his newly converted friends, wonderfully named Faithful Luke, Simon Meek, and Wilson Wang, he began holding student-led prayer meetings in Trinity's chapel. Before long, the room couldn't hold them and their enthusiasm spilled into the streets of Foochow.

The young men found an attention-getting gong and banged it with abandon in the marketplace. As the crowd gathered, the young men sang joyfully and preached the Good News of Jesus Christ.

After his conversion, Watchman threw himself into a profound study of the Bible that few historical heroes of the Christian faith could match. From the age of eighteen on, he consistently employed at least twenty different forms of Bible study, from a general study of all the books of the Bible for an overall view, to the intense study of a particular book to probe its depths; from doing word studies in the original Greek and Hebrew languages, to mining the riches of all the Bible's prophecies; from biographical studies of all the characters of the Bible, to a systematic study of all of its doctrines.

He used several different Bibles for specific types of study. One Bible he saved for writing copious notes in the margins as he grew in knowledge of its contents. Another he purposely kept note-free so that he could receive fresh insight every time he took it up. It was not long before Watchman Nee became known as a young man consumed by God's Word. This one characteristic was to set him apart from less-devoted scholars and preachers for the rest of his life.

The time he invested reading the Bible and great Christian authors soon had a considerable effect on his experience in several key areas, including baptism.

From his daily immersion in the Bible, he came to believe that baptism was for believers who understood what it meant to commit their lives to the lordship of Christ, and that the Bible portrays baptism as an experience of complete immersion; mere sprinkling does not convey the powerful New Testament image of coming up out of the pagan world system into newness of life.

God's timing is always perfect. Just as Watchman settled this crucial matter in his own mind, his mother approached him two days before Easter and characteristically blurted out, "I have given this much thought, my son. The next time you go to White Teeth Rock, I will accompany you. For there I must be baptized!"

With eyes wide, Watchman replied, "My dear mother! I have made the same decision myself. We will be baptized together!"

They left that same day for Miss Barber's mission; and early in the morning on Easter Sunday, March 28, 1921, Watchman and his mother were baptized by immersion in the golden waters of the Min River.

His thorough study of God's Word led Watchman to question how his denomination took communion. He discovered that the Bible said believers should come together often to break bread in remembrance of Christ, but his denomination took communion only four times a year.

Watchman faced the same question that Martin Luther and the other reformers asked four centuries earlier: Should I obey the clear teaching of Scripture or submit to the authority of the church's tradition?

Eventually, most of Watchman's friends and immediate family broke bread together every Lord's Day. When word reached the district superintendent of the Methodist church that the entire Nee family had been baptized by immersion and that many of them were meeting privately to take communion, he came to visit the Nees and registered his concern about their actions.

Not long after the superintendent's visit, Watchman

drafted a bold letter, cosigned by both of his parents, resigning membership in the Methodist church. They were soon visited by their pastor, bishop, several missionaries, the school principal, and many others, trying to dissuade them from taking this drastic step. But the Nees held firm. "The real issue," they said, "is whether or not we will obey the Scriptures."

Full-time Ministry

In 1922, a great revival began in Foochow. Large bands of young men, often sixty to eighty strong, organized and led by Watchman Nee, set out on evangelistic missions throughout the city—and scores of male and female students were converted to Christ.

The movement was energized by an evangelistic crusade led by a visiting preacher from Tientsin, Ruth Lee, a charismatic woman who would become an important influence in Watchman's life. Her powerful testimony—as a former atheist principal of a government school—and her passionate speaking electrified her youthful audience.

So many people were saved at these meetings that the decision was made to continue the crusade even after Ruth Lee left for another city. Watchman and a few of his more gifted friends soon found themselves preaching to larger crowds every evening.

Even during these early days, Watchman showed signs of what later would be the passion of his ministry: discipling those who were being saved and planting local churches.

In his early twenties, Watchman fell deeply in love with Charity Chang, a young woman who had grown up in his neighborhood. He had always viewed her as a friendly pest, but now he couldn't get her off his mind. Unfortunately, her faith was immature and her goals were far from his. After months of praying for her and trying to stop thinking about her, he cried out to God one cold February day, "I will lay her aside! Never will she be mine!" A supernatural peace flooded his spirit.

About this same time, Watchman and his friend Faithful Luke decided not to continue their academic studies and the pursuit of lucrative careers among China's elite. Instead, they would take a vow of poverty and enter full-time Christian ministry.

Leland Wang and other close coworkers politely informed Watchman that he was no longer welcome to worship with them. The anti-Christian movement in China was reaching a new peak, and much of the criticism was focused on Watchman.

Watchman knew in his heart that many church leaders and Western missionaries were being pressured by the government to compromise on several issues. Because these leaders knew that Watchman would never compromise, it was more expedient to push him to the periphery of the movement.

Watchman moved from Foochow to Ma-hsien, a little fishing village not far from White Teeth Rock. He rented a small hut and threw himself into a deeper study of God's Word. He also laid out plans to publish a Christian magazine he called *Revival* to help new believers grow in their faith.

Test of Faith

I n Ma-hsien, Watchman spent long hours gazing at the
Min River and reflecting on his life. His honest self-
analysis eventually led him to recognize his doubt regarding the faith. He read voraciously, but as a self-taught man
in theology and the Scriptures, he couldn't eliminate the
fear that a learned atheist or a brilliant Bible critic could
convince him that God's Word was unreliable.

His fear was put to rest when he heard the story of a
simple tailor named Chen, who lived in Watchman's
province. The only Scriptures that Chen possessed was a
single page he had found, containing the last twelve verses
of the Gospel of Mark. With no way of knowing that the
most trustworthy early manuscripts didn't include these
verses, thus making them unreliable to modern scholars,
the little tailor treasured every word and came to know
Christ Jesus personally through them. He decided after
much prayer to test verse eighteen in his own village. He
began a door-to-door campaign of laying on hands for
healing. God honored his simple faith; and after the
miraculous healing of one of his neighbors, he quietly
returned to his shop to carry on with his tailoring and
daily witnessing to his customers.

Watchman was deeply moved by this story and,

after reflecting upon it, gave the same confident response whenever attacked by liberal scholars and critics of the faith: "Yes," he would calmly reply, "there is a great deal of reason in what you say—but I know my God. That is enough."

The more Watchman observed God's Spirit at work, the less he doubted his faith. Still, he knew that he must deal with a second barrier that was holding him back: his connection to the Westernized and often lifeless form of church that passed for Christianity in China.

The institutional church had lapsed into lukewarm religious secularism. Denominational jealousies and prideful ecclesiastics had practically paralyzed the movement of the Spirit among the churches established by Western missionaries. As a result, anti-Western, anti-Christian nationalism was finding an attentive audience.

Watchman's keen mind and his passion for holiness made him one of the few Christian intellectuals in China to see clearly that the real problem in the church was that the faith of the believers was too shallow. They had no roots in the knowledge of God's Word.

But how could he communicate to his countrymen that Christianity was more than the initial forgiveness of sins or the mere assurance of salvation? He was too busy preaching in the villages to do any serious writing. There was simply no time to put his thoughts into book form.

Then Watchman developed a severe cough and began waking up at night either sweating profusely or chilled to the bone. A trip to the doctor revealed the bad news: tuberculosis. The prognosis was equally grim: Watchman was given six months to live.

At first, he was gripped by severe depression. "Lord, how can the end come when I've only just begun?" he prayed.

After another round of X rays, the doctor told him

there was no hope. Strangely enough, this news settled his spirit and galvanized him into action. Watchman prayed, *If I am to die soon, Lord, let it be while I am writing down all the wonderful things the Holy Spirit has taught me from Your Word.* Thus began his struggle to write *The Spiritual Man,* the magnum opus of his young life.

Eventually, Faithful Luke helped to move Watchman to Margaret Barber's care at White Teeth Rock. It was there that the high fever that often accompanies advanced tuberculosis seized him. He continued to push himself to write, often passing out over his notes, sometimes losing several days, of which he had no memory.

When he was bedridden or unconscious, Margaret would sit by his side and quote the Scriptures to him. "Christ is the victor," she would often remind him. "His strength is made perfect in weakness. He is strengthening you on the inside. Do not give up, my young friend. Christ is the victor."

The raging fever returned, but Watchman refused to give in. Though his skin was hot to the touch, his spirit was hotter. Asking for more ink and paper, he wrote with abandon. When the disease got so bad that he could no longer breathe without pain while lying down, he propped himself up in a high-backed chair, pressed his chest against the desk, and wrote on.

After four months of daily battling, all four volumes of *The Spiritual Man* lay in stacks on the table. Watchman prayed weakly, "Now let Your servant depart in peace."

He was in the throes of death and he knew it. Ruth Lee, who was visiting the mission, gathered several believers from around the compound and led them in a three-day period of fasting and praying.

As Watchman lay on his bed laboring for breath, three verses came clearly to his mind: "By faith ye stand. . ." (2 Corinthians 1:24); "We walk by faith. . ." (2 Corinthians

5:7); and "All things are possible to him that believeth. . ." (Mark 9:23). From that very moment, Watchman believed that God had healed him. Meanwhile, the believers remained in prayer downstairs.

The testing of the truth of those verses came without delay. "By faith you stand," God's Word said to him. He slowly rose from his deathbed and dressed himself for the first time in 176 days. "Walk by faith," he reminded himself. He took two steps and began to faint.

"Where do you want me to go?" he asked the Lord. The answer came: "Go downstairs to Sister Lee's room." With difficulty he crossed the room and opened the door to the stairwell. It was dangerously steep and looked impossible for him to negotiate. "All things are possible," whispered the Holy Spirit, and he began the descent. With each step he cried out, "Walk by faith; walk by faith!" With the twenty-fifth and final step, he realized total healing!

With tears in his eyes, he walked briskly to Ruth Lee's room. When Watchman opened the door, his friends were speechless. A time of sweet celebration and praise followed.

A few days later, Watchman Nee stood up at a Sunday morning worship service and preached with great power for three hours.

Trust

By May 1928, with his health better than it had been in years, Watchman decided to move the base of his ministry to Shanghai, where Ruth Lee lived. Ten years his senior, she was a wonderful evangelist and an accomplished writer. Ruth offered to help him prepare his book for publication and to advise him in launching his new magazine, *The Christian*.

Watchman also saw the potential for the Gospel to make inroads quickly in the corrupt financial capital of Shanghai. After all, hadn't Jesus more success among the notorious sinners of His day than among the respectable citizens?

Soon after he moved his headquarters to Shanghai, Watchman had another spiritual breakthrough. While making a few cosmetic changes on *The Spiritual Man,* he was struck by the pristine power of a passage in Romans that he had only thought he understood before. He was reading Romans one morning when he came to the words: "Knowing this, that our old man was crucified with Him, that the body of sin might be done away, that so we should no longer be in bondage to sin."

Knowing this! Watchman said to himself. *How could I know it?* He prayed, *Lord, open my eyes.* In a flash, the

Lord gave him a tremendous insight. "I had earlier been reading 1 Corinthians 1:30: 'But of him are ye in Christ Jesus,'" he said. "I looked at it again. I thought, *the fact that I am in Christ Jesus is God's doing!* It was amazing! If Christ died, and that is a certain fact, and if God put me into Him, then I must have died too. All at once, I saw my oneness with Christ: that I was in Him, and that when He died, I died. My death to sin was a matter of the past and not of the future."

He later said, "I felt like shouting my discovery through the streets of Shanghai. From that day I have never for one moment doubted the finality of that word: 'I have been crucified with Christ; it is no longer I who live, but Christ who lives in me.'" He later recounted these events in a book called *The Normal Christian Life*.

From this moment on, it became almost impossible to offend him. Why should he retaliate when criticized? He had already died to self-promotion. He made the decision never to defend himself and never to argue when personally rebuked.

As usual, the test came quickly. One day, a younger coworker confronted him and berated him for almost four hours. Watchman sat calmly in his chair, at times even nodding his head in agreement. Little by little, he was becoming a person of the Cross. With a new sense of peace, he learned to accept every problem that came his way as another opportunity to grow spiritually.

He was visiting his mentor, Margaret Barber, for a few days when the fever that had plagued him a few years earlier returned with a vengeance. He had exhausted himself by preaching at every opportunity, and with the return of winter came a violent cough. And although he was not yet aware, Watchman had contracted a heart disease, angina pectoris, that would stalk him for the rest of his life.

In severe pain and suffering again from cold sweats, he

left White Teeth Rock and journeyed home to Foochow to seek the solace of his family. When Peace Nee saw him, she put him to bed immediately, fearing that he would not live long. But early the next morning he rose and left the house.

Few of the townspeople even recognized him as he shuffled through the streets with the help of a walking stick. With a ghostly pallor on his gaunt face, Watchman hardly resembled the virile young man who had graduated from Trinity College not long before.

He had not gone far when he crossed the path of one of his favorite professors from Trinity. The teacher almost walked past him, then stopped and stared impolitely for a moment. Catching himself, the older man gathered himself and asked, "Young Mr. Nee, would you care to join me for some tea?" Tempted to decline self-consciously, Watchman accepted the invitation and soon found himself sitting in silence across the table from his old law professor.

Although the professor didn't say a word, Watchman felt Satan sniping at him from the shadows of the tea shop.

"You had a bright future," the enemy seemed to whisper in his ear. "Full of possibilities, and you gave it up to serve God. That was splendid. Then you had a promising ministry—with your gifts, you were assured of success— and you threw that away too. For what?"

The man across the table appraised Watchman's pathetic frame and said, "What is this? We thought so much of you at Trinity and had hopes that you would achieve something great. Do you mean to say that you are truly like this?"

For a moment, Watchman wilted even further under the man's piercing stare. Tears came to his eyes as he realized that, humanly speaking, his professor was right. He was a sorry figure who inspired more pity than praise.

With his health broken again and the future looking bleak, he surrendered to the oncoming tears. Embarrassed for his student, the Trinity don rose without looking at Watchman and excused himself. "I will leave you alone."

"Alone?" Watchman thought, watching the man leave. The debilitating self-pity within him began to turn to spiritual steel. "I am not alone," he said out loud. "Greater is he that is in me than he that is in the world. If God is for me, who then can be against me?" A passage from 1 Peter rushed back to him: "If ye be reproached for the name of Christ, happy are ye, for the spirit of glory and of God resteth upon you. If any man suffer as a Christian, let him not be ashamed; but let him glorify God on this behalf" (1 Peter 4:14,16). Watchman walked home. He still needed the cane, but his shuffle was less pronounced.

His mother convinced him to seek the counsel of doctors. Their unanimous prescription was a forced rest in the healthier climate of Kuling Mountain, six hundred miles up the Yangtze River.

As he gradually recuperated, he took short walks overlooking the verdant Yangtze Valley. One day he exclaimed, "Lord, you simply must restore me to full health. There is so much work to be done!"

The answer came quickly to his spirit: "This is My affair," said the Lord. "You must trust Me!" Each time that Watchman tried to argue, the same inner voice spoke to him: "You must trust Me, My son. You must let the matter go and trust Me."

One day, repentance washed over Watchman. He found a hefty stick by the path and drove it as deeply into the ground as he could. "Lord, I do trust You!" he cried out. "I have dropped the matter of my healing here!"

But no sooner had he risen to return to his cottage than a wave of anxiety and nausea swept over him. That old cloud of despair began to descend upon his spirit. But before he could fall into that trap, he turned back to the spot where he had impaled the stake and, dramatically pointing to it, announced for Satan and the world to hear, "Lord, I dropped the matter of my healing here. I refuse to take it up again!"

When he forgot about his predicament, his health began to improve and he had the mental energy to rethink his growing faith. He realized that God was simply giving him the opportunity to become more of a person of the Cross.

Out of this experience, 2 Corinthians 4:7 became a theme passage for Watchman's life: "We have this treasure in earthen vessels, that the excellency of the power may be of God, and not of us." Another piece had been added to his spiritual backbone, and his resolve never to be surprised by any circumstance that God allowed to come his way was stronger than ever. As usual, the Lord's timing for such a lesson was perfect. No sooner was he strong enough to descend the mountain steps than he received the news that his beloved mentor, Margaret Barber, had died, at the age of sixty-four, in relative obscurity at White Teeth Rock.

Margaret Barber was both the most honest and humble person he had ever known. She taught him to pay more attention to the quality of his inner life than the visible success of his ministry—that "to be" was more important than "to do." Because of her steady influence, honesty and humility would also characterize Watchman for the rest of his life.

Church Growth

As the crowd gathered for Sunday morning worship at the Hardoon Road church in Shanghai, Watchman observed the congregation from his wooden seat at the side of the platform. Lately, he was aware of how hard they were working at living the impossible Christian life, only to find themselves fighting spiritual dryness and discouragement.

He began his sermon by telling a parable about a centipede who was paralyzed by indecision when he tried to decide which leg to move first. After wrestling with his dilemma for hours, the centipede finally overcame his paralysis when the sun came up and, without thinking, he rushed outside to see the sunrise.

"We all work too hard at being religious," Watchman told the congregation. "[But Paul told] his friends in Ephesus, simply 'walk in His love.' The truth is that the more you try to deal with inner dryness, depression, and flatness, the more you cannot overcome them. These things become an issue because we make them an issue. If you forget about them and let them go, they will disappear."

In response to a question from the congregation, Watchman continued: "Resisting the devil is not the same thing as spiritual dryness. You conquer discouragement and the tyranny of impossible religious expectations by forgetting about them. True faith is not about you trying; it's about you dying. We all must learn to walk in His love."

"Pastor," his coworker and friend John Chang said, "we know that your words are true. But how can we learn to walk in His love?"

"Beloved," Watchman answered, "before my conversion, I devoted my life to accumulating material things: clothing, high marks in school, money, and so forth. And for years after I was saved, I was still in the habit of accumulating things—even though they were now spiritual things: godliness, high morals, wisdom, and patience. But I was still groping in a kind of darkness, seeking to amass the virtues as personal possessions—and getting nowhere in the effort."

Watchman quoted from Philippians 1:19–21, and then repeated Paul's triumphant assertion, "'for to me, to live is Christ.'"

"You see it now, don't you?" he continued. "We labor all our lives to be Christlike, only to find that such a goal was impossible from our first efforts. While we struggle and grow more discouraged daily when it doesn't happen, He simply wants to live out His life within us. For to me, to live is Christ. It is Christ Himself living through us; speaking, witnessing, fathering, befriending, writing, and singing through us!"

Many in the congregation could hardly breathe. They knew that what they were hearing was the key to Christian living. For several of them, this would begin to release them from the grind of working to earn God's favor and set them on the excellent path of learning to live in His grace.

"O the emptiness of things!" Watchman cried. "When they are not an expression of His life within us, they are dead. I don't want to be more like Jesus; I want Jesus to be Himself living within me. Once I saw this truth, it was the beginning of a new life for me. From here on, your daily life can be summed up in one phrase, 'Walk in His love.' "

Watchman had been regularly attending a Bible study in the home of a new friend, Miss Peace Wang, a graduate of Nanking Girls' Seminary and a colleague of Ruth Lee's. Years earlier, as a militant atheist, Ruth Lee had done everything possible to destroy Peace's immature faith. But both young women made radical commitments to the Lordship of Christ and became highly effective itinerant evangelists. Still, something was missing from their ministries.

When Peace Wang met Watchman Nee, she found the something that was missing. "We must do more than evangelism," Watchman passionately stated. "Our Lord poured His life into the twelve disciples for three and one-half years before He told them to go into all the world. We are winning people to Christ without pouring our lives into them."

"But, Brother Nee," said Peace Wang, "the Bible tells us to do the work of an evangelist."

"Yes, friend, but the greatest evangelist of all, next to the Lord Himself, said, 'We were willing to have imparted unto you, not the gospel of God only, but also our own souls' " (1 Thessalonians 2:8), Watchman said, quoting the Apostle Paul. "The believers in China are shallow and rootless. They are clouds without rain. After they come to Christ, someone must help them to grow deeper."

With this new resolve, the finest church movement in China's brief Christian history had its humble beginning. Watchman Nee, Ruth Lee, and Peace and John Wang dedicated themselves to a broader definition of evangelism than had their predecessors. They were convinced that if they followed the primitive, New Testament pattern of evangelism, a strong local church, whose members were being discipled daily, would be the result.

The church in Shanghai began to grow by word of mouth. It had an irrepressible quality of life and spirit, and soon people throughout the province were talking about it.

Watchman's desire for unity among all Christians led him to give the most general terms to every phase of his work. He called the building for their worship services the "assembly hall"; he named his magazine *The Christian;* he spoke of the Christian life as "the way"; and he referred to Christians simply as "believers," because denominationalism was anathema to him.

Watchman was drawn to the Brethren hymnbook entitled *Hymns for the Little Flock.* When he translated the songs for his congregation, he inadvertently left the title on his new church hymnals. Missionary friends took to the name quickly and began to circulate it in their travels. Even though Watchman changed the title as soon as he heard that people were calling the Hardoon Road church, the "Little Flock," it was too late. As much as he detested labels, his ministry would forever be known as the Little Flock movement.

It wasn't long before influential Christian leaders in England picked up news about God's working among the Little Flock. In particular, Charles Barlow, a member of the elitist, ultraconservative "London Group" of Brethren heard about Watchman. He decided to pay him a call when he came to Shanghai on business in the winter of 1931. After a lively ten-day visit, Mr. Barlow wrote home to his Brethren friends about the believers in China.

He was most impressed by Watchman's knowledge of the Bible and the way he communicated it to his congregation. His enthusiasm about Watchman's ministry was boundless. "What is the goal of your work here?" he asked.

"To supply spiritual milk to the young believers," responded Watchman, "and solid food to the older ones. We especially stress the salvation of the Cross. But we are even more concerned with the spiritual condition of the believers. We preach all of God's truth and not just a portion of it."

The visitor from London could not have been more glowing in the reports that he sent back home. The stories about this indigenous group of Chinese Christians sent a wave of spiritual electricity through the London Group of Brethren, such that by October 1932, a deputation team of English-speaking Brethren (representing Great Britain, Australia, and the United States) boarded a ship in England and sailed for China.

Strained Relations

The eight Brethren visitors arrived at Hardoon Road just as Watchman began his morning message. Brand-new chairs had been purchased for the occasion, and Charles Barlow led his delegation into the row reserved for them.

"In John 8:23," Watchman began, "our beloved Lord said to his Jewish congregation, 'Ye are from beneath; I am from above: ye are of this world; I am not of this world.' I wish us to note especially here the use of the words 'from' and 'of.' The Greek word in each case is *ek,* which means 'out of' and implies origin. *Ek tou kosmos* is the expression used: 'from,' or 'out of this world.' So the sense of the passage is: 'Your place of origin is beneath; my place of origin is above. Your place of origin is this world; my place of origin is not this world.' The question is not, Are you a good or bad person? but, What is your place of origin? We do not ask, Is this thing right? or, Is that thing wrong? but, Where did it originate? It is origin that determines everything. 'That which is born of the flesh is flesh; and that which is born of the Spirit is spirit'" (John 3:6).

Charles Barlow turned slightly toward Dr. Powell of California and whispered, "Can you believe this man's depth? And he's only warming up!"

Watchman continued, "So when Jesus turns to His disciples, He can say, using the same Greek preposition, 'If you were of the world (*ek tou kosmos*), the world would love its own: but because you are not of the world, but I chose you out of the world, therefore the world hates you' (John 15:19). Here we have the same expression, 'not of the world,' but in addition we have another and more forceful expression, 'I chose you out of the world.' In this latter instance there is a double emphasis. As before there is an *ek*, 'out of,' but in addition to this, the verb 'to choose,' *eklego*, itself contains another *ek*. Jesus is saying that His disciples have been 'chosen out, out of the world.'

"There is this double *ek* in the life of every believer. Out of that vast organization called the *kosmos*, out of all the great mass of individuals belonging to it and involved in it, out, clean out of all of that, God has called us. And so comes the title 'church,' *ekklesia*, God's 'called-out ones.' If you are a called one, then you are a called-out one."

Watchman measured his audience and delivered the crux of the message: "As the people of God, heaven is not only our destiny but our origin."

Watchman announced with joy, "This is an amazing thing, that in you and me there is an element that is essentially otherworldly. The life we have as God's gift came from heaven and never was in the world at all. It has no correspondence with the world, but is in perfect correspondence with heaven; and though we must mingle with the world daily, it will never let us settle down and feel at home here.

"My beloved friends, have you, like Lot, pitched your tent toward Sodom? Have you so deeply buried your tent stakes that you will not be able to move out in the morning when our Lord returns? Do you feel too much at home in this world, a world that Jesus told us lies in the lap of the evil one?

"Do not be discouraged, dear ones; together we can learn how to stop living between two worlds. Let us not forget," said Watchman, "we serve the One who has 'overcome the world,' and so we can also be 'overcomers.' I want each of you to consider two things before we come together again: where your life intersects too closely with the world, and whether or not you are willing to come out from it. Now let's pray."

After his prayer, Watchman led the congregation in a song from the Little Flock hymnal. When the service was ended, most of the congregation stayed to participate in a meal served in honor of the guests.

After the meal, Charles Barlow said to Watchman, "Pastor Nee, you simply must come to England to speak to the brethren there."

"Your intentions are kind," replied Watchman, "but what makes you think that they would receive me any better than our Lord Himself was received?" Knowing something of his listeners' backgrounds, Watchman added, "I have no interest in Christian societies that build legalistic barriers around themselves to keep unstained from the world. Jesus Christ is our only effective barrier against the world. I have every interest in building His life into the believers He has placed in my charge."

As if he'd only half-heard Watchman's words, Charles Barlow pressed his earlier point. "You simply must come to England. You will be such a blessing to us."

"I will come," replied Watchman, "but I will not be such a blessing."

At the age of thirty, Watchman Nee left his homeland for the first time in his life. The English hospitality was so warm for the initial days of his visit, that it seemed his earlier premonition in China had been wrong. The London Group of Brethren invited him to all of their gatherings and enjoyed introducing this "interesting young man from

China" to their members. In retrospect, Watchman felt that he was mostly a novelty to them and not taken very seriously because of his youthful appearance.

After the novelty wore off, he found himself learning much by listening and observing. From the beginning he was impressed by the breadth of their knowledge on a variety of religious subjects. But Watchman was repeatedly disturbed by their spiritual arrogance when he heard revealing comments like, "Is there anything in the field of spiritual revelation that we Brethren do not have? To read what other Christians have written is a waste of time. What do any of them have that we have not got?"

It was several days later at a Bible conference that his true feelings about the spiritual complacency of his hosts came to the surface. When given the rare opportunity to add his comments to a lengthy doctrinal discussion, Watchman rose to his full height and spoke with conviction.

"My dear brothers, your understanding of the truth is vast, but in my country it would avail you only this much," he said, lifting his right hand and snapping his fingers, "if when the need arose you could not cast out a demon." He later commented to Charles Barlow, "Your people have wonderful light, but oh so little faith."

Of course, Watchman's candor offended many of the Brethren and a parting of the ways seemed inevitable. But for the time being, an open confrontation between his ministry in China and the London Group was put off. Watchman returned home maintaining an uneasy relationship with the Brethren movement.

Missionary Zeal

Watchman could not have returned to China at a more exciting time. In the spring of 1934, under Chiang Kai-shek's aggressive leadership, China was experiencing a brief but unparalleled boom in transportation. New road systems, railways, and even air travel were opening the country up, and Watchman's coworkers in Shanghai joined in his vision to saturate as many provinces as possible with the Gospel message.

Even though Watchman's passion lay in the areas of teaching and discipleship, he sensed the spirit of the times and decided to take this opportunity to reach his homeland for Christ. Gathering the Shanghai believers together, he challenged them to evangelize their countrymen, even if it meant accepting job offers to other cities where they could make their new homes evangelistic centers.

"Because you are not witnessing," he told them, "many have not heard the Gospel. They will be eternally separated from God. What a consequence of our apathy!" His voice rose in pitch and intensity.

"It is absolutely impossible for a person to have light and not to shine. As there is no tooth that does not chew, no fountain that does not flow, so there is no life that does not beget life. Whoever has no interest to help people repent and believe in the Lord may himself need to repent and believe in the Lord."

Many of his listeners began to squirm uncomfortably in their chairs. He continued, "Is it possible for a man to be so advanced spiritually that he is no longer winning souls? I tell you that this is something you cannot out-grow; it is a lifetime undertaking. Some of you who think you are farther along spiritually have been told that it is the mark of a mature believer to be a 'channel of living water.' I do not totally disagree. We need to be joined to the Holy Spirit so that living water may flow through us.

"But let me also say that the channel of life has two ends: one end is open toward the Holy Spirit; but the other end is open toward men. The water of life will not flow if only the end toward the Lord is open. The other end, the end toward the world, must be open too for there to be any flowing. The reason many do not have power before God is due to their either being closed on the end toward the Lord or on the end toward sinners. China can still be won to Christ if we open our hearts to men."

"But we are so few, and our country is so large. You have given us an impossible task," said one of the coworkers.

"I have given you nothing," responded Watchman. "It is the Lord who gives. And it is His task to perform through you. Besides," he added, "I have made some cal-culations that should encourage you: If each of us in this room leads one person to Christ in the next half-year and we disciple that person for the entire six months, then, at the end of that time, both we and our discipled friend win one person apiece and train him for another six months, and so on, we would not only win China to Christ within a generation, but the entire population of the world will have been reached! It is simple geometric progression."

"It is simply God's will," chimed in John Wang.

"Beloved," Watchman continued, "there are two big

days in the life of the believer: the day on which he believes in the Lord—and every day after that when he leads someone to faith in Christ. This is my challenge to you. Witness to at least one person a day. Witness to whomever you meet. It is useless for the Gospel to be preached only from the pulpit. Many can preach, but cannot win souls. If you bring people to them who need the Lord, they are out of their depth. Learn this truth: Only those who know how to deal with souls and lead them to Christ are useful to the church. It is time for us to put feet to our faith."

Days later, Watchman modeled his message by leaving on a dangerous mission to evangelize the remote southwestern provinces of China. He chose as his traveling companion one of his few friends who owned a car, a recently converted businessman called Shepherd Ma, who had more zeal than knowledge when it came to driving. They packed the Model T Ford with full gasoline cans and donated Bibles and set off down the brand-new motor road.

As they drove, Watchman and Shepherd had hours in the car to discuss how to lead people to Christ.

"I am learning much from our journey together, Brother Ma," said Watchman, as the Model T chugged through the Yunnan province.

"What is that, dear To-sheng?" asked Shepherd, always anxious to hear what God was teaching his companion.

"I am learning that impressing upon believers the importance of witnessing is not the same thing as teaching them how to lead people to the Lord—and the lack of such knowledge will render most of their witnessing ineffective."

"I am realizing the 'how' from watching you these several weeks," replied Shepherd.

"And what are your perceptions, my friend?" asked Watchman.

"That you always prepare your heart first before the Father before you try to lead anyone to His Son."

"You are exactly right, Shepherd. Prayer is the basic work of saving souls."

"But there are times when I pray fervently and still see no results," said Shepherd.

"Perhaps it is a matter of God's timing, my friend. Some fruit take longer to ripen than others. It is just as wrong to pick an unripened apple as it is never to go into the orchard at all."

When Watchman returned from this adventure with Shepherd Ma in time for the third annual teaching conference, he received two wonderful messages. The first was that new churches connected to the Little Flock movement were springing up all over the area—partly due to the increased missionary zeal of the believers in Shanghai.

The second piece of news was of a more personal nature and captured Watchman's emotional interest immediately. His childhood friend and sweetheart, Charity Chang, was now in Shanghai, having earned her M.A. in English at Yenching University. He faced a dilemma: Should he contact her, or should he keep his ten-year-old vow to save his heart for the Lord and give it to no woman?

Marriage

Watchman had discreetly followed Charity's school career from afar, and the last he knew she still cared little for spiritual things. But the message he now received from one of his friends was that she had been attending Bible studies, was seeking baptism, and confessed a complete spiritual transformation. Still, second-hand information is often inaccurate, and he knew that he must see her face-to-face. *One look into her eyes and I will know,* he thought.

The next week he arranged to meet with her after a church service. Listening to her talk about her love for the Lord and seeing that she was no longer the worldly girl he had known, Watchman was shaken to the core. He immediately went back to his house to spend time alone with God in prayer.

"Father," he cried out, "what shall I do? I have promised that I would desire nothing on this earth besides You. Is it possible that after all these years I still care for her? Help me to put her out of my mind or give me faith to believe that this is from You."

God's choice was to give him faith, in the form of Faith Chang, who appeared at Watchman's door on a match-making mission. Out of breath, she said, "To-sheng, now that my sister Charity has become an earnest Christian, serving the Lord with steadfast purpose, would you consider marriage with her? I feel sure she would have no objections."

Watchman believed that he had heard from God and, to his delight, Charity accepted his proposal. But there was much opposition to the marriage. Many who looked up to Watchman as a hero of faith were scandalized to think that he, a godly man intent on holiness, would compromise himself by giving unworthy attention to sex and raising a family. They feared that Charity's physical beauty would distract him from spiritual pursuits. On the other side stood Charity's mean-spirited aunt, Mei-chen, who broadcast that the eldest Nee son, a controversial preacher and notoriously poor, was a terrible match for her brilliant niece, Charity.

The young couple would not be deterred, and the wedding went ahead as scheduled. On the afternoon of October 19, 1934, his parents' thirty-fifth wedding anniversary, Watchman and Charity exchanged vows in the company of more than four hundred believers.

Charity's aunt, Mei-chen, expressed her displeasure with the marriage by purchasing advertising space in a national daily newspaper to print a vitriolic attack on Watchman's character. She accused him of shady dealings with foreign investors, gross misrepresentation of himself to her niece, and immoral conduct in his ministry.

Watchman was devastated. He took to his bedroom and refused to see anyone but Charity. One day, she came in and asked him, "What will you do, my love? You have been publicly maligned and your friends await your response."

"My response is not to respond," he answered. "'When a man's ways please the Lord, he maketh even his enemies to be at peace with him' (Proverbs 16:7). But I must tell you, dear one," he said behind tear-swollen eyes, "I cannot pretend this doesn't hurt."

Just then, a missionary friend arrived at their door. "He'll see me," she boldly announced to Charity, "because I have a message for him from God." With her Bible in hand, the woman marched right into Watchman's room, declaring, "'No weapon that is formed against thee shall prosper; and every tongue that shall rise against thee in judgment thou shalt condemn'" (Isaiah 54:17).

Eventually the support of his friends and the tender ministry of his inner being by the Holy Spirit brought Watchman out of his depression—and not a day too soon. Word arrived from the separatist London Group of Brethren that Watchman was being charged with "compromising the fellowship." This came after they discovered that, during his visit to their country, Watchman had taken communion with lesser British Christians who held that "anyone claiming to be a believer was allowed to break bread without regard to the religious and other associations in which he was involved."

The communication from England further informed the church in Shanghai that if they wanted to remain associated with London Group of Brethren, they must cut all connections with other groups and the missionary congregations in particular.

"Let us not forget our official association with the Brethren and that they were the first to recognize the validity of our church," said Y. A. Wu.

"Better that we are recognized by the Holy Spirit," responded Watchman. "The world pays great attention to personal status—to what race I belong, what background I have, and so forth. 'I must maintain my honor,' it says. 'I must protect my status.' But once we become Christians, we should exclude all such discriminations. No one should bring his personal status or position into Christ and the church—the one new man; to do so would be to bring in the old man. Nothing that belongs to the old man should ever be carried over into the church."

"Whether we choose to recognize it or not, Brother Nee," said John Sung, "there will always be differences between nations. What of the English who look down on our ministry even now, or our neighbors, the Japanese, who threaten our very security? Perhaps it is time for us to learn to discern our enemies from our friends."

Watchman looked around the circle of church elders and said gently, "No, my friends. There are no longer any national distinctions. Every time we come to the Lord, we come not as English or Chinese but as Christians. We can never approach the Lord on the basis of our nationality. These outside things must be shut out, for we are united by the life of Christ. Whether some are American, English, Indian, Japanese, or Chinese believers, we are all brothers and sisters in the Lord. No one can divide us as God's children. We cannot have American Christianity; if we insist on having America, we cannot have Christ. The same is true of us in China. If we put our nationalism before our faith, we cannot have Christ."

The Shanghai elders were unanimous in their response that summer to the London Group. Their reply, a courteous and scripturally based appeal to their sponsors in England, showed how far their understanding of the New Testament church had come in the few years that China had been open to the Gospel. Their letter read in part:

It is the Spirit and the Spirit alone, who can decide the question of one's fitness for fellowship. We must receive those whom God has received. This command is clear, decisive and embracing.

The London Group of Brethren responded by with-drawing their support of the Little Flock movement. With a scathing rebuke of Watchman's leadership, they denounced the Chinese church—even going so far as to doubt the sincerity of their love for Christ.

The Shanghai church was deeply shocked and sad-dened by the negative response. Watchman's grief was multiplied when he saw that the letter was signed by his old friend, Charles Barlow. At that moment, the words of the messianic passage in Zechariah 13:6 came to him: "If someone asks the prophet, 'What are these wounds in thine hands?' Then he shall answer, 'Those with which I was wounded in the house of my friends.'"

Anonymity Lost

Watchman and his coworkers threw themselves into the task of planting churches throughout the country. Evangelistic teams were sent out from Shanghai, and soon there were more than thirty new churches. As one of the small fellowships grew, it was given elders to direct its ministry and nurture the little flock.

One of the reasons these local assemblies matured so quickly was that each believer became an active participant. Watchman agreed with Luther that the traditional separation between clergy and laity was inspired by Satan and that the priesthood of all believers was the true *modus operandi* for the church.

He taught that the clergy-laity system with its hierarchy, rank, and position was unscriptural and reduced Christianity to a form of human organization. As it had corrupted the Lord's original plan for His body, the Western church model, with its sophisticated array of salaried clergy, would paralyze the new believers' zeal in China. Watchman and his colleagues determined that there would be no distinction between clergy and laity in the Little Flock churches; all were priests together. They also understood that the real servant of God must live by faith and not be a hired employee depending on a religious organization for a salary.

Although Watchman stayed true to this belief for the remainder of his ministry, he increasingly found himself preoccupied with helping to meet the financial needs of his many coworkers. In his heart, he felt responsible for all of them.

In the summer of 1937, Watchman was invited to preach the Gospel in Manila. While conducting meetings there, he received news that the Japanese had launched a full-scale invasion of China, beginning with their seizure of Peking.

The civil war between Chiang Kai-shek's Nationalist Party and Mao Tse-tung's Communist Party was temporarily suspended when Japanese warplanes bombed Chinese cities on August 14. Highly disciplined and well-equipped troops overran eastern China. The brutality and killing that characterized their sacking of the former Nationalist capital became known as the "rape of Nanking." The Japanese juggernaut then turned its attention toward Shanghai.

Watchman knew that he had little time to rescue his beloved Charity. As Chinese warplanes made reprisal attacks on Japanese ships on the Whangpoo River near the Nees' home, Watchman sneaked back into Shanghai from the south and found his wife safe with the Christian sisters at the Hardoon Road church. Together they made their way through the war-ravaged streets to their home. Finding the house ransacked by the invaders, Watchman and Charity gathered what little they could carry and fled the beleaguered city. Watchman noticed that the Chinese Bible he had given to Charity at their wedding had been stolen.

Taking back roads to avoid the battle areas, the couple eventually reached Hong Kong, where Watchman's parents were living. While there, he was approached by some missionary friends who convinced him that this would be an opportune time for him to accompany them to England. There was a clamoring in Great Britain to have his writings translated into English.

After praying about it with Charity and his family, he knew he must return to London. Late that summer, unaware that his wife was pregnant, Watchman boarded an Anchor Line ship and sailed once again for England. Upon arrival, he joined up with his friend T. Austin-Sparks of the Christian Fellowship Center at Honor Oak Road. They traveled south together to the annual Deepening of the Spiritual Life convention in Keswick. The conference was being chaired by W. H. Aldis, the venerable home director of the China Inland Mission, one of the few missionary associations for which Watchman had high esteem. Earlier in his life he had come under the influence of CIM's legendary founder, J. Hudson Taylor, from whom he had learned much about the matter of abiding in Christ.

He made the Christian Fellowship Center a temporary headquarters for his teaching and writing ministries, planning to return to Charity in Hong Kong after four months of work.

Before he could return, however, he received a letter from Charity, telling him about her pregnancy, but that she had also miscarried. Watchman had no way of knowing that this was the only time his beloved wife would ever conceive. All that he could think of was her suffering without him halfway around the world. But with the escalation of the Sino-Japanese war, he was forced to stay in England more than four months longer than he had planned.

He threw himself into completing and then translating his book *Rethinking the Work,* with help from an English missionary friend named Elizabeth Fischbacher, who years earlier in China had helped him formulate his doctrine of the Holy Spirit.

Watchman wrote the book to examine from Scripture God's guidelines for church life. Its publication was a breath of fresh air and appeared in London to rave reviews from the church. For a man who disdained popularity, he would now find it more difficult than ever to remain anonymous in his homeland.

Business Matters

Japan expected to conquer China within a few years. But in 1939, while the two Asian nations were locked in deadly combat, World War II broke out in Europe. By the middle of the summer, Watchman knew that he must return home no matter what the danger. His original plan was to visit the United States and travel from there directly to China. But word reached him that the Japanese had seized many Pacific ports. Watchman wisely took a British ship to India and finally arrived safely in Shanghai by way of Bombay.

It was good to be home with Charity, but Shanghai hardly resembled the high-spirited, commercial city that he had left. The marketplaces were in ruins and the streets infested with beggars.

On December 8, 1941, the morning after their attack on Pearl Harbor, the Japanese sank the American and British gunboats in Whangpoo Harbor and made a lightning-quick strike against Shanghai's five million citizens.

The church lived in fear and it seemed that things could not get worse. But just a few days later they did. As the Japanese prepared to move against Hong Kong, word reached Watchman that his beloved father, Nee Weng-shiu, had died suddenly from a heart attack.

Brokenhearted over his father's death and fearing for his mother's safety, Watchman secretly traveled to Hong Kong to make the funeral arrangements. This was one of the most difficult times in his life.

When he returned to the church in Shanghai, Watchman faced a financial crisis of the highest magnitude. The Japanese occupation of eastern China had brought commerce to a standstill. Support that church members had been able to give was now almost nonexistent at a time when hundreds of newly planted churches needed funding and thousands of recent converts required expensive Christian education and spiritual care. By this time, the Little Flock movement reportedly embraced seventy thousand members in seven hundred congregations.

Some financial aid arrived from Christian friends in England, but Watchman knew that unless God brought relief from some unexpected source, the Christian movement in China was in trouble. He and Charity prayed relentlessly over the problem and, soon after, an answer came. Whether the answer came from God or not, Watchman was never quite sure. It appeared in the form of his brother George, a research chemist with his own laboratories, who invited Watchman to become his partner in establishing a pharmaceutical company in Shanghai.

There was no way for Watchman to know that joining his brother in this commercial enterprise would eventually lead to his torture and death at the hands of Communist captors. In fact, because of his decision, Watchman began to meet one disaster after another, each one increasingly menacing. But at the time, all Watchman knew was that the opportunity that faced him was a timely one.

In the early months of 1942, the China Biological and Chemical Laboratories (CBC) was launched in Shanghai. One of China's first manufacturers of synthetic drugs, CBC employed many of Watchman's coworkers and apostles part-time, helping them to earn enough to continue their ministries during the rest of the week. As chairman of the newly formed board of directors, Watchman routinely moved back and forth between his business appointments and the work of the church.

Before long, his longtime friend, Faithful Luke, and a delegation of colleagues appeared at Watchman's home for a confrontation. "My dear To-sheng," Faithful Luke said, "why have you left the work of God to go into commerce?"

"I am merely doing what Brother Paul did in Corinth and Ephesus," Watchman replied.

Chen Zexin, one of Watchman's closest coworkers, remarked, "But when Paul made his tents, it was a simple handwork. The business you are doing is a big enterprise. It needs total commitment to run this business well. Because of that, the time left for the Lord and serving the brothers will be reduced accordingly. You must reconsider."

The elders of the church in Shanghai now labeled Watchman as a renegade, citing the verse, "No man, having put his hand to the plough, and looking back, is fit for the kingdom of God" (Luke 9:62). Their judgment was that the one who had helped found the Hardoon Road church was now unfit to preach there. Once again, Watchman was deeply hurt, betrayed by his friends, but he quietly resolved to continue to provide financial support for the coworkers who had come to depend on him.

Believers all over China, and especially those in Shanghai, were shaken by the decision. They did not know what to think and waited to hear Watchman's defense. But Watchman characteristically accepted the action as God's own discipline and chose silence over self-exoneration.

Not only was he excommunicated from preaching in his own church, but his beloved friend, Ruth Lee, who had supported him from the beginning, was convinced by the others to leave him.

But Watchman Nee would not be stopped. He and George moved the factory to Chungking, where he purchased a campsite for the training of lay ministers to spur on the spiritual awakening that was still growing in the provinces not controlled by the Japanese. He was both an itinerant evangelist and the CEO of a highly successful business that employed Christian refugees.

Meanwhile, the Hardoon Road church suffered without Watchman's leadership. The Japanese occupation made it almost impossible to meet as usual. The church held an emergency meeting and decided that the only way they could continue to exist would be to divide into house churches for the time being. Watchman heard of their plight and longed to be there to help them.

When the war finally ended in September 1945, Watchman and Charity move back to his boyhood home in Foochow. There they decided that the small estate would make a perfect training center for more church workers. At the same time, Watchman set in motion his own withdrawal from CBC, turning the operation over to his brother and making certain that future funds would continue to go to various ministries.

About this time he contacted his friend Witness Lee, a fiery preacher for the movement in Chefoo, and asked him move to Shanghai to provide leadership for the Hardoon Road church.

Under Witness Lee's influence, the church in Shanghai soon began to grow again. Families from the many underground house churches began to return to corporate worship, and renewed evangelistic efforts broke out all over the area.

Watchman remained in the shadows, studying his Bible and writing new training manuals for saints he wasn't sure would even read them. Many believers remained confused about the rumors and innuendoes they had heard regarding him. Had he actually misused church funds? Was he really guilty of collusion with the hated Japanese oppressors? Why had he chosen a secular business venture over the church? Because Watchman had never defended himself, few of them knew of his innocence in these matters.

The main body of believers in Shanghai grew more depressed daily by the absence of their founding pastor. Finally, late in 1946, Witness Lee approached the church elders and pointedly asked them, "Were you in the Spirit when you made the decision to reject him?" Their answer was a heartwrenching "no."

With Witness Lee as their liaison, the Shanghai elders sent a message to Watchman at Foochow, inviting him to lead a Bible conference at Hardoon Road in April. His acceptance was immediate and his joy was infectious.

When he stepped onto the platform to address the audience, an assembly hall that comfortably seated only four hundred souls was packed with more than fifteen hundred believers, "hanging from the rafters" just to hear their beloved pastor preach the Word once again.

Accusation Meetings

In March 1947, Chiang Kai-shek's Army of the Nationalist Government launched a major offensive against Mao Tse-tung and the Chinese Communist party, which headquartered in the caves of Yenan. After capturing the city and driving Mao's forces out, the Nationalists broadcast their victory throughout the world. But it was an empty boast. The guerrilla army of the Communists had simply slipped away to poise themselves for a counterattack.

In late June, the People's Liberation Army (PLA) swept across China to the Yangtze Valley, decimating the Nationalist troops and setting the Communist juggernaut in motion. Watchman Nee realized the danger that was coming to the church in China. His closest friends urged him to flee to Taiwan, but he never wavered from his original call: to penetrate all of China with the Gospel of Jesus Christ. He knew that the persecution was coming but thought that God might spare them long enough to win China to Christ.

He and Witness Lee formulated a plan to reach their homeland through "evangelism by migration," a concept they believed was clearly presented in the Book of Acts. "We must not remain stationary," he said to his coworkers, "but must move out and make room for others; for as many will be added as move out."

Soon the "Gospel emigration plan" was set into motion. To the backdrop of civil war erupting all around them, the believers met for urgent training sessions before "emigrant families" would leave Shanghai and Foochow to travel inland to evangelize and plant new fellowships.

The results were remarkable. Hundreds of families moved after their training, and by 1948, more than two hundred new assembly halls had been established. The generosity of the new converts brought uncommon financial prosperity to many of the churches, and the public notoriety began to attract the attention of the Communist party, which was gravely suspicious of anyone who accumulated wealth.

On May 25, the PLA entered Shanghai, and the believers' lives were forever changed. The new premier, Chou En-lai, soon set a devious plan into motion. He feared the thriving young church of China and designed a strategy to enervate it even as he made it work for his own cause. He started by calling three liberal Protestant leaders together in Peking for a late-night, closed-door meeting. There they drafted a document that spelled out the principles of the "new Christian movement."

Their goal was to absorb the church by evacuating all foreign missionaries and making it self-governing, self-supporting, and self-propagating. Of course, offensive names like "God" and "Jesus" could no longer be used, and the only legal Christian publication from now on would be the government periodical *Tien Feng* (*Heavenly Wind*). This eventually would mean the end of Watchman's vast publishing ministry. Time was short and he knew it.

The next several months saw Communism strengthen its grip on China. Local revolutionary committees were formed in most communities, encouraging townspeople to inform on their neighbors. It seemed that the secret police were everywhere. "Tiger hunts" were formed by party leaders to seek out and punish the capitalist tigers who "preyed" upon the wealth of the citizenry.

Then came Black Saturday, April 27, 1951, the day that thousands of Shanghai's intellectuals were arrested and turned over to a program of thought reform. Many believers were taken, among whom were some of Watchman's coworkers. Chou En-lai was building his courage to move against China's most beloved pastor.

Five days later, *Tien Feng* published an order to the Christian church in China to participate in accusation meetings. Churches were required to publicly censure and hand over to the authorities all "imperialist elements and their stooges."

By August 11, *Tien Feng* boasted that sixty-three accusation meetings had already taken place. Each meeting was characterized by emotionally charged accusatory speeches rehearsed by the speaker to defame particular Christians, but with the wider purpose of slandering Christianity itself. This degrading movement gathered momentum with each meeting, and before long, an accusation meeting was scheduled for Watchman Nee's own church.

Before that meeting would be staged, there was still much ministry to be done. Watchman and his coworkers began to work around the clock to prepare biblical materials for the believers who would be left behind. The workers averaged two hours of sleep a night as Watchman dictated new lessons to Ruth Lee and her assistants. He would pace back and forth, expounding God's Word into the early hours of the morning. With little voice left, he would then collapse into bed for a brief nap before rising to take up the task again. This continued until the inevitable footsteps of soldiers sounded in his street and he responded to the loud rap at his door. Watchman embraced Charity, said good-bye to her, and shouted to his friends, "Tell them in Hong Kong to dissociate all secular business enterprise from the church!"

He was arrested by officers of the Department of Public Safety on April 10, 1952, and charged as a lawless capitalist. He was fifty years old and would never know another moment of human freedom.

Time Served

By the time the accusation meeting was scheduled, the authorities had created an indictment 2,296 pages in length. The charges ranged from imperialist intrigue and espionage to counterrevolutionary activities hostile to government policy, gross immorality, and financial irregularities. The Communists did all they could to stir the members of the church into an angry denunciation of their pastor as an enemy of the people. But the few statements they were able to solicit were too preposterous for serious consideration.

The following week saw at least thirty leaders in the Shanghai church taken into custody. A general sweep of Little Flock churches throughout China led to as many as two thousand key believers, being incarcerated, often never to be seen again.

Watchman stood before his government-appointed accusers for twelve long days, listening to page after page of the bogus indictment being read to him. The hours passed, but he remained silent.

After the grueling ordeal, Watchman was taken back to his prison cell, but his public humiliation was far from over. A media onslaught began to inform Christians everywhere of "the crimes of Watchman Nee." *Tien*

Feng ran an eleven-page article exposing Pastor Nee's alleged vices.

There followed a systematic program for "brainwashing" members of the Little Flock churches all over China. Believers were given the opportunity to publicly confess their wrongdoing and join the Three Self movement. Many who refused were arrested and seemingly dropped from existence.

All prayer meetings, Bible studies, and other unauthorized Christian activities in private homes were declared illegal and severely enforced. Itinerant preachers were declared to be outlaws and were rigorously sought by the police.

In the meantime, Charity's name made the "wanted" list. But ill from stress and on the verge of losing her eyesight from hypertension, she was admitted to a hospital and placed under strict medical care and police surveillance. As soon as they deemed her well enough to travel, she was arrested and taken to prison. Because Watchman had no means of communication, he did not know of her suffering.

Watchman settled in for the mind-breaking grind of prison life. His day was divided into eight hours of harsh labor, eight hours of "re-education," and eight hours of dark loneliness in his cell. He froze in the winter and experienced insufferable heat in the summer. Because he was not allowed to communicate with anyone in the outside world, few specifics are known about the suffering he endured for the next twenty years.

Originally sentenced to fifteen years for crimes against the government, Watchman's prison term was extended for an unspecified length of time in 1967.

On April 12, 1972, he completed his twentieth year in chains, suffering from a painful heart condition, and still his captors would not give him freedom. But they did allow him a limited form of communication by this time. Word had reached him that Charity had died, and Watchman took the news hard.

On June 1, 1972, Watchman entered into eternal joy and rejoined Charity. What he had preached so passionately to others was now completely realized in his death: Men go, but the Lord remains. God Himself takes away His workers, but He gives others. Our work suffers, but never His.

THE
ESSENTIAL CHRISTIAN LIBRARY

Books That Stand the Test of Time. . .
Priced as if Time Were Standing Still

Essential reading for every Christian, these hardbound, time-tested classics will form a priceless collection of Christian writing that will bring inspiration and encourage devotion to God for years to come. Beautifully bound, affordably priced at $9.97 each!

Best of Andrew Murray on Prayer, The
Christian's Secret of A Happy Life, The by Hannah Whitall Smith
God Calling, edited by A. J. Russell
Great Sermons, Volume One
Hiding Place, The by Corrie ten Boom
Hinds' Feet on High Places by Hannah Hurnard
In His Steps by Charles M. Sheldon
Morning & Evening by Charles H. Spurgeon
My Utmost for His Highest by Oswald Chambers
Pilgrim's Progress, The by John Bunyan
Prison to Praise by Merlin Carothers
Riches of Bunyan, The
Search for Holy Living, The

Available wherever books are sold.
Or order from:

Barbour Publishing, Inc.
P.O. Box 719
Uhrichsville, OH 44683
http://www.barbourbooks.com

If you order by mail add $2.00 to your order for shipping.
Prices subject to change without notice.

ISBN 1-57748-445-2

9 781577 484455

90000